Rape, Incest, Murder! The Marquis de Sade on Stage

Volume One
Juvenilia and Early Prison Plays

John Franceschina

Rape, Incest, Murder! The Marquis de Sade on Stage
Volume One
Juvenilia and Early Prison Plays

©2013 John Franceschina. All Rights Reserved.
No part of this book may be reproduced in any form or by any means, electronic, mechanical, digital, photocopying or recording, except for the inclusion in a review, without permission in writing from the publisher.

Published in the USA by:
BearManor Media
P O Box 71426
Albany, Georgia 31708
www.bearmanormedia.com

ISBN: 978-1-59393-732-4
Printed in the United States of America
Book design by Robbie Adkins

Contents

Foreword v

Biographical Preface xv

Sadeian Theatricals 3

The Self-Proclaimed Philosopher 23

The Wedding of the Century 41

The Madness of Misfortune 61

The Twins 91

The Freak 131

Henrietta and Saint-Claire 213

Select Bibliography 259

Foreword

Donatien Alphonse François, Marquis de Sade (1740–1814) needs no introduction. As the embodiment of the concept of "sadism" and the author of a number of novels depicting the most lurid of sexual fantasies, Sade is well-known. In the nearly two hundred years since his death, he has been both praised as a literary visionary in his portrayal of man's darkest instincts and condemned as a profligate and pornographer in his often graphic depiction of sexual activity. At the end of Sade's dissolute life, which involved every kind of sexual excess, he was viewed as an immoral atheist whose only mental aberration was an intractable predilection to vice. Yet, the author of *Justine*, *Juliette*, and *The 120 Days of Sodom* also wrote a number of rather conventional, exceedingly moral plays which existed only in manuscript until 1970 when Jean-Jacques Pauvert sought to publish the entire body of Sade's work.

It is not difficult to understand why the plays remained buried. In her *Sade: A Sudden Abyss*, Annie Le Brun suggests that critics tended to disregard this aspect of Sade's creativity "under the curious... pretext that so traditional a theatre could only tarnish the image of a Sade who normally presages much darker forces." Certainly Sade's great biographer Gilbert Lély felt the same way when he argued that publication of Sade's plays "could add nothing to his reputation," adding that Sade's "real drama was not to be found on the stage, but only in his demented notion of being a brilliant playwright." Geoffrey Gorer, writing in 1962, takes Lély's remarks one step further in calling the plays "outstandingly dull, flat and unprofitable, with no apparent merit beyond facility, with practically no original, and certainly no 'shocking' ideas."

Jean-Jacques Brochier, one of the Marquis's most sympathetic critics, emphasizes Gorer's final point in his introduction to Pauvert's 1970 edition of the plays, where he suggests that readers, familiar with *The 120 Days of Sodom*, might be somewhat bewildered by Sade's theatrical writing since "There is neither rape nor torture, no one is murdered, vice appears only so that it can be punished, God is spoken of with respect, society is held in esteem, above all, everyone is very proper." C.R. Dawes, in *The Marquis de Sade: His Biography and Writings*, written in 1927, surprisingly discounts Sade as the author of a 1796 verse play entitled *La France Foutue, tragédie lubrique et royaliste* and issues a typical evaluation of his dramatic work: "On the whole, we are not in a position to appraise the dramatic works of the Marquis de Sade, but it seems fairly safe to assume that they were not of very much importance, from any point of view."

Yet, despite its being in many ways conventional, it is clear that Sade thought very highly of his dramatic work. In his *Descriptive Catalogue of 1788*, Sade put the two completed volumes of plays at the head of his list of works and in a letter written in April 1784 to his teacher, Abbé Amblet, the Marquis brags:

> In my portfolio I have more plays than many of the famous authors of our time and more than twice as many in outline. Had I been given the opportunity, I would have had fifteen plays ready by the time I left prison. They found it more enjoyable to annoy me but time will tell my executioners whether they were right or wrong.

Throughout his career, Sade continually sought to have his plays produced on both the private and professional stage and when those efforts failed, he turned to giving dramatic readings in prison or staging his work at an asylum for the insane. This does not illustrate the activities of a dilettante playwright. Rather, as critics pointing to the theatrical elements in the novels have demonstrated, theatrical activity was central to Sade's life. Annie Le Brun maintains that the plays are "actually much better than is generally made out" and suggests:

> When numerous critics have all pointed to the stunning mastery of dialogue evinced in his novels, to say nothing of the truly theatrical disposition of many of the scenes—erotic or otherwise—this would seem to be linked to the theatrical obsession that persisted so disturbingly throughout his tempestuous existence. Should we not therefore look more closely at this theatre, looming as it does directly over our abyss?

Studying the plays of the Marquis de Sade, however, presents the critic with a trenchant problem. In what creative universe can a group of plays, written in accordance with eighteenth-century conventions, coexist with quasi-pornographic novels which seem far ahead of their time in their depiction of the darker side of the human psyche? The suggestion that the Marquis de Sade has many different facets to his personality and may, like many other writers of the century, experiment with a number of forms is perhaps too glib and inconclusive a response and several critics have offered highly original theories in an attempt to justify the apparent incongruity in de Sade's work.

Looking to psychoanalysis for solutions, Gorer suggests a close relationship between the theatre and sadism. While emphasizing that he is not implying that "actors or dramatists are sexual sadists," he does conclude that "Sadists are failed actors and playwrights." He explains:

> What does a successful playwright or actor do? By his skills, he commands the emotions of his audience, makes them laugh or cry, shudder or exult, as he plans; he produces visible and audible changes in the people who are under his spell. But, in a crude and concrete way, this is precisely what a sadist wishes to do to his victims; in a great number of cases one might say that the sadist is acting out a play with an audience of one.... If I am right in thinking that some sort of theatricality or dramatic ritual was a constant component in Sade's sexual sadomasochism, then it perhaps becomes understandable why he could never admit his incapacity as a professional dramatist. If he could have been a successful playwright, then he would have been able to achieve in a socially acceptable way many of the pleasures which he could otherwise obtain only from dangerously unsocial acts.

Jean-Jacques Brochier offers a different perspective in suggesting that Sade's plays provide the positive norm against which all of his other licentious creations might be appreciated. In his discussion of Sade's drama, *Count Oxtiern*, Graham Rodmell explains Brochier's point of view:

> [T]he important thing is that the sociologically or metaphysically negative cannot exist without the positive, which gives it its value;

scandal cannot exist except by reference to a norm. For Brochier it is the function of Sade's plays to offer this norm, and in his view it is failure to realize this that leads that guru of Sadians, Gilbert Lély, into the mistake of likening Sade's plays to those of the worst scribblers of the eighteenth century: for Brochier, what makes the plays important is their role as a sort of foil to Sade's other, libertarian works.

Rodmell concludes that Brochier is simply desperate to "elevate the value of Sade's plays" and maintains that, regardless of their value as foil, "the conventionality of the plays does seem to stand in direct contradiction to the rest of Sade's writings."

Finally, Annie Le Brun argues that de Sade's traditional approach is not all that strange. Rather, she suggests that "the orthodoxy of his theatre owes much to a certain way of life typical of the ancient régime" and maintains that de Sade "will never rid himself of that divine right to nonchalance" which is characteristic of his upper-class position in society. Stressing the importance of understanding the extent to which de Sade "both refuses and accepts this privileged world, before, during, and after the Revolution," Le Brun concludes that "Sade will always attribute to this world both a very real unreality and a no less unreal reality; one must also realize that his theatre has the requisite qualities to figure in such a world." She goes on to speculate that the Marquis's interest in the French Revolution itself may stem from the inherent theatricality of the situation:

> It is as if theatricalization is the only mode of being Sade finds valid for both the individual and the collectivity; as if the idea of theatricality induces something which is never induced in Sade: the impossible encounter of the individual and the mass. It lasts as long as the performance: just long enough to set up an order and undo it, long enough for a scene to develop and disintegrate, long enough for desire to assume a form and then escape from it. In other words, it lasts as long as desire, which establishes the rhythms of Sade's thought and creates, like a vital necessity, the pattern of scene changes.

Le Brun agrees with Brochier in his view of the normative function of Sade's plays and defends their conventionality, especially given the environment in which the Marquis wrote:

While all else starts to totter with the progress of philosophy, the stage remains, quite oddly, the last refuge of order: a closed space in which traditional figures, stereotyped gestures, and social codes continue to produce meaning, just at a time when men's minds are haunted by an absence of meaning.

If Sade sought to be produced on the eighteenth-century French public stage, governed by the neoclassical rule of verisimilitude, he would have had to create works according to an accepted formula.[1] Tragedy, comedy, and the new bourgeois forms of *comédie larmoyante* and the *drame* all had structural and thematic requirements, while the principle of verisimilitude demanded that plays depict situations that could appear in real life, provide moral lessons, and offer universal truths. Given such parameters, it is not surprising that de Sade's plays are considered conventional, ridden with clichés and overly sentimental.

However, since only *Le Comte Oxtiern* and the first three scenes of *Le Suborneur* (*The Briber*) were ever performed, a closer examination of the plays reveals a different truth. Perhaps they were not conventional enough. Sade's *Julia, or Marriage without Women*, for example, a one-act vaudeville (unfortunately lost), went against the grain since it idealized pederasty. A five-act tragedy, *Jeanne Laisné* broke the rules by the inclusion of a realistic battle scene, continuous action on stage, during the intermission and an indecorous relationship between characters of unequal birth (all elements that would find a place in the melodramas of the next century). In *Le Prévaricateur (The Shyster)*, the eponymous character ridiculed hackneyed theatrical devices and called for the suspension of

---

[1] It is important to note that in addition to the public stage, a number of eighteenth-century French aristocratic private theatres came into existence to produce pornographic plays, free of neoclassical resrictions, with both amateur and professional actors. The chief exponent of the genre, Delisle de Sales (1741–1816), published four volumes of *Théâtre d'amour* in 1780, as Karl Toepfer suggests, "to document the power of theatre to function as an ultimate encyclopedia of lust, perversion, and depravity." In his book, *Theatre, Aristocracy, and Pornocracy*, Toepfer maintains that the second half of the eighteenth century also saw the emergence of taboo words in plays designed for private audiences since "language must transgress a taboo... in order to drive speakers or listeners toward ecstasy." Certainly the Marquis de Sade was aware of such activity; perhaps he even dabbled in the genre. However, the ten plays that head the list in his *Descriptive Catalogue of 1788* clearly indicate that Sade did not choose to create pornographic plays. In associating the clandestine, pornographic theatre with orgy, Toepfer speculates why such a form would not appeal to de Sade:

dramatic rules, the imitation of Shakespeare, onstage torture, and realistic blood effects.

Gorer in *The Devil's Disciple: The Revolutionary Theories of the Marquis de Sade* and Annie Le Brun both cite *La Ruse d'Amour ou Les Six Spectacles (The Tricks of Love; or, The Six Spectacles)* as especially innovative. In his *Descriptive Catalogue*, the Marquis described the effort as an "episodic comedy in six thousand lines of irregular verse and prose, lasting five hours in performance," but in fact, the work was a compilation of five separate genres—*drame*, comedy, *opéra-comique*, pantomime, and ballet—each of which portrayed, from a different point of view, the simple plot of a girl being forced by her father to marry against her will. The Marquis's description of the metatheatrical aspects of the piece displayed a certain amount of originality (which, of course, ultimately rendered the work unproduceable):

> What is unusual about this play is that it has no moments of rest and that the action is continuous, because after each episode the company is supposed to go back into the dressing-rooms to change costumes and rehearse the next scene; but the dressing rooms are actually on stage,... thus the action... is constantly in progress without ever slowing down.

Sade claimed to have introduced yet another structural innovation in *Le Misanthrope par Amour (Love Makes the Misanthrope)*, a five-act, free-verse comedy written before 1785. Citing the authority of Aristotle and Horace, Sade introduced each act with an elaborate pantomime designed to portray the events that happened offstage. Reminiscent of the Elizabethan dumb show, the device clearly owed more to Shakespeare than Racine and anticipated similar devices in post-revolutionary melodrama. While these departures from eighteenth-century theatrical convention might pale compared to the graphic sexual tortures described in *The 120 Days of Sodom*, the fact remains that Sade was not simply pandering to neoclassical

---

Libertine literature constructs an "impossible" realm of fantasy insofar as it is a vigorous critique of a moral system which sets (or "inscribes") limits on the range or magnitude of the "possible," of the desires defining "nature." As Jean-Pierre Dubost observes in relation to Sade's writing, libertine literature emerges out of a profound sense of loneliness. Though it revels in dialogue and theatricalizing rhetoric, libertine literature is pleasure for people who are alone. The writing and reading of it has more to do with solitary masturbation than with orgy.

tradition, but was instead seeking his own distinctive dramatic voice.

Certainly, a kind of fantastic loneliness pervades Sade's theatre. In play after play, characters find themselves faced with the dilemma of either seeking acceptance by the group or going it alone. Though this is hardly an original dramatic device, in the plays of the Marquis de Sade, the decision-making process always involves a reexamination of social values—a sort of debate between private and public codes of behavior—which often results in a reinscription of the social order. In comedies such *Les Jumelles (The Twins)*, the young lover who rejects society's conventions of courtship wins out while the other who embraces them is ridiculed; in *Le Philosophe Soi-Disant (The Self-Proclaimed Philosopher)*, the eponymous, self-styled misanthrope is forced to wear society's trappings as a travesty of his own hypocrisy; and in *Le Boudoir*, the husband finds himself happily facilitating his own cuckolding to prove to society that he was wrongly suspicious of his wife's infidelities.

In the *drames* such as *Franchise et Trahison (Truth and Treason)*, the young lover becomes an unwilling accomplice to wrongdoing in order to secure his beloved. When he chooses to do good, his actions render him worthy of her, but he must give her up to another, even more suitable young man to whom she had previously been pledged. Having embraced his own ethical code of behavior, he finds himself content, but alone and unrewarded socially. In *Henriette et Saint-Clair (Henrietta and Saint-Clair)*, a young man finds himself unknowingly involved in an incestuous relationship with a girl believed to be his sister. He refuses to break off the relationship because his private code of behavior sees nothing wrong with it and in the face of public scandal and the subsequent engagement between his "sister" and his best friend, he decides that death is the only solution. The fact that the girl turns out to be his best friend's sister reinforces the accuracy of the young man's inner feelings and inverts the public ethos, since to avoid incest, society arranges an incestuous match. In every case, the Marquis de Sade appears to be suggesting that morality is a private, not a public, matter.

In Sade's only tragedy, *Jeanne Laisné*, the loneliness of nonconformity pervades the play. The heroic title character alone argues relentlessly against the stereotypical role of women in society; a solitary foreign spy within enemy walls must effect his sovereign's control of the city; after failing to conform to the wishes of the City Council demanding that he alone kill the father of the woman he loves, the young lover must go unaided through enemy territory to warn the allies; finally, the mayor becomes a social outcast in his moral decision to betray his city in order to save it from destruction.

Despite his many self-avowed innovations in theatrical form, Sade does not appear to have been interested in creating particularly original plots. In the introductory essays to many of his plays, he compares his version with that of better-known dramatists and admits to the duplication of ideas. In the preface to *Les Jumelles*, for example, he discusses mistaken identity in plays by Plautus, Molière, Regnard, and Palissot and concludes that "Everything hasn't been said, or it hasn't been enough, because man is not incorrigible; and if virtue does not win him over, it's because it is rarely presented in a way that would attract him." Clearly the Marquis sees himself as a social critic and seeks to correct or control (some would say in a not untypically sadistic fashion) man's social behavior. To the modern reader, his espousal of what is viewed as conventional morality in the plays is certainly less provocative than his sexual flights of fancy in the novels. Yet, viewed from a feminist-historical perspective, his condemnation in the plays of the treatment of women in a male-dominant society clearly demonstrates as far-reaching an imagination. His speaking out in favor of autonomy for women is certainly in step with the libertarian ideas of Beaumarchais, whose *The Marriage of Figaro* was called "the revolution in action" by Napoleon. Yet, when *Figaro* was finally produced at the Comédie Française on 27 April 1784, the feminist scene condemning the subjugation of women by men was omitted because it was considered too *dangerous*. It is not improbable that theatres refused to produce Sade's plays because they found his feminist rhetoric equally dangerous.

This aspect of danger is significant as it demonstrates the power of the stage to influence people, to enrage them, to delight them. The Marquis de Sade was highly appreciative of the (Gorer might suggest "sadistic") potential of controlling people's activities through theatre. In a long letter written in 1799 to a deputy of the French Republic, Sade argues:

> [I]t is at the theatre rather than somewhere else that we must revive the almost extinguished flame of the love that every Frenchman owes his country; there is where he'll be convinced of the dangers that would exist for him should he fall back into the hands of tyranny. He'll carry home the enthusiasm and teach it to his family and its effects will be so much more durable, so much more passionate than the momentary inspirations of a newspaper article or proclamation because at the theatre, he learns the lesson by example, and he remembers it.

Sade was serious about writing for the theatre.[2] He was acutely aware of its requirements as well as its potential. Brochier concludes that he was even more enthusiastic about his dramatic work than his "pornographic" novels, for in a letter dated 12 June 1791 to Reinaud, his lawyer, the Marquis writes:

> At the moment a novel of mine is being printed, but it is too immoral a work to be sent to so circumspect, religious and modest a man as yourself. I needed money, my publisher said he wanted it well-peppered so I gave it to him fit to plague the devil himself. It is called *Justine, or the Misfortunes of Virtue*. If by chance it comes your way, burn it without reading it.

This is the third iteration of my translations of the plays of the Marquis de Sade. Although readers will find much familiar material in these pages, all of the translations, introductions, forewords, and prefaces have been corrected and revised. Except in *The Marriage of the Century*, which exists primarily as a scenario rather than a finished play, I have discarded Sade's use of French scenes dividing the action of the play according to the entrance or exit of a character. This was done to allow the action to flow more easily on the printed page and to render the plays more modern in appearance. Much of Sade's work still resonates in the twenty-first century and I hope that this attempt to contemporize the look of Sade's drama will make the work more appealing and available to readers and performers. As in the earlier editions, the translations are designed

---

[2] The closest the Marquis de Sade comes to disavowing a play is in a letter to his wife dated 26 April 1781 when he begs her not to judge *Le Capricieux* on the merits of *Les Jumelles*.

to be performable and not simply literal transcriptions from the French. Sade's rhymed hexameter verse plays have been rendered in unrhymed iambic and trochaic pentameter in an attempt to mirror, in English, the cadence of the French and differentiate them from the more colloquial prose plays. Also, for the first time, the plays are presented in chronological order (based on best evidence in the case of undated plays) so that the reader might experience and appreciate Sade's development as a playwright.

In the critical morass of speculation regarding the relativity of the Marquis's plays to his non-dramatic works, at least one thing is certain: they deserve to be read. Suggesting that each of the Marquis de Sade's plays is a great work of art is as foolish as claiming that there is no value in any of them. Even critics like Geoffrey Gorer and Gilbert Lély, who dislike Sade's theatre, have found something worthwhile in the plays, if only for their curiosity value. And it must be noted that critics are not always in agreement over the merits of a particular play. Dawes and Rodmell, for example, consider *Oxtiern* "a bad play" of "little significance" while Bloch and Cleugh find it "exciting enough for Verdi or Mascagni... with all the verve and sense of the theatre of which the author was a master" and the only one of the extant plays "worthy of mention." Perhaps it is enough then that, good or bad, the plays provide us with yet another perspective regarding one of the most unorthodox, innovative, and controversial literary minds of the eighteenth century.

John Franceschina, June 2013

Biographical Preface

On 2 June 1740 in the Condé mansion in Paris, the Marquis de Sade was the second child born to Marie-Eleonore de Maillé de Carman, lady-in-waiting to the princess de Condé and Jean-Baptiste-Joseph-François, Count de Sade, lord of the manors of Saumane and La Coste, Lieutenant-General of the provinces of Bresse, Bugey, Valromey, and Gex, and Ambassador from Louis XV to the Elector of Cologne, to the court of Russia, and then to George II of England. On June 3, two servants acted as godparents to the child and misnamed him for the record, a mishap that would plague Sade with the authorities for the rest of his life, especially during the Republic. Supposed to be called Louis-Aldonse-Donatien, he was in fact named Donatien-Alphonse-François. On 24 January 1745, Sade's paternal uncle, a forty-year-old dissolute priest and personal friend of Voltaire, assumed the position of Abbot at the Benedictine monastery of Saint Leger d'Ebreuil and took responsibility for Sade's education.

In 1750, Sade returned to Paris to study at a Jesuit College and four years later, on his father's orders, he entered the cavalry school of the Royal Garde in Versailles. On 14 December 1755, he was appointed sub-lieutenant without pay in the King's Own Infantry Regiment. A little over a year later, on 14 January 1757, he was granted a commission as standard bearer in the Carbine Regiment and participated in the Seven Years' War against Prussia. He was granted leave in 1759 when he returned to Paris to begin living a dissipated life in an attempt to outdo the excesses of his fellow officers in drinking, whoring, and various alternative sexual exploits. At this time, his father, suspicious of Sade's activities, paid one of his son's comrades to spy on him. In spite of his excessive behavior, Sade was promoted to captain in the Burgundy cavalry on 21 April 1759.

In 1760, Sade's mother retired to a Carmelite convent in Paris and his father assigned various estates to his son. In late February 1763, the war came to an end and Sade returned to Paris for a life of sex and debauchery. He was continually involved in gambling debts and duels, was a regular patron of the theatre boudoirs, and did not even consider it necessary to pay the customary respects to the King. As a mark of his profligacy, Sade became engaged to two women simultaneously: Mlle. Laure de Lauris of Avignon, whom he really loved and who ultimately left him for another man; and Renée-Pélagie de Montreuil, who came from a wealthy family tied to the Paris legal and official nobility. In his *Portrait of de Sade*, Walter Lenning suggests that the Marquis's reputation was so bad that the Montreuil family was the only one of means in Paris that would accept him as a son-in-law. Ultimately because of financial problems, Sade was forced by his father to marry Renée de Montreuil on 17 May 1763. The marriage did not prevent Sade from continuing in his dissolute lifestyle and his mother-in-law had him shadowed by Inspector Marais of the Paris police.

On 29 October, by order of the King, Sade was committed to Vincennes Prison for excesses committed in a brothel he had been frequenting for about a month. Jeanne Testard, a prostitute, filed charges against Sade with the Paris police, saying that he had mistreated her, birched her brutally, forced her to commit sodomy, and made her trample on a crucifix and shout at Christ's image, "Fuck off, you bastard!" She went on to say that Sade spoke "countless blasphemies and dreadful oaths, declaring that there was no God and that he could prove it, that he had masturbated and defiled a chalice which he kept for more than two hours in a church chapel, that Jesus Christ was a slippery customer and the Virgin was a bitch." After two weeks, his mother-in-law had him released from prison, but negotiated lettres de cachet[3] with the King, who commanded him to withdraw to Échauffour Manor, a property owned by the Montreuil family in Normandy. From there Sade could not leave except by special permission.

On 4 May 1764, Sade obtained permission to go to Dijon only to remain there long enough to perform in his official capacity as lieutenant-general for the King. He inaugurated a theatre at the Chateau d'Évry with several plays in which he functioned as actor and director. Between July and December, he fell in love with the actress Collette, Mlle. Le Roy, a ballet dancer, and Mlle. Le Clair,

---

[3] Lettres de cachet were documents signed by the king of France by which an individual could be sentenced to prison without trial and the opportunity to defend himself. Wealthy members of society often purchased lettres de cachet to dispose of unwanted relatives or lovers. Such was obviously the case with Sade's mother-in-law.

a supernumerary at the Opera. On 7 December, Police Inspector Marais noted that Sade was in Paris and requested that La Brissualt, a famous Paris madam, "refrain from providing the Marquis with girls to go to any private chambers with him." On 21 December, Marais reported that Collette was a severe financial burden on Sade, who was quickly discovering the amount of money necessary to entertain an actress of the Théâtre Italien.

In January 1765, Sade fell in love with Mlle. Beauvoisin, the twenty-four-year-old lead dancer at the Opera, actress, and prostitute who was also the toast of all the young fops in Paris. He took her to his family chateau at La Coste, where he passed her off at various times as his wife or his wife's cousin and in her honor sponsored many expensive balls and theatrical productions. His uncle the Abbé was a frequent guest at Sade's parties and though he and Mme. Montreuil knew about Sade's affair with the actress, they managed to keep it from his wife. In September, Sade and Beauvoisin returned to Paris, where the affair dissolved in January 1766.

Throughout 1766 Sade traveled, trying to raise money from his various estates. On 4 November, he rented a furnished cottage in the suburbs of Arcueil, which would be the scene of many a sex scandal in the coming years. On 24 January 1767, his father died, leaving his son the marquis as his sole heir. On 16 April, Sade was again promoted in his regiment to captain-commander and ordered to assemble his company without delay. Four days later, under the pretext of going off with his regiment, Sade rejoined Beauvoisin in Lyons, leaving his wife, who was, by this time, five months pregnant (on 27 August his first son, Louis Marie, was born). On 16 October, Inspector Marais reported that Sade had unsuccessfully tried to induce Mlle. Rivière, a ballet dancer at the Opera, to live with him, and on Easter Sunday, 3 April 1768, Sade accosted Rose Keller, the widow of a pastry cook's assistant. A cotton-spinner by trade and out of work for about a month, Rose agreed to accompany Sade to his cottage in Arcueil. There, he threatened her with a knife, ordered her to undress, and flogged her. Then he locked her in a room from which she somehow managed to escape and ran straight to the authorities. On 7 April, Sade's wife and mother-in-law sent emissaries to Rose Keller to obtain her agreement to drop all charges in return for 2400 livres and seven gold louis for dressings and medications. She refused to be bought off and a trial ensued between April and June 1768, during which time the marquis was housed at the somewhat relaxed prison of Pierre-Encise near Lyons.

In August 1769, Sade's wife went to Lyons to be close to her husband, who was released three months later on 16 November by means of a royal pardon. Virtually under house arrest, Sade returned to La Coste, where he produced more theatrical entertainments and ran up more debts. On 27 June, his second son, Donatien-Claude-Armand, was born and, from September through the end of October, the marquis traveled in the Netherlands for unspecified reasons.

The following August 1770, when Sade attempted to resume his military duties as captain-commander in the Burgundy Regiment, he was at once placed under arrest by the deputy commander, who forbade anyone to take orders from the dissolute marquis. After some haggling, the matter was resolved with Sade being reinstated in his duties. On 17 April 1771, his daughter Madeleine-Laure was born and Sade was thrown into debtors' prison late in August on account of the unpaid debts incurred because of his dissolute lifestyle as well as his theatrical activities. To obtain his release, he negotiated a formula for repayment that required the immediate payment of 3000 francs in cash and the balance due in a promissory note dated 15 October. On 7 November, Sade's sister-in-law, Mlle. Anne-Prospère de Launay de Montreuil, joined the family at La Coste and the marquis immediately fell head-over-heels in love with her. On 20 January 1772 at the theatre in La Coste, Sade produced his first play, *The Self-Proclaimed Philosopher*. Later that year in June, the marquis and his valet, a young man named Latour, with whom Sade is said to have practiced sodomy, set out for Marseilles for the purpose of collecting taxes due on his estates.

On 25 June, Sade sent Latour out to find girls with whom they might entertain themselves. Two days later, Latour arranged a rendezvous with four girls between the ages of 18 and 23: Marianne Lavern, Marianette Laugier, Rose Coste, and Mariette Borelly. In the course of the morning, Sade and Latour sequestered themselves with the girls singly, then jointly. At least two of the girls were offered Spanish fly and the orgy continued throughout the day. That night, the last Sade was to spend in Marseilles, Latour found yet another girl, Marguerite Coste, who was also given Spanish fly. On 30 June, Marguerite Coste complained to the Royal Prosecutor of being poisoned and a pharmacist was appointed to examine her. The following day, the four prostitutes accused Sade and Latour of homosexual sodomy and claimed to have refused their unnatural advances. On 4 July, the marquis and Latour, officially informed of their impending arrest, fled to Italy, taking Sade's sister-in-law with them. The following September, Sade and Latour were found guilty of sodomy and poisoning and sentenced to death by decapitation (the marquis's sentence) and hanging (Latour's punishment); and on 12 September, Sade and Latour were executed in effigy. After having traveled under a variety of assumed names, still with Latour and Anne, Sade was finally captured on 8 December at Chambery by his mother-in-law, who persuaded the King of Sardinia to throw Sade into the Miolans fortress in Savoy, where Latour voluntarily joined Sade in prison.

On 30 April 1773 at 8:30 p.m., Sade, the Baron de l'Allée (a fellow prisoner with whom Sade was wont to share an evening meal), and Latour climbed out of the only unbarred window at the fortress and escaped to the French frontier. After having spent some time in Grenoble, Sade rejoined his wife at La Coste, where he tried to have his trial resumed and sentence lifted. On 16 December, after Lady de Montreuil used her lettres de cachet to have the Marquis incarcerated again in the Pierre Encise prison, Sade fled the authorities and wandered between various residences throughout 1774. In November, the "young girls" scandal occurred when the marquis hired seven new servants for the house: a young maid named Nanon, five fifteen-year-old girls, and a young male secretary of about seventeen. In January, three of the children's parents filed a complaint and criminal proceedings were instituted at Lyons, where the marquis tried to hush up the affair. On 21 January 1775, Sade formally refuted the charges, but on 3 May, the President Bruny d'Entrecastaux informed the authorities that he had it on good authority that the Marquis de Sade indulged in excesses of every kind with young people of both sexes, whom he kidnapped particularly from Lyons.

When on 11 May, Nanon, the chambermaid, gave birth to a daughter, the father was rumored to be Sade even though the baptismal record identified the father as Barthélemy Fayere. A week later, the Abbé de Sade requested the capture of his nephew and demanded that he be incarcerated as a madman. In July, with Mme. de Montreuil having threatened new imprisonment with the lettres de cachet, Sade fled once again to Italy under the name of Comte de Mazan, but a year later, Sade returned to France amid rumors that he had become religious and had even been granted an audience with Pope Pius VI. In his new *piety*, Sade engaged the services of a monk, Father Durand, to find him a cook for La Coste. The monk convinced Catherine Treillet's father that La Coste was like a nunnery as far as morals go and, on 2 November, the very pretty twenty-two-year-old was taken to the chateau by the priest. The following December, Sade engaged four new servants, three young women and a young man, who were each seduced by the marquis the night following their arrival and who left the following day, warning Mr. Treillet of the goings-on at the chateau. On 17 January, Mr. Treillet went to La Coste to claim his daughter, who was known there as Justine, and during a heated argument with the Marquis, he fired a shot at Sade point blank, but missed his mark. Later that afternoon, Treillet returned to the chateau with four other men equipped with muskets, who emptied their firearms into the courtyard where Sade was supposed to have been. Having assassinated the wrong man, the five ran away.

Acquitted of the attempted murder and seduction of minors, Sade and his wife went to Paris, where he was arrested by Inspector Marais on 13 February 1777 and formally entered as a prisoner at Vincennes. This continued the series of Sade's incarcerations by means of lettres de cachet and the marquis's extensive prison correspondence described the horror of his situation. He noted that cages should be reserved for savage beasts, not for human beings: "I am in a tower closed in by nineteen iron doors, with light reaching me only through two little windows, each with a score of iron bars." In addition, he complained that, in over two months of imprisonment, he had been allowed only five walks of one hour each "in a sort of tomb about forty feet square surrounded by walls more than fifty feet high."

On 14 June, Sade went to Aix to resume the trial that had pronounced him guilty in 1772. From 7 to 10 July, Sade was cross-examined and, on 14 July, the Court admonished his behavior, ordered him to pay a fine, and prohibited his living in or around Marseilles for a period of three years. In effect, the death sentence had been overturned, but the marquis was still a man in chains due to his imprisonment on 13 February 1777. On 16 July, at an inn where he and his guards stopped for the night, the marquis made his escape, returning to La Coste two days later, where he spent a month with the governess, Dorothée de Rouset. On 26 August, a vigilante mob stormed La Coste and dragged out the marquis, who was returned to Vincennes and locked in Cell No.6 on 7 September.

By 1780, Sade found enjoyment in writing plays in his prison cell and stirring up the other inmates.[4] On 13 July 1781, two months after the death of his sister-in-law Anne, Sade was allowed his first visit from his wife, whom he had not seen in four and a half years, although they were permitted to meet only in the presence of witnesses. A year later on 12 July 1782, Sade completed the manuscript of his *Dialogue between a Priest and a Dying Man*, but on 6 August, Sade was deprived of all his books because prison officials felt that they "overheat his head" and lead him to write "unseemly things." On 3 March 1784, Sade was moved to an octagonal room about fifteen feet wide and nine feet high in the Bastille, where the Marquise de Sade was allowed to visit her husband twice a month. During this early incarceration at the Bastille, an eye doctor was allowed to treat Sade's failing eyesight because of the kindness and goodwill of Le Noir, the Chief of Police in Paris. On 22 October 1785, the marquis began the final revision of *The 120 Days of Sodom; or, The School for Libertines*, which he completed thirty-seven days later on 28 November on one side of a roll of paper twelve meters long. On July 8 1787, Sade completed *Les Infortunes de la Vertu*, a philosophical work of about 138 pages written in two weeks while suffering from eye trouble. The following March (1 March 1788), Sade began work on his short novel, *Eugenie de Franval*, which was completed in six days, and on 1 October, he drew up the *Catalogue raisonné* of his written works (which by this time had amounted to fifteen octavo volumes).

---

[4] One of his most celebrated riots developed out of his dislike for fellow prisoner Honoré Gabriel Riqueti, count de Mirabeau, whom Sade called the commandant's "catamite," suggesting that he might go and "kiss the warden's ass."

On 2 July 1789, the Bastille logbook stated that "The Count de Sade shouted several times from the window of the Bastille that the prisoners were being slaughtered and that the people should come to liberate them." Two days later, he was transferred to Charenton Asylum, an asylum run by the friars known as the *Petits Pères*. Ten days later, on 14 July, the Bastille was stormed and Sade's cell was plundered. His furniture, his suits and linen, his library, and, most significantly, his manuscripts were burned, pillaged, torn up, and carried off. It is important to note that prisons in the eighteenth century permitted inmates the lifestyle to which they were accustomed—for a fee. Sade had to pay 2,400 livres for his "keep" at the Bastille for which he was allowed: a desk, a wardrobe, a full complement of shirts, silk breeches, frock coats, dressing gowns, boots and shoes, family portraits, tapestries, velvet cushions and pillows, candles and oil lamps, and a library of 133 books. The following October, Madame de Sade escaped from Paris accompanied by her daughter and a maid to avoid being dragged out by the women of lower classes to join them in their march to seize the king. She remarked that the King had been brought from Versailles to Paris with the heads of his two bodyguards set on pikes before him and that Paris was in a state of *intoxication*. In much of his dramatic writing, Sade used the term *intoxication* synonymously with madness, passion, and foolishness.

On 2 April 1790, Sade was freed because all lettres de cachet were declared invalid by the Constituent Assembly of the Revolution. The following day, the Marquise de Sade, who had decided to divorce her dissolute husband, entered a convent and, on June 9, a separation order was decreed ordering Sade to restore to his wife 160,842 livres received as a marriage settlement. Now unencumbered by wife or title, Sade returned to the profession of playwright and his *Le Suborneur* (*The Briber*) was accepted for performance by the Comédie-Italien on 3 August 1790. Two weeks later, Sade gave a reading at the Comédie-Française of his one-act play, *The Bedroom*, but the play was rejected. The following 25 August, Sade began an affair with Marie-Constance Quesnet (née Renelle), a young actress who had just been deserted by her husband and left with a small child. This "less than Platonic" union would last for the rest of his life. On 16 September, his five-act sentimental comedy *Love*

Makes the Misanthrope was unanimously accepted by the Comédie-Française and by 5 March 1791, Sade had had five plays accepted by various theatres in Paris.

On 22 October 1791, *Count Oxtiern; or, The Dangers of Debauchery* was given its first performance at the Théâtre Molière. Two weeks later, a second performance incited a riot and plans for further performances of the play were suspended. On 24 November, Sade's Romantic tragedy (anticipating Victor Hugo's *Hernani* by some forty years), *Jeanne Laisné; or, The Siege of Beauvais* was rejected by the Comédie Française by an eight to five vote. The following 5 March, at the Théâtre-Italien, a Jacobin clique, all wearing red caps, made so much noise that the performance of *Le Suborneur* had to be halted after the fourth scene. The following May, after his son deserted from the army, Sade disavowed his son's activities and became actively involved in revolutionary politics. Four months later on 3 September 1792, when ten thousand prisoners were slaughtered throughout Paris, Sade became secretary of his "section" of the city, an act that had little political benefit for him for, two weeks later, an unruly mob of women and children ransacked his chateau at La Coste and destroyed nearly all of the furnishings. Undeterred, Sade continued to be an active member of the political machine during the Terror, writing various political pamphlets and serving as delegate to the National Convention. However, on 8 December 1793, a warrant was issued for his arrest and Sade was imprisoned at Picpus, only a few hundred yards from the guillotine. He narrowly escaped being among those beheaded during the July massacres in 1794 (evidently, the authorities were unable to locate him!), but on 13 October 1794, the Committee of General Safety freed Sade in consideration of his patriotic work and authorized him to reside in his house on the Neuve-des-Mathurins.

In November of 1797, Sade learned that his name had been placed on a list of émigrés, which meant that he was liable to be arrested yet again and all his property and possessions confiscated. He filed a protest with the police department and began a period of hand-to-mouth existence, living in an unheated attic and working at a Versailles theatre for forty sous a day. On 13 December 1799, *Oxtiern; or, The Dangers of Debauchery* (the tile slightly revised, omitting any reference to nobility) was revived under the auspices of the Dramatic Society of Versailles with Sade playing the character of Fabrice. By January 1800, Sade was "dying of cold and hunger," continually writing to friends in an attempt to elicit money. He narrowly escaped debtor's prison in February and the October publication of his novel, *The Crimes of Love*, raised such a furor that he and his publisher were arrested the following March. On 5 April 1801, Sade was incarcerated in Sainte-Pélagie prison, then transferred to Bicêtre prison and finally to the Charenton Asylum, where he was judged to be insane. On 8 September 1801, Dubois, the prefect of police, described Sade as an "incorrigible man" in a state of "constant licentious insanity" and of a character "hostile to any form of restraint."

Beginning in 1803 through 1813, Sade began to stage plays at the asylum, which were patronized by the leading theatre-goers of Paris (as well as the inmates of the asylum). In addition, he produced a number of new prose novels, of which *Histoire d'Émilie* and *Les Journées de Florbelle* are most significant. On 5 June 1807, the manuscripts of several of his works were seized and destroyed, forcing Sade to take immediate action. On 17 June 1808, Sade penned an impassioned plea to Napoleon requesting liberation from the asylum and on 2 August, he was judged to be sane by the Chief Medical Officer of Charenton, who argued that Sade's only madness was vice. It was also rumored that Sade was living in the asylum with a woman (Mme. Quesnet, who had moved into Charenton on her own initiative to be with Sade) whom he passed off as his daughter. The Medical Officer advised that the theatre at Charenton be closed down and that Sade be transferred to some other prison or fortress, a plan that was never implemented. On 18 October, Sade was considered a dangerous influence on the other inmates of Charenton and ordered to be given separate lodging, forbidden to communicate with anyone else and denied the use of pen and paper. The following March, nearly a year after Sade had written to him, Napoleon considered Sade's request for liberty and denied it. On 6 May 1813, all theatrical presentations were forbidden at Charenton and by 1 December 1814, Sade, whose health had been failing gradually, was unable to walk. The following day, the Marquis de Sade died of pulmonary congestion and was buried in the cemetery at Charenton in accordance with the rites of the

Catholic Church, absolutely contrary to the strict instructions of his 1806 will that stated:

> I forbid my body to be opened on any pretext whatever. I demand that it shall be left for forty-eight hours in an open wooden coffin in the room in which I died. Only after these forty-eight hours may the lid of the coffin be nailed down. During this time a message shall be sent as quickly as possible to Monsieur La Normand, wood merchant, of 101 Boulevard de l'Égalité, Versailles, requesting him to come personally with his cart to remove my remains to the forest on my land near Malmaison, in the parish of Emancé near Epernon. My body shall be buried without any ceremony in the first copse on the right-hand side, as seen from the direction of the old chateau. My grave shall be dug by the farmers of Malmaison under the surveillance of Monsieur La Normand, who shall not leave my body until it has been buried as I here describe. If Monsieur La Norman desires, those of my relations and friends who wish to show me this last mark of respect may attend, provided they do not wear mourning clothes. As soon as the grave is filled in, acorns should be planted over it, so that new trees will grow out of it later, and the wood will be thick as it was before. All traces of my grave shall vanish from the face of the earth, as I expect that my memory will vanish from the minds of men. Made at Charenton, Saint-Maurice, in a condition of sanity and health. D.A.F. Sade.

In life, the Marquis de Sade was five feet, six inches tall with blond or light chestnut hair "gathered in a bag" at the back of his head. He was rather stout of build with fair complexion, slightly pitted by smallpox, but with attractive features, a regular nose, a small mouth, pale blue eyes, high forehead, and a rounded chin. His valet, Latour, inseparable companion of his escapades, was somewhat taller, thinner, similarly pockmarked, and had darker hair, worn loose. Unlike his biographers, the Marquis did not consider himself especially debauched. In a letter to his wife dated 20 February 1781, while he was a prisoner of the Bastille, he states:

> I am a libertine, but I am neither a *criminal* nor a *murderer*, and since I am compelled to set my apology next to my vindication,

I shall therefore say that it might well be possible that those, who condemn me as unjustly as I have been, might themselves be unable to offset their infamies by good works as clearly established as those I can contrast to my errors. I am a libertine, but three families residing in your area have for five years lived off my charity, and I have saved them from the deepest depths of poverty. I am a libertine, but I have saved a deserter from death, a deserter abandoned by his entire regiment and by his colonel. I am a libertine, but at Évry, with your whole family looking on, I saved a child—at the risk of my life—who was on the verge of being crushed beneath the wheels of a runaway horse-drawn cart. I am a libertine, but I have never compromised my wife's health. Nor have I been guilty of the other kinds of libertinage so often fatal to children's fortunes: have I ruined them by gambling or by other expenses that might have deprived them of, or even by one day foreshortened, their inheritance? Have I managed my own fortune badly, as long as I had a say in the matter? In a word, did I in my youth herald a heart capable of the atrocities of which today I stand accused?... How therefore do you presume that, from so innocent a childhood and youth, I have suddenly arrived at the ultimate of premeditated horror? No, you do not believe it. And you who today tyrannize me so cruelly, you do not believe it either: your vengeance has beguiled your mind. You have proceeded blindly to tyrannize, but your heart knows mine; it judges it more fairly, and it knows full well it is innocent.

Sadeian Theatricals

Many of the works in this volume represent the Marquis de Sade's interest in amateur theatricals, a practice that had been popular in France throughout the eighteenth century at court, throughout Paris, and in the provinces. Gentlemen of wealth or title were drawn to the theatre as a means of self-promotion and, as Francine du Plessix Gray remarked in *At Home with the Marquis de Sade*, "most every gentleman of substance in France had a theater on his estate." The Marquis de Sade was no exception and early in his married life, he appropriated the private theatre close to his in-laws' country house at Évry, twenty miles from Paris, and built a provincial theatre at his own residence at La Coste.

The theatrical season at Évry began on 17 April 1764 with a short *tribute* (included in this volume) begging tolerance and applause from an audience comprised mostly of Sade's female relatives. According to Maurice Lever, the repertoire at Évry consisted of *Le Retour imprévu (The Unexpected Return)*, a one-act prose comedy by Jean-François Regnard, originally produced by the Théâtre-Français in 1700; *L'Avocat Patelin (Patelin the Lawyer)*, a prose adaptation of the medieval farce *Maistre Pierre Pathelin* by Abbé Brueys and Jean Palaprat, initially produced in 1706; *Heureusement (Thank Goodness!)*, a one-act verse comedy by Rochon de Chabannes, recently performed by the Théâtre-Français in 1762; *Nanine; ou, le Préjugé vaincu (Nanine; or, Prejudice Vanquished)*, a three-act verse comedy by Voltaire, originally produced in 1749; and *Le Méchant (The Wicked Man)*, a five-act verse comedy by Jean-Baptiste-Louis Gresset that premiered in 1747 and in which Sade performed the eponymous role, Cléon. In addition to the marquis, the other performers included Sade's wife, his mother-in-law, Madame d'Évry, Madame de Plissay, Madame de Bourneville, Madame de Mondran, his brother-in-law Monsieur de Launay, Monsieur de Lionne, Monsieur de Ripière, Monsieur de Noinville, and a boy from the Évry household. Clearly, Sade's earliest theatrical ventures were designed to be family entertainments, a practice initially supported by his wife and mother-in-law to keep Sade off the streets of Paris and out of the arms of professional actresses. In fact, the theatrical season at Évry only succeeded in inflaming Sade's passion for theatrical trysts and between July and December 1764, he developed liaisons with Mlle. Colet, an actress at the Théâtre-Italienne, Mlle. Le Roy, a ballet dancer, and Mlle. Le Clair, a supernumerary at the Opéra.

By the early 1770s, Sade's amateur theatricals had blossomed to such a degree that the theatre at la Coste had to be enlarged to seat sixty people comfortably with additional space for sixty standing spectators. Francine du Plessix Gray describes the interior of the theatre:

> Its blue stage curtain was fitted with an intricate mechanism that allowed it to be operated from the lobby; the theatre was lit by sixty-five metal candleholders and twenty-four fairy lights. The permanent scenery represented a salon, as was customary in the eighteenth century but this setting could be altered by adding backdrops of painted canvas (the other two panoramas used at la Coste depicted a town square and, ominously, a prison).

When the 1772 season of performances began on 3 May,[5] Sade had already engaged twelve actors and actresses (including Bourdais and his wife) as performers,[6] put the management of the theatre into Bourdais's hands, and entrusted a man named Bernus with the care and upkeep of the building. Because Sade had decided to produce a festival of plays that alternated at weekly intervals between La Coste and his estate at Mazan (thirty-five miles away), he had to hire stagehands, hairdressers, concessionaires, even two policemen to quell disturbances, as well as the usual complement of candles and heating implements. According to a communication dated 1 April 1772, this would cost the marquis seventy *livres* per performance, a sum exacerbated by Sade's own predacious addiction to sweets and

---

[5] The first production of 1772, scheduled on 20 January, was Sade's first original comedy, *Le Philosophe soi-disant (The Self-Proclaimed Philosopher)*. It, however, was not included in the regular repertory season that began in May.

[6] This group of professional though second-rate actors were to be given room, board, and a salary of 800 *livres*. Evidently Sade's attempt to hire eight professionals from the Comédie-Française was unsuccessful. The *dramatis personae* of Sade's play, *The Wedding of the Century*, believed to have been written for the 1772 theatre season at La Coste, lists the names of several celebrated performers at the Comédie-Française who were expected to participate in Sade's theatrical venture.

the expensive tastes of his wife and visiting sister-in-law, Anne, who demanded custom-made pink silk slippers for their performances on stage. Sade clearly had his hands full, negotiating payment with creditors at one moment, begging for extra money at the next, all the while learning lines and attending rehearsals. The strain on the family—both physical and financial—did not go unnoticed and the Abbé de Sade, the uncle of the marquis, wrote to the marquis's business manager Fage on 11 May 1772:

> I am of your opinion concerning my nephew's passion for plays, which, as you see, is pushed to the extreme, and which would have soon ruined him if it lasted. I have thus far said nothing to him about that, because I was aware of the futility of my opinions. But I see with pleasure that the problems of reconciling the actors with each other, their perpetual scheming and dissension, and the difficulty of finding money to defray the expense of the obstacles that constantly arise in satisfying this passion, begin to dampen it, and I am only awaiting an opportune moment to strike the death blow. It would have already been done had his wife been willing to act in concert with me and less kindly disposed toward her husband's caprices.

Madame de Montreuil, Sade's mother-in-law, echoed the Abbé's sentiments, complaining that the marquis's obsession with the theatre threatened to ruin the family financially and "further compromise his wife and sister-in-law" because of the low class of people who attended the plays. Aware of the financial burden created by his amateur theatricals, Sade left La Coste on 22 June to collect money owed him in Marseilles. There, on 27 June, two days before Sade was due back for performances of *Le Philosophe marié* and *Heureusement* at the theatre at Mazan, Sade and his valet Latour hosted an orgy in which a number of young girls were fed Spanish fly and asked (or forced) to perform a variety of sexual activities. After the marquis returned to Mazan to reprise his roles, the girls complained to the Marseilles police and a warrant was issued for the arrests of both Sade and his valet. On 4 July, during rehearsals for Voltaire's tragedy *Adélaide du Guesclin*, Sade received official notification of the charges and fled to Italy with Latour and his sister-in-law, leaving his theatrical ventures to Bourdais and the other actors.[7]

The theatrical festival at la Coste and Mazan had promised a season from May to October 1772 with a repertory of plays that included old favorites as well as recent successes on the major stages of Paris. Here is the complete program for the series:

3 May	La Coste	*Le Glorieux (The Braggart)* by Destouches *Les Moeurs du temps (The Manners of the Day)* by Saurin
10 May	Mazan	*Le Glorieux (The Braggart)* by Destouches *Les Moeurs du temps (The Manners of the Day)* by Saurin
17 May	La Coste	*Beverly* by Saurin *Le Retour imprévu (The Unexpected Return)* by Regnard
24 May	Mazan	*Beverly* by Saurin *Le Retour imprévu (The Unexpected Return)* by Regnard
12 June	La Coste	*Le Déserteur (The Deserter)* by Sedaine *Le Somnambule (The Sleepwalker)* by Pont-de-Veyle
15 June	Mazan	*Le Déserteur (The Deserter)* by Sedaine *Le Somnambule (The Sleepwalker)* by Pont-de-Veyle
22 June	La Coste	*The Philosophe marié (The Married Philosopher)* by Destouches *Heureusement (Thank Goodness!)* by Rochon de Chabannes
29 June	Mazan	*The Philosophe marié (The Married Philosopher)* by Destouches *Heureusement (Thank Goodness!)* by Rochon de Chabannes
9 July	La Coste	*Adélaide de Guesclin* by Voltaire *L'Amant auteur (The Lover as Author)* by Cérou

---

[7] For a fuller account of Sade's attempts to avoid incarceration, please see Schaeffer, chapters 6–8; Du Plessix Gray, chapters 9–11; Lever, chapter 10; and the general introduction to this series.

13 July	Mazan	*Adélaide de Guesclin* by Voltaire *L'Amant auteur (The Lover as Author)* by Cérou
30 July	La Coste	*Mélanide* by La Chaussée *La Jeune indienne (The Young Indian Girl)* by Champfort
3 August	Mazan	*Mélanide* by La Chaussée *La Jeune indienne (The Young Indian Girl)* by Champfort
13 August	La Coste	*Le Père de famille (The Father of a Family)* by Diderot *La Gageure (The Wager)* by Sedaine[8]
17 August	Mazan	*Le Père de famille (The Father of a Family)* by Diderot *La Gageure (The Wager)* by Sedaine
27 August	La Coste	*Dupuis et Déronais* by Collé *Nanine* by Voltaire
31 August	Mazan	*Dupuis et Déronais* by Collé *Nanine* by Voltaire
10 Sept.	La Coste	*La Gouvernante (The Governess)* by La Chaussée *Zénéide* by Cahusac
14 Sept.	Mazan	*La Gouvernante (The Governess)* by La Chaussée *Zénéide* by Cahusac
24 Sept.	La Coste	*Le Méchant (The Wicked Man)* by Gresset *Les Fausses infidélités (False Infidelities)* by Barthe
28 Sept.	Mazan	*Le Méchant (The Wicked Man)* by Gresset *Les Fausses infidélités (False Infidelities)* by Barthe
8 Oct.	La Coste	*Le Philosophe sans le savoir (The Unconscious Philosopher)* by Sedaine *L'Impertinent (The Impertinent Man)* by Desmahis

---

[8] Sedaine's play is actually titled *La Gageure imprévue (The Unexpected Wager)*. Another play called *La Gageure*, a three-act comedy by Lagrange may have been the play designated here. However, because *La Gageure* was meant as an afterpiece to Diderot's long drama, it is more likely that Sedaine's one-act comedy was the play performed.

| 12 Oct. | Mazan[9] | *Le Philosophe sans le savoir (The Unconscious Philosopher)* by Sedaine
L'Impertinent (The Impertinent Man) by Desmahis |

Only four of the twenty-two scheduled plays for the 1772 festival had been previously staged at Évry, leaving Sade and Bourdais with the monumental task of readying eighteen scripts in less than seven months. It is impossible to comment on the acting values of the productions. Eighteenth-century acting styles were generally presentational and characterization tended to be based on type rather than specificity so even the best performers (and Sade was hardly able to acquire the best performers) would appear stiff and awkward to a twenty-first-century audience used to realism. A brief study of the plays themselves, however, would provide some insight into Sade's dramatic tastes as well as that of his contemporary audience.

Arguably Destouches's masterpiece, *Le Glorieux*, originally produced in 1732, depicts the conflict between the bankrupt nobility and the newly emerging wealthy *bourgeoisie*. It tells the tale of the arrogant Count de Tufière, who conceals his poverty in order to marry Isabelle, daughter of the wealthy *parvenu* Lisimon. Although the count's pretensions are revealed with the unexpected appearance of his penniless father and the discovery that Isabelle's maid is, in reality, his own impoverished sister, all is forgiven and the play ends in his marriage to Isabelle. This exceedingly popular play offered escapist entertainment to noble and peasant, rich and poor alike and provided Sade with a financial trope that would pervade his own plays as well as the name of the noble father in *The Shyster*. Saurin's *Les Moeurs du temps*, produced initially in 1760, offered Sade the time-worn plot of the "forced marriage" in which Julie, who is in love with Dorante, is being forced by her social-climbing aunt to marry a dissolute marquis. Not surprisingly, the marquis's connivances are discovered and the lovers are allowed to marry. Sade's depiction of the dissolute nobility in *Oxtiern, The Madness of*

---

[9] The repertory included one final performance at Mazan on 22 October of *Jenneval* and *La Laitière et les deux chasseurs (The Milkmaid and the Two Hunters)*. I have not included them in the list above because the last two plays did not have a performance at La Coste and therefore did not fit into the festival pattern.

Misfortune, *Truth and Treason*, and *The Dangerous Man* are indebted in some degree to Saurin's play.

Even more important to Sade's development as a playwright was Saurin's *Beverly*, a bourgeois tragedy based on Edward Moore's English play *The Gamester* and first produced in France in 1768. Addicted to gambling in spite of the efforts of his wife and family, Beverly loses all of his money due to the connivance of villains posing as his friends. In jail and despairing of his life, he takes poison only to discover, as he lies dying, that the villains have been caught and his possessions restored to him. Sade made great use of these motifs both in his "English" play, *Fanny*, and *The Madness of Misfortune*. Similarly, Regnard's *Le Retour imprévu* (1700) provided Sade with an almost autobiographical portrait of a son squandering all of his father's money and possessions on fancy entertainments only to find that his sire has returned unexpectedly and wants to examine the son's accounts. Sedaine's musical comedy *Le Déserteur*, produced at the Comédie-Italienne in 1769 with music by Monsigny, turns on a practical joke played on a young military man by his fiancée. Believing her to have betrayed him, Alexis deserts from the army, is caught, incarcerated, and condemned to death—leaving Louise, his fiancée, guilty and distraught. At the moment of her deepest despair, Louise learns that Alexis has been pardoned and the musical ends with the lovers reunited. Sade borrowed some of the serious elements, much of the trickery lazzi, the military motif, and the name of the trickster Louise for his own musical comedy, *The Haunted Tower*.

Cérou's comedy *L'Amant auteur et valet* (1728) provided Sade with another autobiographical sketch, this time of himself as Eraste, an author/lover aided and abetted by Frontin, his valet (Latour). Not only do the valet's machinations anticipate the Marseilles affair, they also suggest the relationship between Philoquet and Barriere in *The Shyster*. La Chaussée's sentimental comedy *Mélanide* (1741) depicts the misfortunes of Count d'Ormancé, who married Mélanide, had a son by her, and then was forced to give her up because of family pressures. Believing that his wife and son are dead, he falls in love again—eighteen years later with a girl of humble birth. Though the girl's mother supports the match, the girl prefers a lad named Darviane, who is, in fact, the count's son, though neither of them are aware of this. Although the count hates Darviane as a rival, even when he learns of his parentage, the eleventh-hour appearance of Mélanide softens d'Ormancé's heart and father and son are reconciled. Here we can see the seeds of Sade's *Henrietta and Saint-Clair* and suggestions of *Love Makes the Misanthrope*. Champfort's *La Jeune indienne* (1764) portrays the fate of a shipwrecked man from Boston who has washed ashore on an uncivilized island. He falls in love with a native girl and, although he has promised to marry another, he marries the native girl instead. The exoticism of Champfort's play anticipates the *Azelis* episode in *The Marriage of the Arts*.

Diderot's groundbreaking *drame Le Père de famille* (1761) spun a complex tale of love and misunderstanding in the household of Mr. Orbesson, who strenuously objects to his son, Saint-Albin, marrying Sophie, a virtuous girl, but of uncertain parentage. To separate the lovers, Orbesson engages the help of his brother-in-law, Commander d'Auvilé, who manages to arrange a *lettre de cachet* against the girl. At the eleventh hour, Sophie is discovered to be Auvilé's niece and the lovers are united. A subplot involves another love affair between Cécile, Orbesson's daughter, and Germeuil, a young man raised in Orbesson's household. In his attempt to save Sophie from the *lettre de cachet*, Germeuil is accused of treachery by his friend (and virtual brother) Saint-Albin, a situation that challenges the course of Germeuil's romance with Cécile. Here are planted the seeds of *Henrietta and Saint-Clair*, the relationship between Valville, Saint-Albon, and Athenais in *The Shyster*, and a not-so-subtle reminder of Sade's relationship with his mother-in-law, who had negotiated her own *lettres de cachet* to curb his outlandish behavior.

La Gageure imprévue (1768), in which a bored marquise seeks the attentions of a military officer who turns out to be her husband's friend; *Dupuis et Déronais* (1768), in which an old man objects to his daughter's marriage on the grounds that she will abandon him in his old age; and *Nanine* (1749), in which a nobleman marries a woman of low birth, all provided Sade with farce lazzi, outpourings of sentiment, and the standard enlightened fare that was the rage in Paris. *La Gouvernante* (1747), about a ruined countess who reappears as her daughter's governess in the household of the people who ruined her, evokes the situation of Lisimon in *The Shyster*. More significant perhaps is *Le Méchant* (1745), in which the eponymous character Cléon (played by Sade at Évry) tries to prevent the marriage of Valère and Chloé using slander and every nefarious means at his disposal. Although Cléon's calumnies are exposed at the end of the play, the mischief-maker remains unabashed and remorseless. The trenchant social satire in the play offered Sade a model for his *The Shyster* and the character of Cléon provided Sade with a template for each of his intelligent, resourceful, Machiavellian villains.

Whether or not Sade consciously drew upon these plays in his own work is a matter of conjecture. That he had access to them is certain: he performed in and directed many of the plays himself. What is perhaps more interesting, however, is the conservative nature of Sade's theatrical taste that seems to be in direct opposition to his profligate lifestyle. Private theatres were not bound by the same regulations that governed the theatres of Paris. In fact, it is known that private pornographic theatres existed in France as early as 1741, where sexual activity was on display either through suggestive dialogue or graphic portrayal of the physical act. Sophie Arnould and Count Grammont were said to have performed the lascivious *L'Air de Mirza* in the actress's bathroom, while Delisle de Sales's *Priapées*, written for the Duc d'Hénin's private theatre, required sexual athletes. Madeleine Guimard, the celebrated dancer at the Opéra, built three such theatres beginning in 1768 with the financial assistance of her lover, Prince Soubise. The first, built inside of one of Soubise's estates, had a stage that was twenty-one feet wide and fifty feet deep with a proscenium opening fifteen feet high and boasted an auditorium equipped for erotic activity when the spectators found themselves too stimulated by the performance on stage. So widespread was this kind of theatrical activity that in 1773, Louis-Sébastien Mercier wrote in his *Du théâtre ou Nouvelle Essai sur l'art dramatique*:

> In so-called 'polite society' in Paris, obscene farces are performed which, unquestionably, possess the merits of being faithful portraits of the dissolute behavior of the debauched spectators who take delight in them, but, in so doing, who show that they have lost all feeling for what is noble, decent and moving.... These social affairs demand a capricious, licentious kind of writing which justly offends the thinking man.... How, in the future, can

spectators who delight in this sort of thing fail to find works of sentimental interest absolutely inane? It is like the corroded taste of an invalid, rejecting all wholesome food as tasteless. Our nobility are sick indeed.

It is a great irony that Delisle de Sales was known as "Sade of the drama" because of his licentious works for the private theatre when Sade himself engaged in much more traditional theatrical fare. Was it because of family pressures that Sade produced a conservative repertory? Or did he feel that a provincial audience, already shocked by his reputation, would shun anything but the most accessible drama? Or was his passion for the theatre too great to allow him to indulge in his baser instincts? The theatrical essays Sade wrote to introduce his plays are clear indications that the marquis took the theatre very seriously: he carefully studied its formal structure, its thematic nuances, its literature. And although many of his plays demonstrate a typical eighteenth-century approach to playwriting in the use of standard themes and characters, *The Marriage of the Arts* does exhibit the experimentation of a highly imaginative playwright who not only understood the conventions of theatrical structure and private performance, but who was able to manipulate them into a metatheatrical event far in advance of anything that was on the Paris stage in the eighteenth century. Perhaps Sade's sights were on the professional theatres of Paris, not on the provincial stages of Évry, Mazan, and La Coste, and he viewed his work in the private sphere as preparatory to his being accepted in Paris. It makes sense, therefore, that he would practice on plays that were part of the accepted repertory rather than indulge in work that would only ever have a clandestine audience. Besides, the marquis did not require any theatrical excuse to practice a profligate lifestyle. In any event, what follows are the Marquis de Sade's earliest attempts at playwriting—beginning with commendatory verses and a short dramatic scene (what the French called a *parade*) that opened the theatre season at Évry on 17 April 1764.

TRIBUTE

Performed 17 April at the opening of the theatre at Évry.

> *The curtain rises and, stage right, we see an author working with a rhyming dictionary. To his left is an actor, half-dressed, studying his lines.*

ACTOR. (*To the technician.*) Well, what does this mean, gentlemen? Raising the curtain like that without anyone telling you to!
AUTHOR. (*Angrily.*) What good-for-nothings! With their cursed carelessness, they made me lose a hemistitch of sixty-three syllables that would have been half the first verse of my tribute.
ACTOR. What! Mr. Dorval, are you taking it upon yourself to write a tribute?
AUTHOR. Yes, it's a little impromptu piece I've been working on for the past three months. But let's get going, Mr. Étoise. Everybody's looking at us. All set to make fun of us. We'll have enough time to collect hisses once we're on stage. Let's not get them beforehand. Besides, it's late. Our ladies are ready and soon the play will begin.
ACTOR. That is if you hammer out the tribute.
AUTHOR. (*Rising.*) Well, yes… yes… yes…
ACTOR. But nevertheless, you should certainly say something sincere to such a nice group of people who come and share our plays and appreciate our feeble abilities. At least you ought to beg their indulgence. There isn't a single one of us who doesn't need it. And I swear to you, frankly, that there's something about our performances that would make me tremble if the desire to please and succeed didn't sustain our courage and arouse our self-esteem.
AUTHOR. For crying out loud! Sir, you've stolen my thought. That's exactly what I was putting in verse. (*Thoughtfully.*) Yet, the material isn't grand enough… it's even a bit trite. There have to be aphorisms in a tribute or some pretty verses. A tribute should be the work of the intellect.
ACTOR. I admit that what I said came only from the heart, but I think that's enough.

AUTHOR. Eh, no! Sir, people don't bother about that. It has to be said properly and in the age in which we live, no matter if it's true or false, if you say something intelligently, people won't ask anything more of you.

ACTOR. Ah! How wrong you are, my dear Mr. Dorval! I assure you, I do, that neither more work nor time is needed and even less trouble is taken when you just say what's on your mind. Besides, honesty, frankness, the virtue that rules over this house, that sincere politeness, that candid naiveté, the symbol of great souls that characterizes so well the masters of these surroundings, succeeds in convincing me more than anything that artifice and its poisonous maxims here give way to all the splendor of truth. Its temple is in the hearts of our kind hosts. Everyone that surrounds them, parents, friends, in short, everyone who is here expresses the same feelings. Let us say, then, what we all think in a simple way without pretty verses and beautiful phrases. Come on. Come on, my dear Dorval, if the mind can make a lie sparkle, simplicity embellishes the truth much better.

(*Here a bell is heard in the wings.*)

AUTHOR. Let's get going. Another bell! Sir, you understand, sir, you have to get dressed.

ACTOR. Yes, that's our only excuse, if one could be had, for not expressing more abundantly the gratitude we owe to such a pleasant group of people for being here today on our behalf. (*To the audience in the orchestra.*) My ladies, to entertain you is our goal; to succeed is our desire. Seeing you here often will be the best proof you could give us that your desires are satisfied. If your applause knows no bounds, we will find ourselves more happy than wise and more to be pitied than censored. If we fail in our hope for success, then we'll have had the desire to please instead of talent. And it is part of a woman's humanity to forgive the one in favor of the other.

Occasional Verse

VERSES

Written for the entertainment that was given on the eve of Madame de Plissay's birthday after the performance of The Wicked Man *and* Thank Goodness![10]

First Verse
(*Sung by Mr. de Sade*)
To the tune: "*It's not a proper celebration without the day after.*"

What a happy omen for us!
If you approve of our amusements,
Their gaiety is only the result
Of these happy surroundings.
Come, prove to us tomorrow
That it's not a proper celebration

Without the day after.

Second Verse
Madame de Mondran leads onstage a little Cupid carrying a basket of flowers. She sings:

Out in the prairie, Cupid
Has picked a basket of flowers
To celebrate Pélagie.[11]
Let us join with the god of hearts;
May the bouquet he carries
Be presented by our hands.
Let us put this god into the celebration

Night and day.

Third Verse

---

[10] Rochon de Chabanne's one-act verse comedy, originally produced at the Théâtre Français in 1762.
[11] That is, Madame de Plissay. Pélagie was her Christian name.

The little Cupid played by the young d'Évry.

To unite with my empire
The sweets of the god of Hymen
Is the goal to which I aspire:
To enrapture every heart…
Let Pélagie lend hers to me
And my victory is certain.
I will adorn the celebration with flowers

Night and day.

Fourth Verse
During the chorus, a peasant enters merrily. Mr. de Rupière, who plays this character, sings while presenting a bouquet of flowers.

In the name of everyone in our village,
I'm here to present you
A small token of our esteem
Which I beg you to accept.
When the celebration comes from the heart,
Whatever is said from the heart is always pleasant,
And the bouquet it brings

Is well received.

Fifth Verse
A drunk played by Mr. de Noinville.

I won't give much,
But that's not what counts the most.
If I don't have any roses,
I don't have any thorns either!
When my head is full of wine
And my heart is filled with friendship.
I certainly know how to keep the celebration going

Until tomorrow.

Sixth Verse
Sung by Madame d'Évry, the mistress of the place.

The dearest offering
Is that of feeling:
In the village, it is sincere,
In the city, rarely.
Artifice haunts the celebration,
But in our house, there is none.
The celebration is in our hearts,

Night and day.

Seventh and Final Verse
Sung by Madame de Montreuil.

If we've been able to please you,
Our desires are in no way betrayed.
You've fulfilled them all;
There's nothing left to do.
Before finishing the celebration,
Always remember rightly
That it's not a proper celebration

Without the day after.

The entertainment was completed by a fireworks display on stage.

VERSES
Sung after the comedy Patelin the Lawyer.[12]

First Verse
(*Sung by Mr. de Sade to Henriette.*)

Let's never lose hope.
Happiness was far away from us;
Now, it is in my heart.
Everything vouches for my fidelity.
You need not be amazed:
It's only a step from bad to good.

Second Verse
(*Sung by Madame de Sade to Valère.*)

If I was frightened of your carelessness
And refused to explain myself,
Dear Valère, a person fears danger
When she senses the power of love;
But I no longer doubt anything;
Let us quickly pass from bad to good.

Third Verse
(*Sung by Mr. Guillaume.*)

Our joy once again becomes the effect
Of the workings of nature.
Ah! How pleased one is to express it
When it is purified by feeling!
With pleasure, we will surely say
It's only a step from bad to good.

Fourth Verse.
(*Sung by Mr. de Lionne.*)

---

[12] A three-act comedy by Palaprat, first produced at the Théâtre Français in 1706. The verses written here were sung after a performance of the play at Évry in October 1764, six months after Sade had been released from Vincennes Prison.

Yes, you're right, Mr. Guillaume, but nevertheless,
Pleasure often follows pain,
But pain follows pleasure.
Alas! Soon it must leave
And forsake being bound to that god.
Ah! Here, one has certainly proven
How one cherishes his ties!

Fifth Verse
(*Sung by Madame de Bourneville.*)

This place is the image of happiness;
The master paints it before our very eyes.
Everything around him is happy;
It's the prerogative of virtue.
Ah! With him one truly tastes
The sweet ties of friendship!

Sixth Verse
(*Sung by Mr. de Rupière to Madame d'Évry.*)

The charming mistress of Évry
Will always be able to captivate hearts;
And her mind full of sweetness
Can please as much as it likes.
In our songs, let's certainly express
That loving her is a blessing to all of us.

Seventh Verse
(*By Mr. de Launay for the audience in the orchestra.*)

I had really lost hope
Of pleasing you any longer;
I despaired of seeing you again.
I had already left the town.
But you never can tell;
It's only a step from bad to good.

Eight and Final Verse
(Sung by Madame de Montreuil to the audience in the orchestra.)

Ladies, it's your indulgence
That can revive our abilities.
Accept our thanks
Dictated by gratitude.
Ah! Leaving you, one knows quite well
That far from you, there's nothing.

The theatre had been closed due to the indisposition of M. de Plissay and was reopened with Nanine[13] *and* Patelin the Lawyer, *after which the above verses were sung.*

VERSES
Sung after the comedy, The Unexpected Return.[14]

CLITANDRE *to his father.*

Deign to excuse the tricks
And the ins and outs of love.
That god perhaps makes one forget
Respect… but not tenderness.
But all at once, everything's restored,
And I feel that in this adventure
It's less necessary to follow nature
Than to know how to refine its laws.

MADAME BERTRAND *to Géronte.*

Forgive that child everything
Since love is his excuse.
But may he be prudent from now on,
And not abuse your forgiveness.
Ah! Just like him, in the past,

---

[13] Voltaire's three-act comedy, originally performed on 16 June 1749.

[14] Regnard's comedy was first produced at the Théâtre Français in 1700. The verses composed here were sung after a performance of the play at Évry in 1764.

We experienced, I'm sure,
How rarely one could extinguish
The voice of nature.
MR. GÉRONTE *to Madame Bertrand.*

That piece of advice was in my heart;
I follow it with confidence.
What happiness it is for a good father
To be lenient.

(To his son.)

Go, go, my dear son. Like you
I have felt love's wounds;
Nature must be forgiven
When one has been subjected to its laws.

THE MARQUIS *to the audience.*

Mr. Géronte truly wants to grant
His indulgence to his son.
Deign to give us a little assurance
Of the same sentiment.
The desire to please is our law,
And it's the only one that puts our minds at ease.
It's here in nature,
Everyone will say so, just like me.

MERLIN *to the audience.*

To encourage our talents
Only requires your presence;
Come and enliven them often,
But come with leniency.
You always have to follow the voice
Of nature's sentiments.
Indulgence is the murmur of nature
That sometimes must be heard.

VERSE

Written for a child in a society comedy who had played the role of Cupid.

In your looks, heavenly child,
One learns the art of pleasing.
When you portray feeling,
Often focus on your mother;
Her eyes, which are always
Expressive of emotion,
Will support your authority.
When Venus seconds Love,
Who could destroy it?

The Self-Proclaimed Philosopher

Introduction

Generally considered to be the Marquis de Sade's first play, *The Self-Proclaimed Philosopher* was probably performed at the manor theatre at La Coste, de Sade's country estate, on 20 January 1772 before an invited audience. The performance celebrated his recent release from debtor's prison, marked the arrival of his sister-in-law, Lady Anne Prospère de Launay (with whom he would fall madly in love), and inaugurated the theatrical season at the manor house, which, under the auspices of Bourdais and his actress wife, would continue sporadically between Easter and November.

The Marquis de Sade always had a great interest in the theatre. Eight years earlier on 17 April 1764, he had founded a private theatre at his wife's uncle's estate, the Chateau d'Evry, where he subsequently produced and acted in Regnard's *The Unexpected Return*, Brueys and Palaprat's *The Crafty Lawyer*, Rochon de Chabanne's *Happily Ever After*, and Gresset's *The Reprobate*. Sade's wife of nearly a year, Renée-Pélagie de Montreuil, and her mother were also regular participants in the theatrical productions, possibly to keep their eyes on the philandering marquis. Their suspicions were justified, for between July and December, Sade fell in love with Collette, an actress at the Théâtre Italien, Mlle. Le Roy, a ballerina, and Mlle. Le Clair, a supernumerary at the Paris Opéra. In January 1765, Mlle. Beauvoisin, the twenty-four-year-old lead dancer at the Opera and toast of all the young fops in Paris, was added to the list of the Marquis's conquests and taken to La Coste, where she was introduced as his wife's cousin and where many expensive masquerade balls and theatrical productions were given in her honor.

Following the premiere of *The Self-Proclaimed Philosopher*, however, Sade's tastes did not incline toward performers. Instead, he and his valet, a young man named Latour, set out for Marseilles to collect taxes due on his estates and to entertain themselves with suburban prostitutes. On 27 June 1772, the last day the pair would spend in Marseilles, Latour arranged a rendezvous with four girls, all between the ages of eighteen and twenty-three. During the course of the day, at least two of the girls were whipped, sodomized, and given Spanish fly, a powder made from tiny ground-up beetles. That evening, Latour found yet another girl, Marguerite Coste, who was also given Spanish fly. Three days later, Coste complained to the Royal Prosecutor of being poisoned by the Marquis and a pharmacist was appointed to examine her. On 1 July, the four young women accused Sade and Latour of homosexual sodomy and claimed to have refused their unnatural advances.

On 4 July, officially informed of their impending arrest, Sade and Latour fled to Italy (taking the Marquis's sister-in-law Anne with them). On 3 September, both Marquis and valet were found guilty in absentia of sodomy and poisoning. Sade was sentenced to death by decapitation, Latour by strangulation (hanging) and nine days later, the pair were executed in effigy. After travelling under a variety of assumed names, the Marquis was finally captured on 8 December at Chambéry by his mother-in-law, who persuaded the King of Sardinia to incarcerate him at Fort Miolans in Sardinia.

While *The Self-Proclaimed Philosopher* is evocative of the games of love with which the Marquis was undoubtedly familiar, the pretense, graft, and manipulation depicted in the play is hardly on the same level as Sade's own romantic adventures during the same period. Rather, the play develops predictably along the lines of traditional French farce in which stock characters engage in a "duper-duped" kind of intrigue. Even though the play has several funny moments (especially the dressing-table scene), it is no wonder that the Marquis de Sade neglected to include it in his *Descriptive Catalogue of 1788*.

The Self-Proclaimed Philosopher
Prose Comedy in One Act

CHARACTERS

Clarice
Madame de Pouval, Widow of the governor
Cleon, in love with Clarice
Ariste, a philosopher
Jasmin, Clarice's manservant
Two Lackeys

(*The action takes place at Clarice's house in the country in an apartment decorated in the Parisian style.*)

CLARICE. Really, Cleon, your philosopher is very nice. But is that man really a philosopher?
CLEON. Madame, in him you'll find a lot of foolishness and stupidity and only a little bit of wit.
CLARICE. Ah! The character will amuse us. That's just what we need in the country and I mean to enjoy myself.
CLEON. Ah! How happy you are to be able to distract yourself and think about pleasant things. As for me, I can only think about love and you treat that very lightly.
CLARICE. Stop that insipid talk, Cleon. Now's not the time to think about such things. Save them, save those mealy-mouthed remarks for all the empty hours we need to fill out here in the country. Now, think only about enjoying the ridiculous character you brought us. Yes, I want to test my charms on a philosopher! My victory would please me a great deal. But don't be concerned, Cleon. I only want to win so that I can crown you with my laurels.
CLEON. Oh! Clarice, can a person be so flirtatious and tender at the same time? Yes, I swear to you…
CLARICE. Stop, stop the sermon. Here's our man now. Try to play your role well.
(Enter ARISTE.)

CLARICE. You're here early, Ariste! I was concerned about you this morning. Your eyes looked as if you'd been up all night.

ARISTE. Madame, this ostentation dazzles me without satisfaction. Luxury exists for the senses and I don't operate on sense. My soul only reflects images like a mirror. Only matters of pure intelligence can affect me strongly. What good are the rich furnishings that fill my room? A fluffy mattress? Those tapestries? Isn't it ridiculous to take such pains just to put a man to sleep? Is that how they sleep in Sparta? A dressing table for me? Oh, Lycurgus, what will you think?

CLARICE. (*Aside.*) What an insipid man! (*Aloud.*) Sir, do you want me to clear out my house for you? It takes a wise man to know how to adapt to every occasion. Listen to me. Enjoy the pleasures of life while they exist. That's the only real philosophy. Sir, would you be so kind to tell me what you believe in?

ARISTE. Detest weakness, stay away from luxury, do good, hate evil. Madame, that's what I believe in.

CLARICE. That's all? The fruit of this wisdom is being happy, isn't it?

ARISTE. And to make others happy, Madame.

CLEON. (*To CLARICE.*) Clarice, you can be a philosopher whenever you want.

CLARICE. (*To CLEON.*) I'll let you share in my wisdom. (*To ARISTE.*) But tell me, Ariste, what do you do to make yourself happy?

ARISTE. That's simple. I have no expectations, I don't depend on anyone, I never change, I don't like anyone, and I say what's on my mind.

CLEON. Not liking anyone doesn't seem to be a very auspicious way of making people happy.

ARISTE. Eh! You don't do good for people you like. Do you like the wretch you help in passing? In the same way, we assist humanity with our wisdom.

CLEON. You make people happy with this wisdom?

ARISTE. Yes, sir, and ourselves, too.

MADAME DE POUVAL. (*Entering, having heard the last words of the philosopher.*) That happiness is rather slight, my dear! Have you no other pleasures in life?

ARISTE. I beg your pardon, Madame. I enjoy scorning all pleasures.

MADAME DE POUVAL. Eh! What do you do with your soul, my poor man?

ARISTE. What should I do? I use it in the only way that's worthy of it: I observe the wonders of nature.

MADAME DE POUVAL. I was just now looking for someone to observe them with me. It's nice out. Come on, Mr. Philosopher, will you give me your arm for a stroll through the park?

CLARICE. Madame de Pouval, take Cleon. Can't you see that I'm taking a class? I want to become a philosopher and the gentleman here is going to teach me the principles of his craft. It's time for my lesson.

CLEON. (*With distress.*) Clarice…

CLARICE. Madame, Cleon will accompany you.

CLEON. (*Going out.*) Ah! You're cruel. You enjoy making me miserable!

MADAME DE POUVAL. (*Going out.*) Clarice, have a nice lesson.

CLARICE. Ariste, I'm looking for reassurance. Our meeting this way isn't dangerous, is it? Answer me. I really want to be instructed. As you are so very determined not to like anyone, have you never found anyone likeable?

ARISTE. I am acquainted with exterior attractions, but I mistrust the inside, Madame.

CLARICE. It remains to be seen if this mistrust is justified.

ARISTE. Oh! Very justified! You can believe me! I've seen enough to convince me that this world is full of fools, scoundrels, and ingrates.

CLARICE. (*With reproach.*) If you'd look a little more closely, you would be less unfair and a lot happier.… Ariste, do you have any pressing business in Paris?

ARISTE. Nothing at all, Madame. A philosopher never has any pressing business.

CLARICE. Very well! I'm going to keep you here. The country should be pleasing to a philosopher and here I promise you solitude, rest, and freedom.

ARISTE. (*In a voice that's tough, but almost tender.*) Freedom, Madame? I'm afraid you're lying to me.

CLARICE. Why such fear, Ariste? Do you think it was wrong of me to have interrupted your freedom, not to allow you to take a stroll with Madame de Pouval? I see it, Ariste. You want to blame me. Your accusations are hard to bear. In revenge, I'm going to throw them back in your face. (*She leaves.*)

ARISTE. (*Alone.*) That woman adores me. That's clear. That little act of jealousy convinced me. There's philosophy compromised with a vengeance! But what can you do? A beautiful woman, a nice house, all the comforts of life… it's all very tempting. Let's see it through to the end. To be sure, I'll be waiting when she casts herself into my net!

(*Enter MADAME DE POUVAL.*)

MADAME DE POUVAL. What's going on, Mr. Philosopher? On the way back, I found Clarice grumbling about you. That woman is a fool. I bet she's upset about what you didn't say to her. She thinks she's beautiful. She's thirty-two years old! Make no mistake about it: she would need a little philosophy to stop her from being such a flirt. But she didn't really want to take advantage of your help. Ariste, would you try your hand at me? I will make you proud, more than you think, because underneath all that you see here is more than a little philosophy.

ARISTE. You, Madame? And what sort of philosophy? Stoicism? Epicureanism?

MADAME DE POUVAL. Oh! gracious me, the name doesn't mean anything. I live on ten thousand a year and I spend it merrily. I drink champagne with my friends. I enjoy myself. Live and let live, that's my motto.

ARISTE. Nicely said, Madame. That's exactly what Epicureus was teaching.

MADAME DE POUVAL. Oh! I tell you, he didn't teach me anything. I came up with it on my own. For the past twenty years, I've read nothing but my wine list and my dinner menu!

ARISTE. In that respect, you ought to be the happiest woman in the world!

MADAME DE POUVAL. Me, happy? I long for a husband who shares my tastes. The governor, may he rest in peace, was a beast. He was good for nothing but the statehouse. He knew about law and order—that was it. I want a man who knows how to love me, who lives for me alone.

ARISTE. (*In a tender voice.*) You'll find a thousand, Madame, and…

MADAME DE POUVAL. Oh! I only want one, but I want him to be good. Whether he's an aristocrat or a beggar, it's all the same to me. I'm attracted only to the individual.

ARISTE. Really, Madame, you astonish me. You're the first woman I've found who thinks this way. Are you really looking for a husband?

MADAME DE POUVAL. Yes, sir, a husband who would belong to me in every way. Lovers cheat us out of our right to complain when they leave us. A husband, on the other hand, belongs to us in front of the whole world and if mine dared to be unfaithful, as the legal spouse I want to be able to beat to a pulp that hussy who dared to steal him away. My actions would be seen as just and honorable.

ARISTE. Certainly, certainly, Madame. Ownership is an inalienable right. Do you know how rare you are? What courage! What strength!

MADAME DE POUVAL. Ah! I've got the strength of a lion. I know that I'm not pretty, but a dowry of ten thousand a year is worth more than the charms of Clarice and her kind. And since love is rare in this day and age, one ought to be able to buy it for ten thousand pieces of silver![15]

(*CLARICE enters.*)

CLARICE. Is it possible, Madame de Pouval, that you've been able to last an hour in conversation with a philosopher? You who always yawn when anyone with intelligence speaks to you?

MADAME DE POUVAL. Really, dear, that's because your intelligence doesn't have any common sense. Ask this wise man here if I'm lacking in wit. We were just talking about what would suit an honest woman and he agreed that a good husband would suit her best.

---

[15] Before the French Revolution, the monetary unit was a silver coin called the *écu* worth between 25 and 30 twenty-first century US dollars. Madame de Pouval's dowry, therefore, would be worth between $250,000 and $300,000.

CLARICE. Fah! Were we created to be slaves? What about freedom, the greatest of all blessings? (*Speaking these words, she looks at ARISTE.*)

ARISTE. Madame, a bond between hearts is nothing less than slavery. If freedom has its good points, it also has its dangers, its stumbling blocks. These happy attachments are a great good and fickleness is so natural to man that, when he experiences a commendable inclination, he must wisely rid himself of his ability to change his mind.

MADAME DE POUVAL. You hear him, Madame? There's a man for you! Without exaggerating in the least, that's what you call a philosopher! Try to seduce him if you can. As for me, I'm leaving under his spell. Goodbye, philosopher. (*Looking at him tenderly.*) I need my rest. I didn't sleep a wink last night. (*She exits.*)

CLARICE. Did you see the look she gave you, Ariste? She's crazy about you!

ARISTE. About me, Madame? Don't you believe it! I don't think our tastes or our personalities are compatible. I drink little, I swear even less, and I don't like the thought of losing my freedom.

CLARICE. Ah! Sir, ten thousand silver pieces a year!

ARISTE. That's an insult for the likes of me.

CLARICE. Ah! For once, that's what I call philosophy! It seems to me that a philosopher doesn't think like another man. Ah! how happy you must be, Ariste, to want to maintain that sweet and joyous freedom! Vainly do I argue against the yoke of matrimony. Whatever attraction your approach has for me, however much I am persuaded that freedom is the one real good, I am reaching the point of giving it up again.

ARISTE. What am I hearing? You're going to form a new attachment?

CLARICE. I don't know.

ARISTE. You don't know?

CLARICE. They want it.

ARISTE. Who, Madame, who? Who are the villains who dare to propose such a thing to you? Furthermore, who is the husband they want you to have?

CLARICE. Cleon.

ARISTE. Cleon, Madame? I no longer have to wonder why he behaves so comfortably around here. He asks questions, he makes decisions, he condescends to be gracious… sometimes. He has that kind of conceited politeness that seems to stoop to our level. One can see that he is a credit to his upbringing and I am aware of all the respect I owe him from now on.

CLARICE. You owe one another a mutual honesty. I intend everyone to be treated as equals at my house.

ARISTE. Is that your intention, Clarice? Ah! Your choice destroys the equality among men and the one who should possess you… Let's not talk about this anymore. I've said too much already. This dwelling was not made for a philosopher. Allow me to take my leave.

CLARICE. No, I need you. You've plunged me into indecision from which you alone can rescue me. You have to admit that philosophy is a very comforting thing. But if a philosopher were a liar, he would be a dangerous friend. Goodbye. I don't want people to see us together so often.… Ariste.… Stay, I demand it! *(She goes out.)*

ARISTE. *(Alone.)* Buck up! Cleon is hanging by a thread. Besides, if I lose Clarice, Madame de Pouval looks as if she'd console me. She has an annuity of ten thousand a year. She's fifty years old, it's true. Yes! But she celebrates with a bottle of champagne every night; that can't take her very far. I would have her consideration, her respect. She's a good woman. She won't be as particular as those finer than she who would deceive you all the time.

(CLARICE enters quickly.)

CLARICE. Ariste! Lucinde is coming to dine with me. She just asked me to go dancing with her afterwards. I want you to escort me. Cleon will take Madame de Pouval. I'm delighted already by the little tryst I'm arranging for the two of them. I want to test the poor boy's chastity.

ARISTE. Madame, it seems you have a bad opinion of Madame de Pouval's virtue. May you have, at least, a better opinion of Cleon's. A person ought to value what he loves; it's the triumph of self-respect. Cleon worships no one but you. Loving anybody else could only degrade him. Once charmed by you, Clarice, he is people-proofed.... But don't trouble yourself, Madame. Let him escort you. Dancing is hardly my cup of tea. That frivolous amusement—the stumbling block to sense—isn't suited to my way of thinking. Allow me the few beliefs that remain, Clarice. I need them more than you think.

CLARICE. Ah! spoken like an angel! But you're coming to the dance. I want it. It's decided and I don't like to be refused. Go on. Get yourself ready. How strange you look! Why don't you dress like everybody else?... Those clothes and that hairdo give you such a vulgar look.... It doesn't look natural.

ARISTE. Eh! Madame, should a person be judged by the way he looks? Do you want me to submit to the popular taste and dress like a marquis?

CLARICE. Why not, sir? Don't you know that everyone is already bored with your aestheticism? More than anything else, that's what weakens your credibility in their minds. As for myself, to give you your due, I need my full powers of concentration. The first glance goes against you and it's often the first glance that decides these things. Why not give virtue all the beauty you can?

ARISTE. No, Madame. Virtue does not wear a mask. The more naked it is, the more beautiful. In seeking to adorn it, you misrepresent it.

CLARICE. Very well, sir, I'll leave virtue to its own devices. As far as I'm concerned, this shabby rustic look is awful to look at. Isn't it odd that someone who was born with such a nice body should take so much pleasure in defacing it?

ARISTE. Eh! Madame, what would you say if a philosopher took the trouble to deck himself out? And...

CLARICE. (*Interrupting him.*) I'd say that he was trying to please and that he was succeeding. Don't deceive yourself, Ariste. It takes a lot of trouble to be pleasing.

ARISTE. Eh! I desire nothing more than to succeed in your eyes.

CLARICE. If you're serious about this, give me at least a quarter of an hour. That's not all. I'm harder to please than you think. Our clothes clash. That's not the way to go to a dance. I'm going to go in a rose-colored domino. I want you to follow me there... dressed the same way.

ARISTE. (*Astonished.*) Ah! Ah! Ah!
CLARICE. Ariste…
ARISTE. Madame…
CLARICE. That's what I want.
ARISTE. Ah! Madame, at least allow me to maintain the seriousness of my profession.
CLARICE. No! No! There's no time to argue. I've just sent someone to look for the elegant outfit I want you to wear. Please tell me… what fantastic notion are you holding on to? I heartily approve of wisdom, but it seems to me that knowledge comes in every color. Are Mr. William's chestnuts more natural than the color of sky blue pink? What fancy makes you dress like a chestnut rather than a rose petal or a spray of lilacs in spring? I tell you, in my opinion, the color of pink is lovely to look at. It has, I don't know, such a tender quality about it that goes straight to the soul. You'll be lovely dressed in a rose-colored domino.
ARISTE. Rose-colored, Madame? A rose-colored philosopher?
CLARICE. Yes, sir, the pale pink color of a rose. What do you want? It's a passion of mine. What? Do you refuse to come to the dance in a domino similar to mine? It's very odd that you deny me this trifle. The importance you place upon it warns me to be on my guard regarding other, more serious, matters.
ARISTE. But, Madame, this extravagance will cost me my reputation.
CLARICE. A happy misfortune: when you lose one reputation, you gain another. Come on, come on. You'll profit by the exchange.
ARISTE. Madame, I hate to displease you, but…
CLARICE. I'm losing my patience with you! I've told you already, I don't like being refused. I'm going to start by giving you a new hairdo. Jasmin, come style the gentleman's hair and spare no pains. Goodbye…. Ariste, I'm counting on you.
(*A dressing table is brought on stage. Two LACKEYS enter.*)
ARISTE. Heavens! What am I in for and what will they say? (*He sits at the dressing table.*) My friend, do with me what you will.
JASMIN. Sir, allow me to inspect your face. We have rules in our art just like you have in yours. (*He stares him in the face.*) Horned-rimmed glasses, yes, horned-rimmed glasses. That's what the

gentleman needs.... A long nose, a large forehead, small eyes.... Yes, nothing but horned-rimmed glasses can change the gentleman's face.... Madame told me to spare no pains. I hope that you and she will be satisfied.

ARISTE. My friend, your diligence alone can satisfy me. For heaven's sake, let's be done with this quickly. For me, time spent at the dressing table is time lost. I've never been able to understand how sensible men can participate in customs that are as foolish as they are vain and ridiculous.

JASMIN. Sir, it is in your best interest that your ideas don't catch on.

ARISTE. (*At the dressing table.*) A philosopher at the dressing table! Yes, here I am! Love, love! What do you do to men? In vain does philosophy resist you. You only establish yourself in the hearts that most distrust your hateful illusions. The more a person tries to escape your torch, the more you enflame it, the more you make known your power. You only offer men the path toward delusion, but, cruelly, you know how to strew the way with flowers so that men prefer it to the road of good sense!

(*A LACKEY enters with the domino.*)

THE LACKEY. With Madame's compliments.

ARISTE. (*Still at the dressing table getting ready, looking in the mirror, having considered the domino.*) What a ridiculous costume! Frivolous man, what are you thinking? You should have invented masks to hide your faults! Too bad! Your vanity conceals from you the need. At any rate, you know that it's the least you can do to show your respect. Give me the domino, since it's what she wants. (*He takes it and looks at himself in the mirror; the dressing table is removed; the LACKEYS exit. Wearing the domino, he crosses to the edge of the stage.*) You have to agree that society paints a pretty picture. If I were gallant, eager, obliging, and likeable, who would give me a moment's notice? You see that sort of man everywhere and a woman's vanity is tired of those prodigal sons. But to tame a bear, to housebreak a philosopher, to bend his pride, to soften his soul, that's a triumph that's difficult and rare and one that strokes their pride. Let's go catch up with Clarice in this bizarre costume. (*He starts to go. CLEON enters.*)

CLEON. (*Looking at him indignantly.*) Sir, if I had a disagreement with a man of the world, I would propose that we try to slit each other's throats. But I'm talking to a philosopher and I only want to assault him with sincerity and truth.

ARISTE. (*Dumbfounded.*) What do you mean by this, sir? Your words surprise me.

CLEON. I loved Clarice, sir, and she loved me. We were going to be married. I don't know what's come over her all of a sudden, but she no longer wants to hear any talk of love and marriage. Before, I only suspected the cause of her about-face, but seeing you in that domino confirms my suspicions. You're going to the dance with her tonight. Pink is her favorite color. You're wearing pink. The die is cast, sir. You are my rival!

ARISTE. Me, sir?

CLEON. No doubt about it. And all the events that prove it are crowding my brain. Your little meetings, your secret strolls, the whispers, the furtive glances, the words you drop here and there, especially her dislike for Madame de Pouval, they all betray you and reveal everything to me. Here, then, sir, is what I propose. Clearly it is necessary for one of us to give way to the other. Violence is the wrong way to go. Generosity will settle everything. I love… I idolize Clarice. Without you, I was happy. I can be happy again. My attentions, the passage of time, and your absence can return her to me. If, on the other hand, you make me give her up, you'll see a man on the edge of despair and death will be my only hope. Ariste, you decide whether or not you're in the same situation and give me an answer. If your happiness depends upon my giving way to you, I won't argue with you. I'll leave.

ARISTE. Come on, sir. You'll not be more generous than Ariste. No matter what the price, I'll prove to you that I'm worthy of such behavior.

CLEON. I am content, sir. I'm depending on you. Say nothing of our agreement. Making it public would be useless. I'll leave you alone. I don't want to make her suspicious. *(He exits.)*

ARISTE. (*Alone.*) At last, here's an opportunity to be a hero! Ah, you men of the world, you'll learn to admire us.… Perhaps they all don't know what's going on. Oh, of course they do. Clarice mentioned it to one of her friends. She told it to some others.

The love affair is unusual enough to cause a stir. Worst come to worst, I'll start the rumor myself. It only needs to be well-known; it doesn't matter how it got started. Our age needs this kind of example; it's a good lesson for humanity. Nevertheless, let's not be virtuous foolishly and let go of Clarice without being sure of Madame de Pouval. Here she comes. Let's find out what she's thinking.

(MADAME DE POUVAL enters.)

MADAME DE POUVAL. Ah! Philosopher, how handsome you look! But what do I see? Oh, heavens! I recognize Clarice's color. You are quite attentive to her tastes. Go on, Ariste, take advantage of the pains you're taking to please her. Certainly they will merit their reward.

ARISTE. My natural simplicity does not allow me to lie to you. In choosing this color, I was only satisfying the lady's whim. I will go even farther, Madame. I will swear that my intention was to look pleasing in the lady's eyes. The wisest man isn't without his weakness and when a woman takes a liking to us, it's hard not to get involved. How feeble is my confession. I blame myself for everything, Madame, and you ought to blame me likewise.

MADAME DE POUVAL. Ah! philosopher, that isn't true! The domino just confused me.

ARISTE. Very well, Madame. I put it on unwillingly. I'll gladly take it off. If my natural simplicity . . .

MADAME DE POUVAL. No, leave it on. I find it charming. What am I saying? How happy you must be to look so handsome, Ariste. If only I were pretty.

ARISTE. What? Madame, don't you know that beauty is in the eyes of the beholder? Nothing is beautiful or ugly in itself. Different men have different tastes.

MADAME DE POUVAL. (*Mincing.*) You flatter me, philosopher, but I know the only beautiful thing about me is my soul.

ARISTE. Well? Isn't that the sublimest beauty, the only one worthy of touching a man's heart?

MADAME DE POUVAL. Ariste, believe me, that beauty alone is hardly attractive.

ARISTE. Hardly attractive for the rabble, perhaps, but once again, you're not reduced to that. What about a noble expression?

An imposing look? A face full of character? And since when has stateliness not been the hallmark of elegance?

MADAME DE POUVAL. I'm a little overweight. What do you think about that?

ARISTE. Ah, Madame, what we consider obese is regarded as beautiful in Asia. Can you imagine the Turks not having an eye for women? Well, all the pretty asses we admire in Paris wouldn't find their way into the emir's harem and the emir's no fool. In a word, good health is the mother of pleasure and plumpness is the sign of good health.

MADAME DE POUVAL. You've succeeded in convincing me that my fat is not unbecoming. But what about my nose? It doesn't come to a point. It just sticks out in front of my face.

ARISTE. Good Lord! What are you complaining about? Did Roman women have noses that come to a point? Look at all the antique busts.

MADAME DE POUVAL. At least they didn't have a big mouth and thick lips.

ARISTE. Madame, thick lips are the attractions of African beauties. They're like two pillows on which rests a sweet and tender voluptuousness. As for your gaping mouth, I know of nothing that makes a face look more open and happy.

MADAME DE POUVAL. That's true when you've got good teeth. Unfortunately…

ARISTE. Go to Siam: there, people are ashamed of having good teeth. What a person calls beautiful is whatever attracts him.

MADAME DE POUVAL. (*Covering her face with her fan.*) Could I be what attracts you, my dear philosopher?

ARISTE. Excuse me, Madame, if I hesitate. My sensitive nature makes me timid. Though I am speaking impartially, you don't know me well enough not to be suspicious. You mentioned ten thousand silver pieces a year and that's what makes me nervous.

MADAME DE POUVAL. Come on, sir, you don't really suspect me of suspicions so base. It's Clarice who makes you hesitate. I see your tricks. Leave me alone. (*She starts to leave.*)

ARISTE. (*Holding her back quickly*) What injustice, Madame. Stop. You won't accuse me when you hear my plan. Cleon's engagement was broken off. He came to me and complained and

I promised to convince Clarice to give him her hand in marriage. Now, how can you believe that I'm in love with her?
MADAME DE POUVAL. (*Quickly.*) Goodbye. I'll wait for you. Don't disappoint me. Tonight, we're leaving the country. We'll fly to Paris and get married. (*She exits in a great hurry.*)
(*Enter CLARICE and CLEON.*)
CLARICE. Ah! What a pretty domino. Come closer so I can see it. Cleon, isn't it lovely? I'm the one who chose it.
CLEON. (*Very seriously.*) I know that all too well, Madame.
ARISTE. Let's talk about more important matters, Madame, no more chit-chat. I'm here to vindicate myself and to conclude an important task. Cleon loves you and you used to love him. He lost your heart and I'm the reason why.
CLARICE. Yes, sir, what's the point of being mysterious? I just told him as much.
ARISTE. Madame, I... I tell you that I will not bring about the unhappiness of such a worthy gentleman who deserves you and who will die if he doesn't possess you. I love you as much as he does. I admit that without shame. But more than mine, his passion has the force of habit and perhaps I will find within myself the ability to get over you in time... an ability which he is lacking...
CLEON. Ah, sir. What a man! You're delightful! Ah, you amaze me! What can I do...
ARISTE. Nothing, sir. Isn't it payment enough just to see you happy? Your generosity set the example. I simply imitated it.
CLARICE. Where is Madame de Pouval? Ah! Lucinde, why haven't you arrived? I want the whole world to see the triumph of philosophy.
ARISTE. (*Taking CLARICE's and CLEON's hands, he joins them.*) Be happy and stop being amazed at an endeavor which, however painful, is its own reward. (*Tenderly to CLARICE.*) Clarice, enjoy your good fortune and leave me alone. (*He exits.*)
(*As soon as ARISTE has gone, they both start to laugh.*)
CLARICE. He's going to seek consolation in the arms of Madame de Pouval. She took the thing too seriously.
CLEON. I really think so, Madame. I can hardly wait to see the outcome of this scene. What's that I hear?

(*MADAME DE POUVAL and ARISTE appear upstage of CLARICE and CLEON.*)
MADAME DE POUVAL. (*To the PHILOSOPHER.*) You've come back to me, philosopher! Ah, come, let me embrace you! (*She ties a pink ribbon around his neck.*) Let me enjoy my victory!
ARISTE. Ah! Madame, what sort of control do you have over me? Oh, Socrates! Oh, Plato! What has become of your disciple? Do you recognize him in these humiliating circumstances?
MADAME DE POUVAL. (*Dragging him downstage.*) Lovely, lovely.
ARISTE. Merciful heavens! Madame, spare me the humiliation.
MADAME DE POUVAL. What do you mean by humiliation? I want you to pride yourself on belonging to me and bearing my insignia.
CLARICE. It wasn't designed to make you ashamed.
CLEON. It was fastened by the hands of love.
MADAME DE POUVAL. Look at him. Look at him. A man so proud, he's crawling at my feet, aching for a look at my treasure! You can have him; my role is played out.
(*Peals of laughter return.*)
CLARICE. There he is: the philosopher unmasked!
ARISTE. (*Tearing himself away from the crowd that surrounds him, he throws off the domino.*) Abominable sex! I have every reason to despise you. Yes, I curse you forever. I'll triumph over your injuries. Far from alarming me, your little joke reaffirms the dominion of my sound judgment. What would become of philosophy if virtue didn't know how to cover up for it in everything?
CLARICE. Look at him, the duper duped! Let him be the man who wanted to set an example for mankind! Cleon, I'm afraid you acted your role too true to nature. You're going to be jealous, I can see it.…I give you my hand.
CLEON. Ah, Clarice, I take the object of my adoration seriously so that suspicions like the ones I had might never disgrace her in my eyes. Yes, I am the happiest of men.
MADAME DE POUVAL. Very well, very well! I'm the one who ended up looking like a fool in this adventure, but I'll get over it. Go on, be happy! At my age, I can only participate in the pleasures of others. Your happiness is my greatest joy.

CLARICE. My dear friend, increase your joy by coming to our wedding and sharing in our happiness forever.

THE END

The Wedding of the Century
Introduction

What exists of *The Wedding of the Century*, considered lost for nearly two hundred years, lies in four notebooks and a loose sheet of paper discovered by Count Xavier de Sade and published by Jean-Jacques Pauvert in the 1970 edition of Sade's plays. The first two notebooks (the A and B Texts) contain synopses of the play, though the second notebook is missing the first act. The third (the C Text) contains a rough draft of dialogue for the first act, while the fourth (the D Text) offers only the first two scenes of act two. Like *Fanny; or, The Effects of Despair* and *Truth and Treason*, this play appears to be a melodrama in the "English style," a genre of which Sade was especially fond (see the introduction to *Fanny* in this series and Sade's own in discussion of Shakespeare and the importance of showing real action onstage in Act Two of *The Shyster*).

Sade's scenario owes a great deal to Gotthold Ephraim Lessing's bourgeois tragedy *Miss Sara Sampson* (1755), which has a virtually identical plot and denouement. By the time Sade began writing *The Wedding of the Century*, Lessing's play had been translated into French and performed with great success in Paris. There is little doubt that Sade was aware of *Miss Sara Sampson* and used the play as a structural model for *The Wedding of the Century*. Lessing's tragic lover, Sara Sampson, becomes Sade's Pauline; Mellefont, Sara's lover, becomes Count Castelli; Marwood, Mellefont's vengeful former mistress, becomes Destournelle; Sir William Sampson, Sara's father, becomes the Baron Saint-Pré, Pauline's guardian; and Betty, Sara's maid, becomes Sophie. Sade ignores the rest of the dramatis personae of Lessing's play (Marwood's daughter Arabella, the servants Waitwell, Norton, and Hannah), replacing them with a single character, the Knight of Castelli, who functions as a foil to his brother, the count. The passion, posturing, and poison plot of Sade's play clearly reflect the influence of *Miss Sara Sampson*, even in the ending where Castelli falls, dying of grief, over Pauline's body.

In Lessing's play, Mellefont stabs himself before falling atop Sara's dead body. In both cases, the attempt at pathos is the same.

Perhaps even more fascinating than the play itself is the loose sheet of paper which suggests a cast breakdown that includes the name of the actor Bourdais, whom, along with his actress wife, Sade employed on 25 February 1772 to perform at his theatres at La Coste and Mazan from Easter to All Saints' Day. It seems certain that the play was composed during this period. Sade's contract with Bourdais promised the actor and his wife a sum of 800 *livres*[16] as well as room, board, and travel expenses. In addition to acting in the roles assigned them by Sade, Bourdais was charged with the function of *régisseur*, the director of the company. In that function, Bourdais wrote on 1 April 1772:

> I, the undersigned, on behalf of the Marquis de Sade, promise and pledge to provide at each performance of the plays scheduled to be done in this town of Mazan eighty tallow candles which I will distribute in the theatre, the foyer, the orchestra, and the boxes as well as twelve additional wax candles of which eight will be placed in the auditorium and four in the boxes. In addition, I pledge to provide two policemen to *Prévent* disturbances, to light a fire in the foyer when necessary, to stock two bottles of fruit cordial in the foyer and furnish said foyer with two tables, decanters of water and goblets, enough to provide for a dozen people. Finally, I promise to have two stagehands available to change the scenery when necessary and also to snuff out the lights between acts… to provide a wig maker responsible for those members of the company pointed out to him during the day; to keep the theatre clean and, in a word, to respond in general to whatever happens—taking care of the keys—in return for seventy livres French money, a figure that barely covers the total cost, damages, and interest, which sum will be paid to me by the Marquis de Sade after each performance. In good faith of which, I sign my name, at Mazan, this 1st of April, 1772.
>
> *Bourdais*

Sade was obviously serious in his attempt to establish viable theatres at Mazan and La Coste. He planned to produce plays by

---

[16] A *livre* was a French paper currency in the eighteenth century worth about one-sixth of an *écu*, or about $5 in twenty-first century US currency.

Voltaire, Chamfort, Gresset, Regnard, Sedaine, Collé, Diderot, and Destouches; and, in addition to the Bourdais, he hired an impressive list of actors and musicians that included Du Tilleul and his wife (leading performers of comedy and tragedy), Rostand (a comedian), Madame Nini Blazore (a soubrette), Bernet and Madame Aline (romantic leads), and Achard and Madame Claire (character actors).

It is not known if Sade ever completed *The Wedding of the Century*. Sade's mother-in-law, the Présidente de Montreuil, began complaining about the high cost of running a theatre and about the unsettling effect the theatricals had on her daughters, Sade's wife and sister-in-law, both of whom performed in the plays. It is not unlikely that the Présidente sensed Sade's attraction to actresses and the danger that could present to his marriage. As Arthur Maria Rabenalt has stated in *Theatrum Sadicum: Der Marquis de Sade und das Theater*:

> The Marquis has a hobby… which he shared with the entire feudal aristocracy, with the tax-collectors and land-owners, with the entire European, French-influenced society. He loved the theatre above all and in every form: as literature, as a domain of changeable existence, as a fundamental and double-faced masked play, as an erotic atmosphere, as a social catalyst. He loved the theatre and the theatre world of women, the comedies and the comedians.… He ran after the theatre princesses like Goldoni who stated in his memoirs that he could never resist a soubrette, that such was his fate.… Sade was a '*ballettranttenfänger*' (Pied Piper of the chorus girls).[17]

While Sade appeared to take little stock in the recriminations of his mother-in-law, he did cease to participate actively in the theatre at the end of June when he and his servant Latour set out to collect taxes in Marseilles. By 4 July, Sade's tax collecting had led to an arraignment for sodomy and attempted poisoning, but Sade was back at La Coste, busily producing a double bill of *Adelaide of Guesclin* (a tragedy in five acts by Voltaire) and *The Author in Love* (a one-act prose comedy by Cérou) for a performance on 9 July.

[17] (*Theatrum Sadicum: Der Marquis de Sade und das Theater*, 1963, pp. 10-11, noted by Annetta Foster in "The Place of Theatre and Drama in the Life of the Marquis de Sade, *Homme de Lettres Extraordinaire*," 1975, p. 408.)

Warned of their impending arrests, Sade and Latour fled to Italy along with Sade's sister-in-law, Anne, and the Marquis's theatrical activities were suspended for a time.

The Wedding of the Century

CHARACTERS

ACTORS OF THE COMÉDIE-FRANÇAISE[18]

The Baron Saint-Pré—Mr. Brissaut
Pauline—Miss Doligni
Count Castelli—Mr. Molé
The Knight of Castelli—Mr. Chevalier
Sophie—Miss Lucie
Destournelle—Madame Préville

ACTORS AT SADE'S THEATRE AT LA COSTE

The Baron Saint-Pré —Mr. Bourdais
Pauline—Miss de Launay
Count Castelli—Marquis de Sade
The Knight of Castelli—Marchais
Sophie—Marquise de Sade
Destournelle—an actress

The action takes place at Saint-Pré's estate (in the manuscript, Sade adds, "in Pauline's residence, not Saint-Pré's") *in the forest of Fountainbleau.*

ACT ONE

Scene One[19]

In the A text, probably an earlier outline of the play, Sade describes the initial scene as follows:

---

[18] Sade's aspirations for the play must have been high since he earmarked roles for actors currently under contract at the Comédie-Française.
[19] Because most of *The Wedding of the Century* exists only in outline, for clarity's sake I have maintained Sade's original division of acts into French scenes.

The first scene is a conversation between Saint-Pré and Pauline. She is working at her loom; Mr. Saint-Pré, at the edge of his fireplace, was reading a magazine and he stops abruptly. He tries to make Pauline understand the arrangements he has fashioned for her, emphasizing the advantages he believes are to be found in a union with Mr. Castelli, leaving her, nevertheless, free to choose as she likes. Saint-Pré exits, Sophie enters.

Add to this first act a scene about the Knight of Castelli that would let us get to know him. This will be a scene with his brother in which, while praising the virtues of his wife, he'll make him promise never to see Destournelle again. This scene will be interrupted by the arrival of the letter written by Destournelle upon her coming into town.

The setting is a room, elegantly furnished. SAINT-PRÉ is finishing a letter at the chiffonier; PAULINE is working at her loom. When the letter is sealed, SAINT-PRÉ looks at his watch and says (the following dialogue is derived from the C text):

SAINT-PRÉ. It's six o'clock. What could be keeping him? He knows very well that we have a lot to take care of the day after a wedding!
PAULINE. *(Working at her loom.)* Alas! If Castelli loved me, you'd see it in his attentiveness. He hasn't made an appearance the entire day! Yet my heart forgives him even though my head condemns him all the more. *(She stops working and, about to embrace SAINT-PRÉ, she says to him with tears in her eyes.)* My father! *(Hugging him.)* Ah, my father! *(They take stage.)*
SAINT-PRÉ. My daughter, my beloved daughter! How pleased is my affection for you by that title so dear to me. If nature hasn't given me the actual right to it, you can at least believe that I feel all its tenderness. *(He embraces her.)* Your youth prevented you from feeling the loss you experienced in the best of fathers and my dearest friend. His last wish was for me to accept the title of your guardian. I did it. Your education was the delight of my old age. In you, I saw all of your father's virtues delicately recreated; your happiness became my only concern. Rich, beautiful, and

virtuous… all Paris cast its eyes on you. Soon my house was filled with the brightest young people from the court and the city. They were lavish in their praise: each spoke his mind, saying, "This is a heart that belongs to Pauline!" You knew how to disregard correctly the customary insipid declarations that express obscenity rather than sentiment, degrading whoever receives them as much as they demean the one who makes use of them. You asked me to disperse this crowd in which your eyes saw nothing but vice and absurdity. Count Castelli and his brother were the only exceptions. Your heart hesitated for a long time, but at last, your choice was made: your preference lies with the count. You marry him and the very day after you've taken your vows, you're trembling… your heart is quivering…your senses are disturbed… your eyes are filled with tears. Ah! My daughter, what terrifying premonitions!

PAULINE. *(Sighing and wiping her eyes.)* Without a doubt, they're terrifying, father! No matter. I know how to smother them: they'll yield to the object of my love. Castelli loves me, I don't doubt that. Ah! Why wouldn't he love me? I adore him. My only pleasure lies in letting him catch a glimpse of all my affection. Why would he want to betray it?

SAINT-PRÉ. Wipe your tears, my girl. Dispel the misconceptions that are troubling you. I see your husband coming. *(The COUNT appears.)* Go on, your happiness is written in his eyes.

Scene Two

The A text indicates the following action:

Second scene. Continuing to work at the loom, Pauline relays to Sophie part of the conversation with her guardian. Sophie draws a parallel between the description of the count and that of the knight; she seems to lean strongly in favor of the knight. A servant announces Madame Destournelle, who has the conversation with Pauline detailed on pages 38 and 39 (all dialogue pages referred to in this draft are believed to be lost).

Count Castelli, very richly attired, Saint-Pré, Pauline

COUNT CASTELLI. Ah! My dear Pauline. Some responsibilities… some business affairs… some useless concerns, more annoying than necessary, but which had to be taken care of nevertheless, have kept me away from you all day. I lamented them… I cursed them a hundred times… I was boiling with the desire to be at your feet. Well, here I am, dear friend. Ah! May we be able never to be apart from one another! *(He embraces her.)*
SAINT-PRÉ. All right, my children, I'm leaving. Devote yourselves, without reservation, to the feelings that will become the delight of your lives. May this tender union also become the delight of my days and spread over the rest of my life the divine happiness of having made the one I love happy. *(With tears in his eyes.)* Goodbye, Pauline. Goodbye, daughter. *(In a low voice so that CASTELLI does not hear him.)* You see, you see. You'll be happy. It's my heart that tells me so.

Scene Three

Pauline, Castelli (The A text gives this scene to Pauline and Madame Destournelle.)

CASTELLI. Dear Pauline, you seem awfully sad to me. Ah! Good heavens! I see tears flowing from those charming eyes where I'd prefer to see only love. What's wrong? Will you hide the reason for your sadness from me? Do you still have some secret to tell me? Pauline, why are you running away from me?
PAULINE. *(Trying to leave. Wiping her eyes, she is in the depths of despair.)* Leave me alone. Ah! God! You must! *(Interrupted by sobs.)* When I thought he was the most sincere… when everything was coming together to make our marriage perfect… the dirty liar…
CASTELLI. *(Beside himself.)* Pauline, explain yourself. You're driving me to despair, sweetheart, my beloved bride.
PAULINE. Your bride? Me, your bride! You dare to call me that without blushing. You wanted to seduce me just so you could deceive me! What kind of triumph were you expecting from your treachery? The kind that belongs to all the dirty liars like you who

only delight in defiling the holiest bonds of nature. Just like all the young men of your age, you look at marriage as a matter of self-interest and custom in which the settlement is only concerned with property and not at all about people. Maybe you could say that "I really have to tell this poor little girl that I love her out of politeness. So long as she believes it, what does it matter!" There's nothing wrong in deceiving a woman and coloring, in this way, the most hideous of vices with so much smugness. You would have committed your crime in cold blood if your accomplice herself hadn't betrayed you. *(Firmly.)* Here! Read this.

CASTELLI. *(Trembling, reads with difficulty and bewilderment.)* Undoubtedly you do not know, miss, what kind of scoundrel you're about to marry. For the past five years, he has been in my captivity and I've no greater inclination to release him than he has of trying to escape. Besides, you're the second woman this month he's attached himself to. Miss Dorbessan accepted his proposal and expects to marry him next week. That's the kind of man you're dealing with. Don't thank me for writing. You owe it only to my rage. Stay on the edge of the precipice and be careful not to plunge into it. You've still got time, I know it… and if you disregard my advice, at least be in mortal fear of my revenge. Destournelle.

PAULINE. Your bride. Yes, that's what I've become. There's no more time. Heaven, you allowed it to happen. The monster! He deceived me. I'm dying! *(She falls, faint, into a chair.)*

CASTELLI. *(All ablaze, throws himself down on his knees before his wife, takes one of her hands, and says.)* Dear friend, explain yourself, I implore you. I've not deceived you in any way. You alone I adore. Pauline, see your husband at your feet, in tears, begging you to listen to him or at least make him aware of his mistakes. What have I done?

PAULINE. *(Opens her eyes and sharply frees herself from the count's hand.)* Get out of my sight. *(All the rest is spoken through tears.)* Monster, then it was only to deceive me that you tried to seduce me. Ah! Well, what reward have you reaped from your treachery? Was it for the sight of a woman wretched for the rest of her life that you wanted to indulge your cruelty? Study her at your convenience. Study the victim of your wickedness. But you won't enjoy it long. I know how to break the bonds that you weren't afraid to create. I'll go looking for a place of refuge, far from the world and far from you, where I'll be able to lament, for the rest of my miserable life, the misfortune of having loved you.

CASTELLI. *(Still on his knees.)* Dear friend, you're breaking my heart. Show me my mistakes. I can accept them close to you… close to you whom I adore… close to my beloved Pauline, whom I've never stopped loving since I met her and whom I'll adore for the rest of my life.

PAULINE. Mistakes! Monster. Mistakes! Liars, when they've deceived a woman… when they've succeeded in defiling the most respectable of bonds through the practice they have of ridiculing nature's most holy laws… that's what they call mistakes! Here, read this, and see your mistakes… or your crimes. *(She hands him a note.)*

CASTELLI. *(Reads with difficulty, fear, and surprise.)* If there's still time, postpone the knots that are about to unite you. Castelli is a monster who's unfaithful to three women at the same time. He's promised his hand to Miss Dorbessan and I've shared his life for some time now. I found out about your wedding only two hours ago. I'm not wasting a moment. But maybe I've run out of time. Let's join forces to destroy the villain. Above all, let none of the three of us become his victim. Destournelle. *(At a loss, he falls into a chair.)*

PAULINE. Well, sir, how do you explain this mistake?

CASTELLI. Ah! My beloved Pauline, can you possibly believe the tricks of a wicked, domineering woman whose charms, I admit, once captivated me, but which your loveliness has completely erased… erased in my heart. Stop believing what she tells you. It's true. I was in love with her… but ever since I fell in love with you, her image no longer appears to me except as something loathsome. And I swear to you that she's infecting you with the same loathsome ideas. I hardly knew Miss Dorbessan and I've never been linked with her to the point of asking her to marry me. I like to think that I've never even had the idea. Set your mind at ease, beautiful Pauline, and have faith that my perseverance and my increased attentions will succeed perhaps in destroying what the most hateful of women is trying to do.

PAULINE. Ah! If only I could deceive myself in such a way. But all I can see are the images of fear and of a terrifying future. Goodbye, sir. Allow me, for a moment, to shed in private the involuntary tears that I cannot hold back. *(She tries to leave.)*
CASTELLI. Ah! Stay with me…
PAULINE. Let me go.
CASTELLI. Pauline.
PAULINE. It's what I want.

Scene Four

(The A Text provides a very different scenario for this scene: *In the fourth scene, Pauline argues with Sophie over the oddness of Madame Destournelle's visit and the fifth scene is completed by Miss Dorbesan. The conversation will be the one from page 40 to 43. The description of Castelli is found on page 44 and following. Sophie is the one who'll bring it up in the second scene and Pauline will reply with what is said on pages 48 and 49. Mr. Saint-Pré will say what is written at the beginning of page 50 in the first scene to Pauline to make her see the advantage of marrying the count.*)

CASTELLI. *(Alone.)* What a predicament I'm in. I see myself on the verge of making the most virtuous of wives unhappy. When I married her, I thought I was in control of my passions. It seemed that her charms had effectively destroyed every other object in my heart. Oh, dire influence of a passion improperly extinguished! I've seen Destournelle again and everything's forgotten. Good God, I'm unhappy! Down into what abyss is she going to pull me? Will I have the strength? No, no, I won't be able to resist her. In vain do I arm myself with weapons and courage; one of her looks destroys them all. Oh, heaven! I was born just to be the perpetual plaything of the most violent of passions! How deceitful she is! She hid that note from me. It's breaking Pauline's heart. She wants me to meet her tonight in the park… to open up my own house to her… to take her in. Good Lord, but I've got to do it. What a mess! Why didn't I delay the bonds that would bring eternal misfortune upon the woman most worthy of honor and respect!

Scene Five
Servant, Count Castelli

SERVANT. *(In disguise, carries a letter.)* Sir, someone who just arrived in town ordered me to bring you this note.
CASTELLI. Ah! God, it's from her. Let me read it: I've arrived and I'm counting on you to keep your promise. You will not always deceive me. The most passionate love leads me to you. Let us see if you'll be false-hearted to the end! *(CASTELLI falls into a chair.)* Ah! God. *(To the SERVANT.)* Go on, my friend. Everything's fine. Give this key to the woman who gave you the letter and tell her that what she desires will be done. My emotions have gotten the better of me.... I can't control them. God almighty, guide this fatal day! *(He exits.)*

(The A Text adds a sixth scene before the end of the act: *The sixth scene is occupied with Mr. Saint-Pré leading Count Castelli to Pauline's feet. Pauline surrenders, the count is enraptured; the three of them exit, saying that they are going to make preparations for the wedding* [or, as Sade writes, "that happy moment"]. *Saint-Pré tells the count from now on to think of his house [Saint-Pré's] as his own.*)

END OF ACT ONE

ACT TWO

Scene One

(It is night.)

(The A Text begins the second act with the following scene: *First scene. Preparations for a festival. A monologue for Destournelle, who announces that she's going to avenge herself and that she's waiting for the count, who is about to go into his wife's room.*)

The scene is set in a park.

(The dialogue for a fragment of Act Two is found in the D Text.)

DESTOURNELLE. *(Rushing between the men and the count and speaking simultaneously with him.)* Stop. Stop. Allow me the pleasure of silencing him beforehand and of punishing him myself to the limit of his treachery. Come, villain, come confess your crime. Speak, speak if you dare… what became of your vows, your promises? What became of the honor you pledged to me? I admit it… I plotted against your life. *(Showing him the armed men, who afterwards withdraw.)* See. See what my fury had dared to attempt. Your blood was supposed to appease my jealous rage. The sight of you has calmed my anger, or rather, to take inhumanity to a new extreme, I had chosen to overwhelm you rather than punish you. Dare to confess your crime, vindicate it, or make amends for it in my eyes.
CASTELLI. *(With tears in his eyes.)* Make amends… can I? The deadly influence that you have over me… Destournelle, I loved you.… I still love you.… I dare to swear for the last time in my life that it was only your impetuous behavior that could have made me consider marrying someone else.

(Here the D Text ends. The B Text offers a somewhat fuller description of the final result of the action: *The second act opens with a monologue for Destournelle, who stations her men at various locations onstage. The count arrives. Destournelle is behind him. The count wards off the blows; he's overwhelmed with accusations. She throws away the dagger and gives in to a scene of tenderness during which she completely becomes the mistress of Castelli's heart and soul. At the end of the scene, Castelli is more in love with her than ever.*)

Scene Two

(The A Text adds a second scene in act two: *The count crosses the stage. Destournelle raises her arm to stab him.*)

Scene Three
Castelli, Destournelle, The Knight of Castelli

The third scene opens with the knight interrupting the conversation between Castelli and Destournelle, separating them and crushing them both with accusations. Destournelle exits spitefully. (The A Text gives the following scenario: *Scene three, enter Miss Dorbessan, who holds back Destournelle's arm. At the count's cry for help, Pauline comes out of her room. She faints at the sight.*)

Scene Four
Count Castelli, The Knight of Castelli

The fourth scene is between the two brothers in which the knight will threaten to bring about a separation and the count will say that his motives are clouded by jealousy. The count exits spitefully. (The A Text: Scene four. *Furious at having missed her mark, Destournelle escapes after having spoken the speech at the beginning of page 56.*)

Scene Five

The Knight of Castelli (Alone.)

The knight, alone onstage, has a monologue in which he considers what he's going to do. Saint-Pré finds him and forces him to explain himself. (Scene five is missing in the A Text.)

Scene Six
The Knight of Castelli, Saint-Pré

The knight tells Saint-Pré about everything that has happened. Saint-Pré is astonished and asks to join forces with him to break the marriage bonds. They decide to work together. (In the A Text: *Scene six begins with what Miss Dorbessan says (pages 56 and 57) and she shows Pauline the note which Destournelle had thrown on the ground during her escape. She connects it with the one she had received and reads it as well to Pauline. The count, seized with terror, has disappeared. Pauline has a monologue when Miss Dorbessan exits (pages 60 and 61) which constitutes the seventh scene.*)

Scene Eight
(From the A Text) *Mr. Saint-Pré and Pauline*

They have the conversation detailed on page 64 and following. Pauline's despair, Saint-Pré's remorse. The two of them exit to go to the aid of the count, whom Destournelle has wounded before leaving. When he has left the stage, what the count has just learned from Pauline's narrative. She goes out saying something very tender about the baneful misfortune of this particular day.

ACT THREE

(The apartment.)

Scene One
Count Castelli, A Valet

The count orders his valet to remove Madame Destournelle from the house in which she is living in town and bring her into this apartment by such and such a door… and that she is to be there alone and in safety. The valet exits. (The A Text: *Pauline and the Knight of Castelli. Pauline opens with a monologue and announces that the Knight of Castelli is coming to speak to her.*)

Scene Two

Count Castelli (Alone.)

Monologue from the count, who is a little suspicious of his brother's feelings and his desire to lend himself to the break-up. (The A Text: *The Knight of Castelli informs Pauline that, under the pretense of going to bed for the night, when he (the count) had put his wife to bed, it was only to let in Destournelle, who had spent the night in his apartment. The conversation is on pages 76, 77, and following. He shows Pauline the note (page 82) and at the moment when he throws himself at her feet to beg her to excuse his brother's offense, Castelli enters, all bandaged up.)*

*Scene Three
Destournelle, Count Castelli*

Destournelle convinces the count of the affair between the knight and his wife. She uses every trick possible. The count struggles. Destournelle insists and ends up persuading and provoking the count. Then she tells him that every step she takes dishonors her, that she knows that he is likewise plotting against her, and that all that remains for the count is to do everything in his power to marry her. She leaves him alone to think it over. (In the A Text: *Scene three is a dialogue created from the conversation on page 85 and following. The knight shows his brother Destournelle's note, which Pauline had dropped. Castelli grabs a sword to cut down his brother. The knight answers with what is on page 87. The rest of this scene is the dialogue on page 88. Throughout the scene, Pauline is faint.)*

Scene Four

Count Castelli (Alone.)

The count's monologue in which the count resolves to clear everything up. (While the A Text gives no scene numbers for the rest of the act, it does provide the following synopsis: *The knight has gone out. The count curses his wife, saying that he is a hundred times tempted to stab her while she is unconscious. He leaves only after entrusting her to his men in his apartment. Pauline's monologue and scene between Pauline and Sophie. The count returns and says that he has just learned all that his brother and Saint-Pré are plotting against him. He accuses Pauline of the plot (pages 94, 95, 96). He is no longer himself. He drags Pauline by the hair and hurls her into the wings.)*

*Scene Five
Castelli, Pauline*

Enter Pauline, whom the count receives indifferently and to whom he discloses his accusations. Pauline rejects them with dignity, sweetness, and affection. The count exits, accusing her of being in favor of a divorce.

Scene Six

Pauline (Alone.)

Pauline's monologue in which she is in despair over the way her husband thinks and her inability to change his mind.

Scene Seven
Pauline, The Knight of Castelli

Enter the Knight of Castelli. Pauline complains to him about her husband's coldness. The knight informs her that the evil woman was in the park all night with armed men; that she is plotting some crime; that he cannot help thinking that it might be against her; that he is imploring her to go back to Paris and to spare his brother from committing a crime. Pauline forgives her husband; the knight rushes and casts himself at Pauline's feet.

Scene Eight

Castelli, Knight of Castelli, Pauline

Scene eight opens with Castelli, who enters, shocked, furious, and heaping the bloodiest accusations upon his wife and brother; here read page 84. He grabs a sword and attacks his brother. Pauline rushes between them and forces the knight to withdraw, which he does, saying: "I'm leaving, but tremble. Your life will answer to me for your wife's" and page 88. The count comes back onstage with his wife. His anger remains the same. He blames her for having trembled prodigiously on behalf of his brother's life and concludes by dragging her by the hair into a dungeon.

END OF ACT THREE

ACT FOUR

(The setting is in a dungeon.)
The scene opens with Pauline's monologue, interrupted by the knight who is coming to recommend that she file for divorce. She opposes it and says that she doesn't even want to leave her dungeon cell… that Castelli himself couldn't drag her from it. Castelli enters, acts contrite, and his humanity returns to him. He appears to admit to his mistakes and asks his brother to leave him alone with his wife. His brother exits. (The A Text paints a similar portrait: The scene is set in a repulsive dungeon. Pauline is there, her hair disheveled. Monologue. Sophie enters completely terrified and announces to Pauline that her death had been decided by Destournelle and the count. She relates everything that is on pages 101 and 102. Castelli, conqueror of those who he believes are after his wife's honor, enters the prison like a madman. He softens, nevertheless, at the sight of the wretched state to which he sees his wife reduced. "Madame," he tells her, "I am ready to remedy all that I've done if you will be willing to deny, in writing, all the false accusations made to the ministry by Saint-Pré and my brother, all those made against Miss Destournelle, whose case cannot be separate in this affair." Pauline signs without hesitation. One can barely see the entrance of Saint-Pré, who is supporting himself with difficulty. Castelli withdraws upon seeing him, turning pale with terror. This scene takes place still in the prison. It is on page 139 and following. A servant comes to give Pauline Castelli's letter: page 147. The only alteration that might be made here is that Castelli is being followed, about to be arrested, and forced to flee.)

Scene between the husband and his wife, the husband's insincerity, the wife's affection. A moment later, the knight returns absolutely terrified; he is coming to inform Pauline about the duel between her husband and Saint-Pré because Saint-Pré wanted to annul the marriage. Saint-Pré is carried into the prison; he asks to see Pauline. Saint-Pré's death; Pauline's despair. Accusations from the knight, who drags Pauline out of prison. (In the A Text, Sophie arrives and sets her free. Pauline goes to the ministry to ask pardon for her husband.)

END OF ACT FOUR

ACT FIVE

First scene between Destournelle and Pauline: the former admits to her crimes, begs Pauline to forgive her, and asks for her friendship; the latter acts in good faith and embraces her. The count enters, finds them together, and at Destournelle's request, he is genuinely reconciled with his wife. She begins getting hot flashes; Castelli is concerned; Destournelle grows bolder; the vapors increase, the signs of poison are showing. "I am avenged," says Destournelle. The wife dies with a virtuous resignation, weeping over her husband, lamenting him, loving him, and forgiving Destournelle.

(Neither the A or B Texts indicate specific French scenes in Act Five. The A Text runs as follows: *Pauline enters with her husband's pardon. Destournelle enters in a rage and tells her everything that is specified on page 43 and following. She informs her that Castelli has fought with his brother over Miss Dorbessan, whom he wanted to kidnap and with whom he is in love. Destournelle leaves Pauline in sorrow. She runs to look for her husband, who enters after a short monologue. Destournelle enters and she and the count have a scene copied on page 109 which the countess hears because, looking for her husband, she sees them and cannot help but hear them… an interesting scene to relate that which is on pages 129, 130, and following. They exit on opposite sides. Pauline enters, monologue copied on page 138. In the scene between Destournelle and the count, the former having convinced him of his wife's infidelity, she presents him with the idea of getting rid of her by means of poison; they part company, the count having agreed to it. The count is all the more convinced of his wife's infidelity when Destournelle reads him aloud a counterfeit love letter. After Pauline's monologue, a servant brings her a letter from the count, page 165. Pauline's terror and despair. She faints. An interesting monologue in which she makes known that she thinks she has been poisoned. Enter Destournelle, who is coming, she says, to look upon her victim.*)

The count cannot tolerate this excess of horror; he stabs Destournelle. The knight enters. His brother does not recognize him; he is out of his mind. The knight tries to bring him back to his senses; he goes mad and stabs himself over his wife's body. (In the A Text: *The count is moved by compassion and remorse. He stabs Destournelle, who dies saying that she is finally punished for her crimes. The count is alone onstage between Destournelle's corpse and his dying wife. The latter embraces him and dies saying to him all the most tender things imaginable. The count, alone, has a terrifying monologue set up by the 'scene in the English style' in which all of his crimes springing to mind cause his hair to stand on end. He is seized with despair. He falls and dies of grief upon his wife's body. He should in no way appear to consent to the poisoning of his wife.)*

END OF ACT FIVE

The Madness of Misfortune

Introduction

The Marquis de Sade put *The Madness of Misfortune; or, The Virtuous Criminal*, a three-act drama in prose, at the head of his first volume of plays listed in the *Descriptive Catalogue of 1788*. In his examination of Sade's work, Gilbert Lély suggests that the play (then lost) was written in Vincennes Prison sometime before 1781. Jean-Jacques Brochier, however, cites the discovery of two notebooks dated 1808 that contain Sade's final revisions of the play along with directions to the copyist. This "good rough draft," as Sade called it, is significant in dating the play more accurately. On the inside cover of one of the notebooks, Sade crossed out an inscription from Voltaire's tragedy *Alzire*, Act II, Scene ii, which read,

> Woe to ungrateful hearts, born for crime,
> Unmoved by the misfortunes of others.

and added a phrase in black ink, "There are, after all, crimes that a person cannot condemn" as well as the date 1772 in Roman Numerals. On 15 January 1772, Sade invited Girard de Lourmain to attend a performance of an original play (perhaps *The Self-Proclaimed Philosopher*) scheduled for 20 January at the manor theatre of La Coste, his country estate. The following February, the Marquis hired Bourdais and his wife, both professional actors, to perform at La Coste between Easter and November 1772. Because of the highly demanding roles in *The Madness of Misfortune*, it is probable that the professional actors were hired for a performance of that play.

A loose page appended to the manuscript, written in Sade's hand, indicates that as of 30 October 1790, *The Madness of Misfortune* had been offered to the Théâtre du Palais Royal. Below it, in a different color ink, Sade added, "Withdrawn at the time of my quarrel with Gaillard and given to the Théâtre Molière where it was accepted."

What the quarrel with Gaillard, the manager of the Palais Royal, was about we may only guess from a note dated 18 November 1790:

> If Mr. de Sade would take the time to spend a morning at the administration desk of the Théâtre du Palais Royal, someone will provide a critique of his play, *The Madness of Misfortune*. Should he agree with our opinions, and subsequently make the necessary changes, the play could be performed in the future at the Théâtre du Palais Royal.

Almost certainly, the play was submitted to the Théâtre Molière after 6 March 1791 since on that date, the Marquis wrote to Reinaud, his lawyer, telling him that the play had been accepted for performance at the Palais Royal. If Sade had provided the necessary alterations to the play to insure its acceptance, the fact that it was not performed suggests an even deeper, perhaps more personal, disagreement between the author and the theatre manager. There is no record of a subsequent performance of the play at the Théâtre Molière.

It is hardly surprising that a man of the Marquis de Sade's personality would be argumentative, especially at this point in his life. On 13 June 1790, his wife Renée de Montreuil sued for divorce; in August, the Marquis began a liaison with a young actress named Marie Renelle; on 23 September, the divorce settlement revealed that Sade owed his wife a total of 160,842 *livres* to be paid in annual increments; and in November, he set up house with Marie Constance Quesnet, a "decent, kindly, matronly woman." The Marquis de Sade's personal life certainly evoked the melodrama as well as the madness and misfortune of his play.

In 2003, the Belligerent Muse Company undertook a production of *The Madness of Misfortune* in a church hall in Philadelphia. In an attempt to recreate Sade's productions at La Coste, the actors portrayed the Marquis, his wife, sister-in-law, and servant Latour, performing the roles of the Chevalier de Merville, Cecile, Marianne, and Derval. Although audiences were taken with the concept, reviewers were unimpressed:

> I am astonished to be able to report that a show that involves wrist-slashing, two women making love, executioners in black shiny zippered-up-the-back bikinis, two occasions of masturbation to

orgasm and various other hoo-ha is, simply and stupefyingly, *boring*.

The same critic went on to report that "the thing is, people confuse plays *about* Sade with plays *by* Sade. The decadent French aristocrat who spent much of his life in prison wrote the graphic, sexually perverse novels (*Justine* is the most famous/notorious) that gave his name to sadism. But alas, and not to mention alack: His drama is cloying rubbish, full of sentimental scenes and cliché language. He explains that women in distress turn him on, and this play makes the old silent movie *The Perils of Pauline* look sophisticated—and this play isn't silent, not by a long shot, more's the pity."

It is not surprising that, 230 years after *The Madness of Misfortune* was written, critics would find fault with the play. In its own century, the management of the Théâtre du Palais Royal and Théâtre Molière did not see fit to produce it. Nonetheless, Sade placed it at the top of his list of original works, certainly an indication of his perceived value of the work. Julia Chandler Hayes argued in her dissertation, "The Representation of the Self in the Theater of La Chaussée, Diderot, and Sade" that "these works from the first half of Sade's literary career show us the formation of a strong and disruptive literary sensibility, which has not yet found its ideal form of expression. Consciously or not, in his plays Sade is taking all the commonplaces of his period and distorting them just slightly.... [W]hat results is largely incoherent, lacking any definite standards, casting doubt on the meaningfulness or value of the *système de rapports* [the social structure]."

Perhaps *The Madness of Misfortune* has not stood the test of time on the stage, but it is an important document in the development of the Marquis de Sade as a revolutionary writer and in its pages can be seen the seeds of *Justine*, *Juliette*, and *The 120 Days of Sodom*. As Janine Cey Hartman concluded in "The Politics of Decadence: The Political and Social Ideas of Sade. Gautier, Baudelaire, and Flaubert," "Sade existed chiefly as a writer determined to present a private alternate view of the universe. Despite his rank and acts, Sade was valued more for his ideas and willingness to challenge and transcend all accepted values."

The Madness of Misfortune
Drama in Three Acts

CHARACTERS
Derval
Old Merville
The Chevalier de Merville
Cecile, Derval's wife
Marianne, Cecile's companion
A policeman
Two bailiffs

(The play takes place in London.)

COSTUMES

DERVAL should be in the most wretched disarray, without a sword, nobility nowhere but in his face.
CECILE and MARIANNE are dressed very simply with little distinction between their clothes. They could be either in faded French clothes that are out of style or in the simplest of English dresses that are somewhat more up-to-date.
OLD MERVILLE is in a fur-lined coat in the second act since it is a winter night. In the third act, he wears black or brown velour embroidered with gold.
The CHEVALIER is very elegantly dressed in the first act in contrast with the women's clothes. In the third act, he wears a frockcoat.
The Policeman and the bailiffs wear typical English clothing.

ACT ONE

(The scene is a ramshackle apartment. Everything indicates the most extreme misery; the only furniture in the room is an ugly table and two unpolished, worn old chairs. A lamp is burning on the table. CECILE and MARIANNE come out of a small side room where

Cecile's son is resting. Both of them are pale, downtrodden, and depressed.)

MARIANNE. Mr. Derval has been gone four hours and he's not come back. Ah, dear mistress, what a sorry plight you're in! You who could have been, if you so desired, the wife of one of the richest men in France… living in luxury and opulence in the company of the rich and famous. But here you are, abandoned by everyone, without any money, plunged into the most hideous misery, and reduced to live in the humiliation of taking charity… In England! In a strange country, where every reason you have to hide your name and your birthright only serves to make your life poorer and more difficult. Ah! Madame, is love worth this?

CECILE. Oh, my sweet Marianne, I shed my tears for you, not for myself. Happy with Derval, whom I adore, in spite of everything, my heart is satisfied… but you who have sacrificed everything to share in my sad fortune, to follow my unhappy fate, the state brought about by my own husband which is killing that poor child, the sign of his *love… (She cries.)* Ah! Marianne, Marianne, these are the terrible deeds that are ripping me apart. Let death, in carrying me away first, promptly seize from my eyes the horrible spectacle of my distress. *(In the greatest distress, she falls next to the table.)*

MARIANNE. Oh! heavenly mistress, live, live, I beg of you. Let strength and courage run through your senses already numbed by sadness. If you love Mr. Derval, if you cherish that child, save yourself for those who are so precious and dear to you.

CECILE. Alas, what can I do for them? Without me, Derval would have less to sigh about. When he has to share the meager gifts he carries home from the generous old Frenchman who used to come and visit us… when he has to share them, I tell you, the paltry portion he keeps for himself can scarcely provide him with the strength necessary to go out again and beg for more. Alone, he will live better, he'll have less to trouble him; he will not abandon his child. No, Marianne, he will not abandon him! Ah! My dear friend, heaven is rejecting me. It refuses me my daily bread. Why do I seek to prolong the agony? Does it not show me its will? Is it not opening the door to the grave? How many times did the sun begin and finish its course before the most meager

nourishment came into our miserable household? Today, aren't we in the same situation? We've done without for three days. Ah! Marianne, what a terrible fate we have!
MARIANNE. *(Quickly.)* Ah! What a horrible situation! Derval, you're to blame for all of this. You're the one who carried her away; your love has ruined her. Why couldn't you leave her in the care of her family? Wouldn't it be better to have given her up forever than to keep her at such a terrible cost?
CECILE. What are you saying? What would life be without him? I wanted him. For the sweetest of all loves, he gave up a brilliant fortune which was his birthright; he plunged a father, an entire family into sorrow and desolation. The innumerable difficulties and insurmountable obstacles that my family raised against our marriage made him even more determined to marry me at any cost. He made all of the sacrifices. Don't I have everything in the world I wanted? Derval, my heart is as capable of blaming you in the smallest way as it is to stop loving you. Heaven is my witness that I make no accusations. Ah! I am only distressed by seeing him reduced to the misery that engulfs him because of me. Every moment I tremble to see regret on his lips or in his heart; and if ever I had the smallest proof of it, I would not survive, you can be sure of it. I don't mind that we have nothing. As long as Derval lives and loves me, I'll never be unhappy.
MARIANNE. If Derval has sacrificed the treasures of a fortune, he has acquired nature's most precious treasure. Yes, dear mistress, I am forever attached to your fate. I want to live and die with you... but allow me to suggest an idea. Do you think that the French ambassador would be unsympathetic to your circumstances if you approached him? And wouldn't he be a resource to draw upon in these terrible times when you're reduced to poverty?
CECILE. We'd have to tell him who we were and isn't that what we're afraid of? Maybe he already has secret orders in his hands; we know that he's a friend of my father-in-law... Our separation would be certain twenty times over. We considered the idea, but the certainty of being torn from one another made us reject it immediately. Derval and I would rather suffer the cruelest misfortune if it could be softened by our love... by the attraction of

participating in it together, instead of the life intended for each of us, which we could only enjoy separately. On the very eve of my marriage to a man I couldn't love, to whom I had been promised, Derval offered me an escape. By revealing my identity, wouldn't I be breaking the ties that are dearer to me than life only to form others under which unhappy Cecile wouldn't survive an instant?

MARIANNE. Eh! I don't know a lot of things… but… this young Frenchman you know… his soul moved by the excess of your misery… feeling generous, he might give you some token if he knew your situation. Frivolity may numb the mind, but it doesn't stifle the sentiments of the heart. Perhaps…

CECILE. Ah! He's a monster; stop talking about him. Marianne, have you forgotten what price this scoundrel places on the services he offers? How I blush to have been deceived by the tricks he used to get close to me from the very beginning. I should have spoken to Derval about it, but I admit that I feared my husband's violent temper. I was forced to see him a second time. Though I blame myself for the whole situation, I hope, nevertheless, that the way I treated him the last time will have discouraged him from coming again. I'd rather die a thousand deaths than accept his generosity. What's the use of seeking assistance? There is nothing left for us. Even the feeble labor of our hands is scorned. Remember how tired you became working day and night last month? It's not the work that bothers me, you know, it's just that there's nothing to do anymore. Our misery is at its worst. There's not even the slightest hope! Not even the smallest resource! It's all used up! *(Despairingly.)* God, what a horrible plight! *(Getting up with difficulty.)* I've never been so depressed. A terrible weakness has come over me… Derval isn't back yet. Has he abandoned his wife? Has his son stopped being dear to him? Everything disturbs me. Everything is making me nervous… I hear a noise. Go see how my son is doing.

(Derval enters.)

DERVAL. *(Dressed miserably and behaving with the greatest agitation.)* Oh, God of my heart, there is nothing left us now but death. I've carried home nothing… not any relief at all. Those happy people who scarcely know misery close both their hearts and their ears to the doleful sounds of misfortune. There is nothing

I haven't done, nothing I haven't tried. Would you believe it, beloved? I almost threw myself at the feet of a famous banker whom I saw coming out of the stock exchange with several sacks full of money. He hardly cast a glance at me. It seems that the gold of the rich builds a fortress in their heart that rejects and repels the humble supplications of the unfortunate. Immediately following, thinking that a Frenchman would be more sympathetic, I tried to interest two of them in the street. The same attempt, the same refusal. Finally, humiliated, impatient, dying of cold, having spent the whole day out of doors begging for the feeblest sustenance, bread, alas! Bread drenched by my tears. I've returned empty-handed and can only propose, my sweet Cecile, that we die together and terminate the terrible days which unhappiness, oppression, and misery have taught us to surrender to the cruel being who has prolonged them far too long.

CECILE. Dear and tender supporter of my ills, remember all the courage and perseverance which have served us up to now. Save yourself for your child and let me die first. My days arc a burden to you; I am ready to make the sacrifice, only, alas! Promise to save yourself.

DERVAL. *(Holding her in his arms.)* Oh, beloved wife, what are you suggesting? What in the world would I do without you? Who would befriend me? If I had some kind of trade… but the frivolous education of the nobility offers no resource for misfortune. In France, at least, I could serve my King… but here, to carry arms against my country… no, Cecile, no, I will not betray, in that way, all of the feelings in my heart.

CECILE. Ah! I will not allow it!

DERVAL. Alas, what will become of us? Everything has abandoned us altogether; our sanity is failing and disappearing before our own eyes. Pale and beaten, the bloom that used to adorn your face reproaches my inhuman behavior as it fades away. And I was the one who wanted it, who took you away from a family happy to have you under their roof. And where? Good God! To the most frightful and horrible hovel in England; is that a sanctuary for beauty, for virtue? If my father were at least able to know about our terrible situation, he would have pity on us. We would cast

ourselves at his feet. He is good. He's a father. I daresay we could expect his forgiveness.
CECILE. Couldn't we write to him?
DERVAL. I don't know where he's living these days. You know as well as I the latest news I've received from France. After a long period of lamenting my loss, he was reconciled with his second son, the brother whom I've never known, with whom my father had been so unhappy for these many years. Now they're traveling together. Who could tell me where they are? If I knew my brother, I would try to interest him on our behalf so that he could put in a good word with my father. He would not be so callous to refuse me.
CECILE. Ah! If only we could find them both.
DERVAL. *(Extremely discouraged.)* Sadness, despair, and remorse are suddenly assaulting my heart. Abandon me, Cecile. Get away from me. I am an unfortunate man; my heart leads me astray. Leave me, I tell you. Everything has been taken away from me except the ability to prolong your life. People refuse me; they don't even listen to me. Your beauty will melt their hearts. Go, use every attraction you have. Don't think about anything but you and your son. Forget about me. Forget me. When you return, I'll no longer exist. *(In extreme despair, he falls into a chair.)*
CECILE. Derval, do you dare talk to me like that?
DERVAL. *(Getting up suddenly after a terrible silence.)* Listen, there is a way. God, what madness! Oh, my Cecile, let's die. Let's die instead. How could that be any crueler for you? Here, I'll give you an example: let's not permit hunger, devouring hunger, to force us to die in misery and pain! Let a death, sweeter and less frightening, return us to the bosom of that miserly nature which refuses to nourish its children!
CECILE. Oh, my friend, let's try something else. I am willing to die with you, but let's prolong, if we can, the life of our child. Who will sustain his feeble days if we abandon him? My friend, my husband, I beg you on his behalf.
DERVAL. *(Firmly.)* Weak woman, you don't dare take him into the coffin with us. Very well! See him die of misery; hear his painful cries asking you either for life or the end of an existence you are unable to prolong. Just like an abandoned young plant, watch

him fade as he springs up and blame us for the unhappy days of sadness and suffering we gave him.

CECILE. Ah! God! What a sight. Derval, do you want your words to destroy me completely? Is that the courage you made me believe in? Coward! It didn't cost you anything to promise courage in the lap of luxury; but the moment you find yourself in trouble here, blinded by love, you become weak. *(Firmly.)* Derval, another attempt, I implore you, one more, only one more attempt for this child. I don't need anything for myself. A little water satisfies me, but in the name of our love, do not abandon that unhappy creature.

DERVAL. *(Frantically.)* If it's what you want, I'll do it! I'm on my way. I'm hurrying. But tremble, unhappy woman. You're going to answer to… no, I'm going, my dear friend. It's late. What does it matter… maybe I'll find something…

(Marianne enters.)

MARIANNE. *(In tears, deliriously.)* Madame, Madame, come quickly. Your son just fainted. He was pale and contorted while I held him. *(CECILE flies to her son with a frightening shriek.)*

MARIANNE. *(Quickly.)* Ah! Sir, try to get some help. Without it, this night will carry away your wife and son. In the name of God, find some relief for their misfortunes.

DERVAL. *(Distracted and distraught.)* Yes, I'm going. I'll find something. Marianne, assure your mistress of that fact. I'll find something. I will not return without it. It will be difficult for us, perhaps… but after all, in our situation, don't we have to take what we can get? Marianne, take care of her… take care of my son. Soon… ah! merciful God… *(He exits like a madman.)*

MARIANNE. Has anyone endured a more terrible plight? Love, what do you do to men? How she's changed, my poor mistress. What a difference. I don't dare tell her, but it's easy to see how sadness, misery, and worry will lead her to the grave. I'll follow her there; I owe everything to her; I will never abandon her. I feel less sadness in sharing it with her. Ah, God, there's that villain again! What can be done to keep Cecile from the real horror she feels in his presence?

(De Merville enters.)

DE MERVILLE. And good day to you, my lovely little angel. What's your pretty mistress doing leaving you all by yourself here?
MARIANNE. At the moment, more wretched than ever, she is at the bedside of her son, who has been overcome by a violent seizure. Ah! Sir, she is hardly in the mood to welcome you today; every day, her situation grows more frightening.
DE MERVILLE. *(Almost touched.)* That's terrible! *(Continuing ironically.)* But it's your fault, too. Why didn't you tell me about it? A person can't always be a mind-reader in this country. I am not without means and if I were able to prevent all these little trifles… Why didn't you let me know? I'm not going to hide the fact that it's also your mistress' fault. She's arrogant when she's miserable: she needs to be humbled a bit. I ask for nothing more than to help her, but she must bend at least to the gratitude I require. Isn't that right, my child? You wouldn't be so proud, would you?
MARIANNE. There is little nobility and generosity in that way of thinking, sir. What would become of the poor if the ears of the rich hardened, closing off the plaintive cries of their misery?
DE MERVILLE. Talk! That's all talk, my pretty slut. People really only want to lend a helping hand if the outcome is favorable. That, you will agree. It's a matter of making good investments. I am very rich… but I like to spend wisely. Truly, you know in your heart that your dear lady would not be too happy if…
MARIANNE. *(Breaking in quickly)* Ah! You're frightening me. You don't know her, sir, you don't know her. She is poor, but she is proud. The blood in her veins runs true. Adversity may have withered her beauty, but it has spared her heart. She has the noble sentiments of her birth, sir; she only regrets that she hasn't the means to sustain them. Moreover, she has a husband she loves and death would seem a thousand times sweeter to them both than the despicable help you dare to propose. *(Aside)* Ah! God! Does this monster come here just to humiliate us?
DE MERVILLE. *(Sarcastically.)* Very well, my child, let her stay with her beloved husband. I in no way want to corrupt the peace of the marriage bond. She's right. Infidelity is a hideous thing. And then this dear husband… certainly he doesn't deserve to be offended.

MARIANNE. *(Crying.)* No, sir, he doesn't deserve it. Happier in the virtues of his heart than you are in your wealth, he would not exchange his soul for all of your money. Keep it. Keep it, sir. It would humiliate us to accept it at your price. My mistress may die of misery, but she'll never die of shame.

DE MERVILLE. Shame! For God's sake, my dear, it is I who should blush a little for carrying so much money with me. I should hold on to it vigorously in so frightening a neighborhood and at this time of night. But your mistress arouses feelings within me that are so strong that I cannot resist coming here, to a house such as this. If anyone knew about this, it would hurt my reputation. Ah! Damn it. I want you to speak well about all that I'm going through for her… But here she comes.

(Cecile enters.)

CECILE. What brings you here, sir? I was hoping that what had happened the last time I was honored by your presence might have discouraged any future visits. They're a burden to me, sir, I cannot hide that from you. Not being able to receive your visits as would befit my situation and not wanting to permit them in any other way, I think, sir, it would be prudent and noble of you to stop coming here.

DE MERVILLE. The feelings that I have for you, Madame, may serve as excuses for my behavior. I had thought that so much love on one side, so much misfortune on the other, might soften that heart where a pride, unfit for poverty, forever reigns.

MARIANNE. Ah! Madame, if you only knew all that the Chevalier dared to tell me in your absence.

CECILE. *(To MARIANNE.)* His improper remarks only disgrace himself. *(To DE MERVILLE.)* They shame you, sir. I understand that the respect of a poor woman such as I is of little worth to you, but has the voice of your conscience ceased to be of any value? Search inside yourself, sir, and see if it agrees with you.

DE MERVILLE. Always talking virtue! Grand words! Honor! You are incorrigible. Why not condescend to share in the magnificent fortune I offer you in exchange for your heart. Yes, that's all I'm after… that alone will make me happy. Leave this wretched hovel. Never was Venus so badly enshrined. Leave that poor bastard who abandons you all the time. Leave that child who is good for nothing and follow me. Then you can count on getting everything you desire and the most tender and magnificent lover will be eager to anticipate your every wish.

CECILE. My wishes are reduced to a single one, sir, which you can easily satisfy and that is for you to leave immediately. Stop insulting an unfortunate woman whom you bring to despair with your sordid talk. A person can do without everything, sir. Happy is he whom Heaven blesses with wealth! But does he have the right to offend those crushed by misery? The heart of a man could be insensitive to misery; nature did not endow all beings with organs of similar response. But it is only villains who treat with contempt the sadness of others and laugh at the bitterness of their tears. May heaven preserve you forever from the misfortunes you dare to defy. Whoever can view them with a cold heart would not have the courage to endure them. Get out, sir, get out, I beg you. Do not carry me beyond despair. My grief and my tears crush me enough without having to suffer again the excruciating offenses that ravage my heart. Get out, you most wicked of all men. *(She weeps.)*

DE MERVILLE. *(Ironically.)* Madame, excuse me, I did not think that offering you help would offend you. With all due respect, if I offer a fortune, it is reasonable that I desire something in return. Goodbye, Madame, I'm leaving. *(Aside.)* You will remember this last refusal, Madame Derval. *(To MARIANNE.)* Goodbye, lovely queen. Ah! Please make my peace with your mistress. What misplaced prudishness! *(Aside, tossing a purse of gold into his hand.)* Oh! Sooner or later, she'll be caught in this net; it's the graveyard of all virtue.

(During this aside, CECILE leans on the table, engulfed in her grief. Having heard what the CHEVALIER said to her, MARIANNE approaches CECILE to console her. The women neither see nor hear the final actions or words of the CHEVALIER.)

CECILE. What a monster, my friend! Is it possible that there are hearts like that on earth? What a contrast with the honest old man who helps us out of kindness.

MARIANNE. The last time he came, Madame, finding no one here but me, he forbade me to tell you he was here bringing gifts. "Go on, Marianne," he said to me, "let her be happy, that's all I want. If she's happy, I'll be content. Don't tell her it's me; a kindness revealed loses most of its value. She will owe me nothing. She will be spared the recognition and I will enjoy myself more." Alas! Why doesn't he come by more often? It disturbs me. Has he left London without coming to see us one last time?

CECILE. I don't know, dear.

MARIANNE. How was your son when you left, Madame?

CECILE. A little better, thanks. He only fainted from hunger. I gave him a crust of black bread that Derval brought home the other day. He responded rather well to this meager gift. He seemed to know that it was a sacrifice. My husband… what's become of him?

MARIANNE. He left the moment before the Chevalier arrived, but with a mad look in his eyes. He said he wouldn't return without…

CECILE. *(Disturbed.)* Ah, God! Why did you let him go out at this hour? You don't understand him, Marianne. Knowing that his son… his wife… he is capable of anything. We would have spent tonight well enough. I must hurry to find him. I'm filled with terrible apprehension! Stay close to my son. Ah! Marianne, I fear the worst. *(She exits, terrified.)*

MARIANNE. All-powerful God, if virtue is precious and dear to you, save her. Save her from the madness of misfortune!

END OF ACT ONE

ACT TWO

(Night. The setting depicts a secluded street in the outskirts of London not far from DERVAL's house. We can see snow falling and collecting on the street.)

DERVAL. *(Alone.)* What a night! The shadows seem to magnify the horror of my plans. Oh, tender half of my being… no, I will not return without the help I promised you. *(He wanders through the street like a madman.)* The first one who passes by

will provide the grim assistance whether he wants to or not. Necessity—cruel necessity—if you are able, stifle the terrible cry of my conscience. Sacred voice of nature, I have to obey you, yet you seem to despise my crime. My soul is filled with fear. Need, honor, love, and virtue assault it. They tear at it one by one and leave it in the most overwhelming uncertainty. *(Like a man terrified.)* God, I hear the sharp cries of my son dying of hunger; I hear the groans of his mother; I see her trembling at my feet begging for life. It's done. I've decided. Cruel laws, give life to those you seek to overcome or deal gently with him who dares to disobey you every now and again to keep what he holds most dear. Nobody's coming… too bad for the one… *(Silence.)* Tomorrow, led into a foul prison, thrown together with horrible criminals… I will have nothing more than my conscience. God, what terrifying remorse I may find there! Love will soften it at least. She's the reason that I'm doing all of this. In the midst of the horrors that surround me, she alone, alas, will sustain my courage. I'll imagine myself in the bosom of my beloved Cecile; there, I'll feel her completely and find consolation. A deadly chill fills me… I think I hear a noise. Good Lord, how far am I from the fearless ferocity of a criminal. Ah, I wasn't born for crime! No, I will never dare to do it. But I must. Let's go. *(He goes off to the wings and returns distracted and trembling.)* It was no one. Still nothing. Calm yourself, Derval. You're still innocent, enjoy the last moments of virtue that remain. You are still worthy of your Cecile; you are still as pure as she is. There's no mistaking this noise. Someone's coming. It's a man. I'll hide behind this house to catch him by surprise. *(He hides so that he is unseen by the audience.)*
(Old Merville enters.)

OLD MERVILLE. It's been awhile since I've looked in on the poor needy family that lives in the neighborhood. It's all because of my business affairs. Alas, should they have been more important to me than doing a good deed? *(At this point, DERVAL comes forward a bit, draws back in fright, and fades into the background.)* It is enough to know that my son may be one of those unfortunates. God! If I could find him! There would be no greater satisfaction. Heaven is my witness that the real motive behind the trips that I take at my age is simply to try and find that beloved child. Oh, providence so benign, will you resist my impatience? If only I could embrace him again, I would return to my homeland and die a happy man.

(DERVAL suddenly comes out from behind the house, his eyes distracted, his hat pulled down over his eyes, not looking in the direction of the person he is about to attack. He speaks very quickly.)

DERVAL. Whoever you are, help me. I am an unfortunate man reduced to doing what you see. Don't blame me; don't try to discourage me from committing a crime I don't want to commit, a crime which is contrary to my heart and conscience. It's about bread. I'm doing it for bread.

OLD MERVILLE. Ah! Unhappy man, you're looking for trouble! Get away or I'll cry for help.

DERVAL. Cry. Cry. I'll take everything from you in an instant. Quickly, quickly, give me everything you have or fear for your life. There's not a moment to lose. *(He takes him by the collar.)*

OLD MERVILLE. Help! Help! Heavens, what unwarranted violence! *(Throwing him his purse.)* Take it, villain, that's all I have. *(Going away.)* I don't regret the loss of this money; I regret being unable to use it as I intended. *(He exits.)*

DERVAL. *(Alone, in the greatest disarray, leaving the purse on the ground.)* It's done. In an instant, I've overcome the distance between crime and virtue. You will live, my son! You will live, my beloved and noble wife. I will no longer hear your cries; I will no longer fear your accusations; I will be content! Content! Heavens, can I be content after committing such a terrible deed? What despicable cruelty! Perhaps this money was also the last resort of my unhappy victim. All right! I'll report it. *(He picks up the money.)* What am I saying? The dreadful deed is done; let's enjoy it. It cost me a great deal! Here, then, is the fruit of crime! The terrible remorse that pierces my heart becomes my most frightening torment. Nature, take it away, or furnish me with another means of keeping those I love alive. *(He trembles.)* I feel like I still hear the cries of the old man! The sound of his voice stabs my heart and cuts it to pieces. Seductive voices coming to lead me astray, I will not hear you! Oh, my father, my father, what has become of my very cultivated upbringing, my well-established beliefs? What would you say, oh respectable author of my life, if you saw your unhappy son in this situation? You raised him to be an honest man and he has become nothing but a criminal! Someone's coming. My grief makes it hard for me to think. I don't know where I am anymore. *(He trembles. He exits and reappears.)* I'll hide. *(He flees in the direction where his wife is entering; she recognizes him. In meeting her, DERVAL utters a cry and continues walking.)*

CECILE. What do I see? Oh, my friend, pale, distorted, trembling, what could you be doing here at this hour? Horribly distressed at the way you left us, I couldn't help but fly after you. You're not saying anything. Everything frightens me… everything disturbs me. Your silence and the look in your eyes make me tremble. Please speak to me.

DERVAL. *(Away from her, trying to appear calm.)* It's nothing. It's nothing, my beloved friend. I had come to look for some sustenance. I've found it. Here it is. *(He gives her the purse.)* Here is what I've achieved. I trust we'll be happy now?

CECILE. *(Firmly.)* Happy! Derval, you're not happy at this moment. You don't dare look your wife in the eye. Why are you running from me? Stop. *(She tries to take him in her arms. DESVAL, totally bewildered, doesn't recognize her.)*

DERVAL. What do you want? You're preventing me… Very well! Lead me… I am covered with blood… I've just had a bad fall… that scaffold there… I was climbing it. You'll tell my wife… no, don't tell her anything. Let her know nothing. If only you'd carry me, my son!

CECILE. *(In tears.)* Ah! my dear husband! What unbelievable madness. Don't you recognize your Cecile?

DERVAL. *(Still far from her.)* Cecile… I've lost her. *(Opening his eyes, going to her, and throwing himself into his wife's arms.)* Oh, my divine friend. *(After a silence.)* Your husband isn't worthy of you. Go away, virtuous wife, go away and let me submit to my fate.

CECILE. Ah! Cruel… Derval, run and report this money. We should die a thousand times rather than owe our lives to a crime. Then come back, come back to die in the arms of your wife. She'll be waiting for you. Heavens! My husband a murderer!

DERVAL. What! Above and beyond the hideous reproaches of my conscience, now I'll have to bear yours. It's too much and

I don't deserve them. Please spare my breaking heart. Forgive a crime that love has committed. See in him his excuse: he did it for you.

CECILE. Can it be less hateful when honor accuses you? Weak man, rather than offer your son bread tainted with the blood of an unfortunate victim, give him your own blood. Soon mine would be mixed with it. We would have nourished him with our own lives and you would still be an honest man!

DERVAL. *(Quickly.)* Ah, God, what are you saying? I've not even dirtied my hands. Dear wife, listen to me. The one I dared to attack is still alive. Cecile, oh, my Cecile! As my accuser, you're the one to make my blood flow, drop by drop. May your son drink with it the courage that it inspires in you. May he live, may he adore you, and let me die! I want to meet death here. Leave me alone. I will not move from this place. *(He throws himself like a madman onto the steps of a house as if he were trying to knock his head on the stones.)*

POLICEMAN. *(Enters with TWO BAILIFFS on either side of him. To CECILE.)* Isn't this the place, Madame, where a robbery was committed tonight? Undoubtedly this house belongs to you… and you ought to have heard the commotion that occurred not too long ago…

CECILE. *(Throwing herself at the POLICEMAN'S feet, she hides DERVAL's body, which she reveals in getting up.)* Sir, sir, I beg of you. Alas, have pity on us. We are unfortunate strangers who have no money. It was to keep his wife alive… his son. Ah! Sir, do you understand pity?

POLICEMAN. It cannot offset the deed. Your words enlighten me. You have betrayed yourself. Stand up, Madame. Undoubtedly, here is the guilty party. You both have to follow me.

DERVAL. *(Getting up quickly.)* Stop, sir, stop. I was the only one. Leave this woman alone; she is not guilty in the least. I'm the one who committed the crime, I'm the one who should be punished. Leave her alone, I tell you, or you'll force me to kill myself. *(Flying into the arms of CECILE.)* Ah! Worthy and tender wife, this is the greatest service you could render me in my life. Here, hide this money. Maybe they won't ask for it back. Save my son, prolong your days. Alone with that dear child, your life

will become much easier. Think of me every now and then. Oh, my beloved friend. For the last time, feel my heart beating next to yours. *(He embraces her.)* Forgive your husband, give him your respect and your heart. He is still worthy of it. Don't let him carry to the grave the terrifying thought of your hating him. *(To the POLICEMAN.)* All right, sir, lead on. And above all, don't let her follow me.
CECILE. *(Flinging herself into her husband's arms and dragging herself along with him.)* No, I'm not leaving you. *(To the POLICEMAN.)* Sir, sir, here's the money. *(She throws him the purse.)* Let them imprison us and kill us together if they have to. *(One of the BAILIFFS picks up the purse and the curtain fall)*

END OF ACT TWO

ACT THREE

(The setting is a prison.) This entire scene was crossed out by Sade.
CECILE. Ah, Marianne, I'm the one who ruined him; without me, he would have been able to save himself. I will have his death on my conscience. Dear husband, I will not survive you very long. I want to find the justice of the peace and make him see my position. He will understand the reasons for such a terrible crime. Marianne, if he has a heart, he will not be unsympathetic. I'll take my son to him. I'll set him at his feet, weakened by hunger and misery. Will he be able to remain unmoved by such an awful sight?
MARIANNE. Ah, my dear mistress, the habit of seeing unfortunate men renders immovable the hearts of judges who are accustomed to condemn criminals, to withstand their tears and their repentance. The law is all that they have against you and since it is often unnatural, judges are forced to stifle the voice of nature. They groan… but they condemn. Believe me, Madame, you don't want to degrade yourself to the point of bowing before the "idol." Don't lose the few moments you have been granted to

be with your husband. What's he doing now? God, how I long to see him…

CECILE. I just left him. More than anything, he wants to write to his father and make me the bearer of the sad news. Ah, can he believe that I will survive him? How moving his letter is! After reading the first few lines, my eyes let loose a flood of tears. If he knew the situation we're in, perhaps that tender father who so cherished his son might act on our behalf. Ah, my dear friend, what an uncertain and unsteady comfort. Have you brought my son? What is he doing?

MARIANNE. The poor child is sleeping over there on a little bit of straw; his beautiful eyes turned languidly toward me seemed to be asking for his mother. Ah, Madame, that he will have learned misery at so young an age! Do you want to hold him?

CECILE. No. I'd rather give up the sweetness of holding him than risk the effect the sight of him would have on his father. Marianne, will they be so inhuman to refuse me the right to die at his side? If they drag him to the grave, I'll follow him there. I want the same wound to reunite us in the tomb. What! Am I not as guilty as he? I hear him. Hide your tears, my dear friend, and spare yourself the sadness of seeing him.

(MARIANNE leaves reluctantly. She sees DERVAL enter and looks at him with tears in her eyes. She starts to move toward him, but stops herself.)[The end of Sade's deletion.]

(CECILE is seated next to her husband, looking very depressed. He is likewise seated and holds her hand. The child is sleeping on a bit of straw.)

DERVAL. *(Calmly.)* Let's make the most of the moments that remain. They will be brief. I've just learned that they are moving quickly on my execution. Some secret enemies… People are even jealous of adversity!

CECILE. *(Crying, she throws herself into her husband's arms.)* God, how I know. Dear husband, I will follow you.

DERVAL. Stop your crying, Cecile. I do not fear the moment of death. For a long time now, my misery has accustomed me to being cold-blooded. My only regrets are for you. What will become of you, my beloved friend? Alone, without support, without protection, without help, in a country absolutely unknown to you. The brink of disaster presents itself on all sides and the worst misery surrounds you. You will take this letter to my father. Do the impossible and find him someday… so that in hearing of my misfortunes, he may soften yours. *(CECILE takes DERVAL's hand, the one carrying the letter, and begins to cry.)* This hand you hold today, in a few days, maybe in a few hours, will feel nothing more. It will be mixed with the bloody remains of this fragile body and returned to nature's bosom. While the rigorous laws of men dishonored it, tarnished it, ripped it to pieces, their just or unjust vengeance will not touch my soul. It is pure, a being more radiant than they will judge it in a little while. As always, it is on deposit in your soul and were it possible, I wish they could only judge them together. The virtues of the one will outweigh the errors of the other in their eyes. And as far as you're concerned, oh, my God, I would owe my happiness to my Cecile.

CECILE. *(Throwing herself in a chair and crying.)* Ah! Dear, unhappy husband, may our souls be separated and reunited, both at the same time.

DEKVAL. *(Sitting next to CECILE.)* No, Cecile, remember that the heavy burden of life has become a duty for you. Don't try to commit suicide. You owe it to that beloved child, the sacred pledge of our mutual love. A few involuntary tears are escaping in spite of my attempt to control them. A tender memory of the past will remove them. Oh! happy days when my Cecile, surrounded by a family who adored her, was hardly deserving of the caresses that destroyed her… and it's my fault… my miserable fault! Oh! deadly passion… *(Up to this point, CECILE is overwhelmed with sadness; her head rests on DERVAL's lap.)* Turn your eyes toward me, Cecile. I need to see them so I won't curse them. *(CECILE turns to look at him with her eyes full of tears.)* One day, tell your beloved family all about it. Inform your parents that I, the object of their overwhelming hatred, died trying to conceal my crime from them. Maybe they will forgive you. *(He draws his child close to him.)* Take them this child. Let his feeble arms beg forgiveness at your mother's feet. Let him teach them what you have suffered. Raise him well. Above all, teach him to master his passions. Look, Cecile. See their deadly effects! If he is able to do without love…

ah! What am I saying? Isn't his heart our responsibility? May your goodness at least pass into his soul; your features are already imprinted on his face. *(Seeing that this idea bothers CECILE.)* No, Cecile, what I mean to say is that in addition to yours, nature has given him my features. May he remind you of them now and again, my dear friend. *(He puts his son down.)* Holding him every day, you will think about the unfortunate father who gave him life. At the end of a long life, come and find my ashes in this country. They will come to life again for you. Let me take the thought of this mournful reunion to the grave with me. *(To his son.)* Oh, my child, you will be a consolation to your mother.
THE CHILD. Papa, why are you leaving us?
DERVAL. *(To his wife.)* Take him away from me. I cannot bear any more of this. *(A sound is heard.)* Someone's coming. *(The prison door opens noisily; CECILE and DERVAL rise. The CHILD, frightened, runs back to the pile of straw.)*
CECILE. God, here they are!
(The Chevalier enters.)
THE CHEVALIER. In spite of your rudeness and ill treatment of me, Madame, you see that I have not forgotten you. The person whom your so-called husband tried to kill so cowardly this evening was my father. When I heard it was an émigré, I was sure that it could only be him. *(Looking at DERVAL with righteous indignation.)* I went to the judges. I asked in the capacity of a fellow countryman for permission to clear up this affair. In no time at all, they answered me: the man is guilty, he must die, and that will not be long in coming. Of course, my wealth has no greater influence than in prison. My gold has made me the master of the situation. With a single word, I can save him. I am able, therefore, to speak the sentence that will either cost him or give him his life. You hear me, Madame, you know what price I put on his liberty.
DERVAL. What price? God, what do I hear? Monster, do you dare to take such advantage of the misfortune that oppresses us? Is yet a new grave being prepared for us by his presence? Give up, get out, and thank God that I am unarmed.
CHEVALIER. So much pride astonishes me in a vile criminal. Do you know that I am the master of your life?

DERVAL. Perhaps, but what does it matter. If you are, it's because of the vilest of all rights: he who is strongest. Almost always, it's a case of villainy over virtue. Yes, you can be the master of my life, but you will never be the master of my soul.
CECILE. Oh, my beloved, please don't anger him.
CHEVALIER. Make this man shut up, Madame. He wearies me. He's taking advantage of my good nature. I'm losing patience.
CECILE. *(To the CHEVALIER.)* Ah! Sir, forgive him. He is distressed.
DERVAL. *(To his wife, quickly.)* Cecile, do you want to dishonor my last moments?
CHEVALIER. *(Ironically.)* Dishonor! What a wonderful word! He deserves a mouth full of gold. Too bad he wasn't guided by such lovely sentiments tonight!
DERVAL. *(Fiercely.)* Stop condemning me for the hideous madness to which I was led by necessity in spite of my heart and my mind. Criminal though I am, I believe I am better than you. Love made me forget virtues you've never known. Whoever such a violent passion leads into the abyss is undoubtedly the unhappiest of men, but whoever plunges him there through villainy or just watches him in the abyss without offering a helping hand, he is the more wicked.
CHEVALIER. Madame, you see how he treats me. This too much! Tremble, traitor. *(He takes a piece of paper out of his pocket.)* You're ruined!
DERVAL. That name suits you better than it does me. Whoever sold you my death warrant is just like you. I scorn you both! Execute your orders. Go on. Now, since my life depends on you, I want to die. *(He sees that the CHEVALIER is troubled.)* Nature has avenged me. You're trembling and I am calm.
CECILE. *(Who throughout the scene stood between the CHEVALIER and her husband now falls to the CHEVALIER's feet.)* Sir, sir, save my husband. Don't listen to what he says. Oh! Sir, don't listen to him.
DERVAL. *(Lifting his wife up quickly.)* What are you doing, Cecile? Get up, I order you. Why present this monster with a victory? You don't know the souls of villains. They enjoy your tears.

Hide them from him, Cecile, come and shed them here. *(He takes her in his arms.)*
CECILE. *(To her husband)* My friend. *(To the CHEVALIER.)* Sir, sir, have pity on my tears.
CHEVALIER. Ah! Cecile, must I remind you of my passion now? I adore you. I'll give you everything, but leave that man this instant.
DERVAL. *(Placing himself between his wife and the CHEVALIER.)* Leave me, leave me! Come on, come on, try to pull her out of my arms. If you can, take this heart imprinted with her image and tear it to pieces with your hands. Act as my executioner. Your cruel and base soul will be delighted perhaps by this new excess of horror. *(He forms a fortress around his wife's body.)* Make my blood gush out all over her; tear away my life little by little, but you can be sure that she will be only the prize of my last dying breath.
CHEVALIER. This is too much. Gentlemen, *(To the guards at the rear of the stage.)* do your duty. Take him to the justice of the peace and from there to the grave.
CECILE. *(Frantically running from one to the other, grabbing her son and carrying him to the CHEVALIER as if to move him.)* Sir, sir, at least have pity on this child.
CHEVALIER. *(Making another gesture to the guards.)* No mercy, Madame. *(The guards drag off DERVAL. He stops them for a moment to speak to his wife.)*
DERVAL. Let me embrace you for the last time. *(He pulls her aside and gives her a dagger.)* Take this. I'm making this sacrifice for you. Here is the weapon that would have protected me from the blade that awaits me. Place my son in the hands of Marianne. Commend him to her. And don't let that monster be rewarded for his crimes. *(He exits. One of the guards leads away the child.)*
CECILE. So be it. I'm going to stab myself before your very eyes. *(She lifts her arm to stab herself. The CHEVALIER runs to her and holds her back.)*
CHEVALIER. *(To Cecile, holding her.)* What are you doing?
CECILE. *(Quickly.)* My duty! I'm sparing you a crime. *(The CHEVALIER disarms her and throws away the knife.)*

OLD MERVILLE. *(Entering by the side opposite the one DERVAL has just used to exit and seeing the catastrophe.)* What do I see? Good Lord!
CHEVALIER. My father?
CECILE. *(Throwing herself at OLD MERVILLE's feet.)* Oh, generous old man… save me from that monster. Let me die beside my husband, who is being led away.
OLD MERVILLE. *(Raising her up.)* Calm yourself, Madame. Here is his freedom. I'm the one, alas, he attacked tonight without knowing it.
CECILE. *(Beside herself)* His freedom, ah! My gratitude… read it in my heart. I cannot express it. Forgive me, I must fly to him. My tears… joy makes them flow. Ah! Sir, let me embrace you. *(She exits intoxicated with joy.)* Derval, our worries are over.
OLD MERVILLE. The trouble I just saw you in, sir, and what I learned from the justice of the peace all convince me of your villainy. You seek to take advantage of people. You're an obscene bastard! Get out of my sight!
CHEVALIER. Father, let's be reasonable about this. It was love…
OLD MERVILLE. Love?
CHEVALIER. All right, Father, a fancy, I admit it… a simple amusement.
OLD MERVILLE. One that causes trouble! What a soul! Didn't you know with whom you were dealing? Didn't her virtue hold you back?
CHEVALIER. *(Feebly. He gives in gradually.)* I know I did wrong and the damage is irreparable. At least believe that the feeling that led me there was pure.
OLD MERVILLE. That woman was married; you knew that.
CHEVALIER. *(Troubled and contrite.)* I ignored it. I attributed the title of "marriage" to the unhappiness they shared… so I thought…
OLD MERVILLE. The real proof of your wrongs is the difficulty you have in justifying them.
CHEVALIER. *(Confused, suddenly giving up.)* Please forgive me. Your generosity enlightens me, your accusations confuse me. You rekindle in me the feelings that my mistakes had stifled.

(He throws himself at his father's feet.) Ah! Father, give me another chance to become an honest man.

OLD MERVILLE. I do not believe you are so corrupt, sir, to express a repentance that you would not live up to. That lie would only crown your treachery. Be your own judge. If you apologize in good faith, get up. I forgive you.

CHEVALIER. Good Lord! This moment should serve me as an example forever. Ah! Father, how virtue appears sweet to him who has had the misfortune of abandoning it even for a moment. *(DERVAL and CECILE stand in the distance. CECILE holds her child by the hand.)*

CECILE. Oh, my friend, run to the feet of your savior.

DERVAL. *(Still next to his wife and in the distance.)* Heavens, I'm trembling. It's him. I don't dare approach him. *(He turns his eyes and throws himself into CECILE's arms.)*

OLD MERVILLE. Yes, it's me. How terrible your misery must have been to reduce you to the awful activities of tonight! Alas, I was going to comfort your wife and to apologize for letting my business force me to neglect her for such a long time… but what distress the sight of you brings to my senses. I can hardly speak… my heart can only guess… *(He approaches DERVAL.)* Imprudent young man, when did you leave your country?

DERVAL. *(Troubled.)* For five years, I've been separated from a father I loved. Cecile, it's him. *(Undecided, held by the fear that his father might be angry.)* What crime have I committed! *(Throwing himself into his father's arms.)* Oh, my father, who would have known that I should find you in such a horrible place?

MERVILLE. *(Throwing his arms around his son.)* My son!

CHEVALIER and CECILE. His father!

CHEVALIER. *(Very quickly.)* Ah! Father, could you ever forgive me? I am a monster. Madame, my father. Forgive me. Tell them to forgive me.

DERVAL. Embrace me, brother, and all is forgotten.

OLD MERVILLE. *(To DERVAL.)* How happy I am at having found you. God, what an event! Son, you owe me your imprisonment and your release. When you stole my money, I had the police make out a warrant for your arrest. Soon after, I found out that the unfortunate man was none other than the husband of this poor woman whom I had occasionally assisted. I used everything in my power to save him. I had happy premonitions: it seemed that nature spoke to me in the depths of my heart. My influence with the French ambassador enabled me to get what I wanted. Arriving before the justice of the peace with letters in your favor, I learned of the activities of my other son. They were hideous, Chevalier!

CHEVALIER. Ah, father.

OLD MERVILLE. I worked quickly. I was afraid there wasn't enough time. Fortune blessed my endeavors. *(To DERVAL.)* Son, will you tell me about your misfortunes? My friend, how miserable you must be to have so quickly forgotten so many of your sacred duties!

DERVAL. *(Embracing his father.)* Father, you will hear about everything... *(Presenting his wife and son.)* And there is my excuse.

OLD MERVILLE. That's her, then, son, the beloved wife for whom you abandoned everything.

DERVAL. *(Enraptured.)* Yes, there she is. Look at her, Father. And she's the one who sacrificed everything. I owe her everything. We have suffered a lot... but, alas, that's all in the past.

CECILE. Too generous and too kind father, how do I acknowledge so much generosity, so much kindness? Ah, please embrace this child. It's your blood that flows through his veins.

DERVAL. *(Still filled with joy.)* That's not all, father. I have a proof of his love that you will enjoy... that you will cherish. The child is named after you. You are living again in another me.

OLD MERVILLE. *(Embracing the child.)* Come here, let me embrace him! Come here, my children... how happy I am! What a joyous moment for me! Derval, I have found you. I want to make peace with your parents, my dear girl. Will you give me their names? *(He embraces her.)* Let us make haste to return to France. You, Chevalier, with a conduct forever beyond reproach, make amends to your brother and sister-in-law for all the repulsive things you've done. Children, *(He takes DERVAL and CECILE by the hand.)* you see that you can never leave the path of duty without being punished. It alone leads to real happiness. You can buy your way out of it only at the expense of your conscience. *(Quickly.)* Oh, virtue, my soul's most cherished sentiment… Yes! The heart of man is your sanctuary since he cannot remove you without remorse.

END OF THE THIRD AND FINAL ACT

The Twins

Introduction

The Twins; or, Difficult Choices must certainly have been written before April 1781, for, in a letter dated 26 April 1781, the Marquis de Sade wrote his wife asking her not to judge his play *The Inconstant Man* by *The Twins*.[20] Composed during Sade's incarceration at Vincennes Prison, the manuscript, in a copyist's handwriting, bears the date of October 20 on the title page and the number 8 on the cover. Pasted on the inside cover are the words, "Me Quesnet, chez M. Vailant, rue de Clery des Menuisiers, n 33." As Madame Quesnet was the Marquis de Sade's companion at the Charenton Asylum, it is likely that the manuscript was revised by the author during his stay there between 1803 and 1814.

The preface to the play (believed to have been written at Charenton) is indicative of the breadth of Sade's literary knowledge and his tendency to compare himself to already established writers. As Julia Chandler Hayes noted in "The Representation of the Self in the Theatre of La Chaussée, Diderot, and Sade":

> Sade's prefaces, in most case written long after the plays which they accompany, are a fascinating document of his account of himself as a dramatist, and of his status in his own view with respect to other dramatists.... [T]hese chatty little pieces are perhaps mnost revelatory for what they say about Sade's view of himself in relation to his literary world. The prefaces have in common an overwhelming sense of alterity, a sense that all one can say is being said or has already been said by others, and an urgent need to establish some sort of relationship between

---

[20] A letter from Marie-Dorothée de Rousset to Sade dated 1 April 1781 also mentions *The Twins* (called the *Two Twins* in the letter since Sade's original concept was to have two sets of twins) in reference to a manuscript Sade sent to Rousset for commentary. Marie-Dorothée de Rousset was the daughter of Sade's notary who was hired as a governess in Sade's household. Like the Marquis, she had a great interest in the theatre.

oneself and the others in order to guarantee one's own place in the hierarchy.

In the preface to *The Twins*, Sade compares *The Menaechmi* by Plautus, Moliere's *Amphitryon*, and Regnard's *The Twins* with his own attempt to create a play based on mistaken identity. After admitting the difficulty of establishing the convention of identical twins, the Marquis goes on to argue that his simple plot in which a lady's maid runs interference between her twin mistresses and their rival suitors could not but "produce a definite impression, perhaps even a highly original one." To those who suggest that he has produced merely the outline of a play, Sade replies that he "would be happy to see such a project in worthier hands" and continues with a comparison between his work and Regnard's.

Confessing that he lacks Regnard's "inimitable grace... easy versification... cleverness... and wit," Sade argues that the character differences in Regnard's play render the convention of twins unbelievable. On the other hand, he expresses concern that the maintenance of identical personalities in his own play might lead to monotony and would certainly be difficult to perform. He reminds the reader that Colatto unsuccessfully tried to solve the problem of verisimilitude by having a single actor portray three roles in his production of the play *The Twin Boys* and suggests that Palissot had more success in his *New Menaechmi* by "uniting the two personalities into a single one that replenished both of them."

Finally, the author expresses concern that the last scene of the first act might be considered "too episodic and thrown in, as you might say, without any real reason" and justifies its inclusion as a means to develop the relationship between the two lovers and "to justify Adelaide's preference for Durval, since, without it, her motives would have been very mysterious." Not untypically, the Marquis ends his preface with a social commentary:

> Have our young men become more honest in spite of everything that's been said? Have they stopped looking at those charming objects filled with precious attributes more like flowers offered to their passions than like beings almost always superior to them, and possessing uncontestable claims to their respect? No.

Everything hasn't been said, or it hasn't been said enough, because man is not incorrigible; and if virtue does not win him over, it's because it is rarely presented in a way that would attract him. Someone will ask me, "Do you think you've been any more successful?" I haven't the conceit to think so, and I turn it all over to the severest critic, convinced that it is through his flame that talent is purified or seen to blossom.

Although Lély considered the play "one of Sade's most insignificant works," its portrayal of late eighteenth-century feminist attitudes in the polemical discussion between Damis and Durval is quite important, for it shows the author of *Justine* and *Juliette* working from a highly enlightened moral perspective. Although the physical comedy in the play is lively, it certainly offers nothing new to the stage and it is probable that the Marquis de Sade himself considered *The Twins* an early exercise as there is no evidence that he ever sought to have the play produced.

The Twins
Foreword

After *Amphitryon*[21] and *The Menaechmi*,[22] to put on stage a play that, like those masterpieces, consists only in a conventional likeness, which, to my way of thinking, even in nature could never be exact enough to produce a complete illusion, is a bold thing to do. I admit it, so much that it has frightened me, and instead of creating an immense tableau, which was my original conception, I have contented myself with a very simple sketch. Nevertheless, even after the models I just cited, there might remain some glory to claim in this genre.

A comedy artistically managed in which a maid as shrewd and ingenious as the Valentin of *The Menaechmi* would keep the lively and energetic passions of two young rival lovers in suspense alternately between those two mistresses who look alike; scenes pulled off successfully, incidents naturally arising from so vast a subject could only produce a definite effect and perhaps even one that is completely original despite everything our masters were able to take away from us in that regard. May these remarks cause others to carry out that of which I have ventured to create only the idea. I would truly enjoy seeing such an endeavor in more skillful hands. Perhaps, I admit, had I risked more, I might have thought it possible, like Regnard, to establish in my *Twins* the same difference of character with which he shaded his *Twins*. But not sensing in myself the talents of that immortal artist to veil such an inconsistency by means of such great masterstrokes, I am, in spite of myself, restrained within more limited boundaries. One would have to have the inimitable gifts of that delightful author, his fluent versification, his charm, his gaiety, all the wit, in a word, of his blessed genius to make a play shine like him. That alone creates the play's main flaw. The contempt of nearly all the characters in that comedy, Isabelle, the Marquis de Coquelet, Finette, Araminte, that old fool whom the experience

---

[21] A free verse comedy in three acts by Molière (1622–1673), based on Plautus's *Amphitruo* and produced in 1668.

[22] A comedy by Jean-François Regnard (1655–1709), based on Plautus's *Menaechmi* and produced in 1705.

should have at least made more tactful—is all that contempt, I say, natural? Is it conceivable from the moment a difference exists within the characters? A difference, or rather, a contrast of temperament as striking as what Regnard created in his *The Menaechmi*? Yet it is from this contrast that he draws the greatest charm from his play, to such a degree that one could almost blame him for having sacrificed the probability of the whole to a single role.

But someone will perhaps say to me, "Haven't you likewise created that difference? And isn't it that difference that decides Durval's choice?" Think about it for a moment: the difference that Durval thinks he notices is only the fruit of his feelings, strengthened by those that Adelaide displays toward him, and more than anything else, strengthened by the powerful effects of pride. Between two women equally lovable, or perfectly similar, we will always lean toward the one we think loves us best, the maxim is quite certain. But have I developed this difference elsewhere? Does one notice the slightest trace of it? And can the one whom Marton informs add a shade more to the picture? Be that as it may, such a project will always be very hard to carry out for whoever wants to drive it to its fulfillment and perfection. And of all the kinds of plots onstage, although this might be one of the most attractive, it is nevertheless the one that always seems to me the most difficult to accomplish. If the similarities are exact, as in what one is about to read, that's monotonous; if they aren't precise, as in Regnard, that's improbable. Falling into this last defect, Colalto[23] tried to remedy it by having the three roles of his *Twins* played by the same actor. But if it appears to be a disadvantage to one, the other did not endure it less in its entirety; moreover, I don't know whether similar business would be terribly successful on the French stage.

Palissot[24] did better in his *New Menaechmi* by combining the two characters into a single one that satisfied both of them. It was the height of art.

I've thought occasionally that one might find the last scene of the first act a bit too episodic and thrown in, so to speak, for no real reason. Nevertheless, it seems to me that it develops the character of

---

[23] An actor at the Comédie-Italienne who wrote a number of farces based on commedia dell'arte models.

[24] Charles Palissot de Montenoy (1730–1814), dramatist who attacked the philosophers and encyclopedists and wrote a number of controversial social satires.

the two lovers and justifies the preference *Adelaide* grants *Durval*, the motives of which would have been very obscure without that. But a lot has already been spoken about the women—I agree—and it's possible that all there is to say about their qualities still might not have been said. This subject is like their charms… inexhaustible. Have our young men become more decent in spite of everything that's been said? Have they stopped looking at those charming objects filled with precious attributes, more like flowers offered to their passions than beings almost always superior to them, and possessing uncontestable claims to their respect? No! Everything hasn't been said or hasn't been said enough because man is not incorrigible. And if virtue does not win him over, it's because it is rarely presented in a way that would attract him. Someone will ask me, "Do you think you've been any more successful?" I haven't the conceit to think so, and I turn it all over to the severest critic, convinced that it is through his flame that talent is purified or seen to blossom.

The Twins
or
Difficult Choices

Verse Comedy in Two Acts

CHARACTERS

Damis, lover of the twins
Durval, friend and secret lover of Adelaide
Dumont, valet to Damis
Célise, the mother of the twins
Adelaide, Julie, twin sisters
Marton, a maid
Lafleur, a household servant

(The action takes place at Célise's country home ten or twelve miles outside of Paris.)

ACT ONE

DUMONT. (*Alone. Carrying the mail, in the wings, to the postman who has just dropped it off.*) That should do it… and three books of stamps.
(*During the following lines, he puts his wallet back in his pocket, puts down his parcels, and tosses his whip into a corner.*)
Those rascals are so terribly fond of money,
They're not content until they break us all.
(*Entering and looking around.*)
Now who to talk to? Hello! One of the servants…
But it's too early in the morning… (*Noticing MARTON entering.*)
Ah! That pretty face will do.
Now things are looking up. Why, she's an angel!

I can't remember ever having seen
So many lovely features. Oh, she sees me!
The devil take me... I know that girl.
(*Taking a letter from his pocket, he gives it to MARTON; he is quite distracted, more concerned with remembering who she is than with what he is saying.*)
This letter from the castle. I'm supposed to give
To Madame Célise. (*Recognizing her.*) Oh, it's really Marton.
MARTON. It's really me; and you, my dear Dumont,
How long have you been here?
DUMONT. I've just arrived,
You see, my child, entrusted with the letter,
Which in my opinion... but tell me, please,
Since we should speak about ourselves before all else,
How did you come to leave Hortense's service?
MARTON. At length, worn out by inconsistency,
Her meddling, and her insincerity
(Provoking everyone who gathers round her),
I seized the opportunity on whim
To liberate myself from her employ.
The change is for the better. In this house,
Where amiable wisdom and good judgment
Makes felt the heavenly power of happiness,
I'm better off a thousand times.
DUMONT. Agreed.
But what about your boyfriends? Bourguignon and Deschamps,
Frontin, Basque, Germon, la Violette, and Champagne?
They can't all follow you out to the country.
MARTON. You only numbered seven, my dear, a trifle!
And you should never stop on an odd number...
Give credit where it's due: a lover entertains me,
His looks and conversation... I forgive him all...
Should he get serious? I toss him out like that!
I fear too much the sighs of pining love...
They say you're not supposed to when attracted
To someone. Me... I prefer a good night's sleep.
DUMONT. (*Emphatically.*) Ah! Enchanting lips! Impressive eyes!

Mischievous feet! (*Taking her hand.*) White and creamy skin!
Beholding that, a person couldn't sleep,
Or toss and turn so badly, that the dawn
Would catch him in the imagined arms of his beloved.
MARTON. What's that, a tragedy?
DUMONT. Yes, it's what I do best.
If you could only see me when I soar!
MARTON. (*Interrupting him.*) Incidentally,
Who is your master and what brings you here?
DUMONT. You're full of curiosity, my queen,
But there's nothing to hide from one's beloved!
Besides, a valet talks. It would be wrong
For servants not to satirize a master
Just among themselves.
MARTON. Their troubles are
Their problem… and our lot to laugh at them.
If that's any consolation.
DUMONT. What a charming system!
But to be truthful, dear, portraying faults
Is not exactly what I'm here to do
And Damis has a few that might offend us.
Adoring without knowing, playing without loving,
Immediately enraptured by a pretty face,
And tossing it aside for yet another
While fluttering, fluttering endlessly about.
In two words, that's the man, since Marton asked.
If you'd add indiscretion to the list,
You'd have him trait for trait: a perfect fit.
MARTON. The reason for this journey?
DUMONT. Is the letter
That I'm supposed to give to Madame Célise
And which contains, unless I am mistaken,
A formal marriage offer from our dear
Papa… As for the rest, here take a look
If you like. (*He gives her the letter as if to encourage her to open it.*)
MARTON. What? Unseal the letter?
Dishonesty like this can't be allowed;
It's an offense against man's sacred rights

Which nothing can legitimize and which
At no time and in no case can be excused.
He who abuses such a holy bond
To satisfy his curiosity
Deserves the selfsame treatment from another.
DUMONT. I willingly admit my indiscretion;
Your eyes, the cause. I thought they wanted it…
And who can disobey the least request
Read in two eyes as beautiful as yours?
All duty disappears before your eyes.
MARTON. You're making me delirious! All right.
Excused by all the foolish things you've said,
You tell me what you think is in the letter.
DUMONT. (*Mysteriously*.) The letter tells the judgment of Germeuil
About the late departure of his son
And finally, a request to either one
Of your two mistresses, for as I'm told,
Since good Germeuil is bored with doughty deeds
Which, four times every day without success,
Make him begin to act the father-in-law,
He wants to bind us here through holy wedlock.
The young man has agreed and does consent
To undertake the duties of the household,
Provided that the god of love is able
To join him with the god of matrimony.
For once, he wants to see the girl; he knows
Your mistress has two personalities
And wants to choose between them… it excites him!
His father agreed to it without protest.
(*MARTON begins to laugh quietly.*)
And seriously, the purpose of the letter
Is to obtain from all the family here
A similar consent, to guarantee
That, having picked the most attractive girl,
My master won't regret the choice he's made.
(*MARTON laughs openly.*)
Well! Why the laughter? Are you scolding me?

(*Her laughter increases.*)
Please tell me, have you gone hysterical?
The devil take me if I'm talking nonsense!
I, too, am going to laugh, and then we'll see
Which of us two creates the greater noise.
MARTON. (*Laughing at the top of her voice*)
The choice, it's just the choice that makes me laugh
Since you don't know a thing about it.
(*She laughs again hysterically.*)
DUMONT. Well,
Instead of all the laughter, I'd prefer
If you would kindly let me in on it.
MARTON. (*Gradually returning to normal*)
It's just that it's impossible to tell
The slightest difference between the two;
Never did nature, in its strangest whims,
Give birth, at once, to two so much alike
That I who serve them can't tell them apart
And more than twenty times a day, their mother
Is in the selfsame mess. The only cure,
The only means of solving the confusion,
Is to distinguish them by different clothes,
A flower, or a ribbon, or some other thing.
Now, knowing this, see if your master's choice
Won't make you laugh.
DUMONT. I've got a secret way
To tell the two apart.
MARTON. For friendship's sake,
I can excuse you, but around this house,
I wouldn't breathe a word if I were you.
DUMONT. And so you claim the twins are so alike
That they could be considered turtledoves.
MARTON. Nothing is closer to the truth, my dear.
Same looks, same frame of mind, same tone of voice.
See, everything about them is seductive,
Misleading, and confusing.
DUMONT. Alike in personality?
MARTON. Without the slightest contradiction, dear.

One, however, Julie, is less serious,
More frank and innocent than Adelaide.
To understand these subtle nuances,
To spot so little difference, in a word,
It would take months and should your eager master
Expect to get to the heart of the matter
In less time, you can bet he's in for trouble.
DUMONT. I'm well prepared for Damis's recklessness.
I know he'll get confused in the resemblance…
Enough of all this talk! Tell me, my dear,
Who is that noble fellow in the courtyard?
Is it another suitor?
MARTON. He could be.
He's certainly well known to your Damis.
It's Durval.
DUMONT. (*With the gestures and tone of recognition.*)
Every year we meet in Paris.
Why, I could hardly recognize the man
From such a distance. He's a worthy fellow,
Much brighter than my lord, yet very kind.
Old Germeuil used to hope his prudent conduct
Might set a good example for his son.
Well, that may come in time. I guess he's here
To see one of the twins?
MARTON. Good lord! I'm not
Inclined to satisfy your curiosity.
If there's something between them, it's between them!
You think that I know all there is know,
Or better yet, that I predict the rest.
You give me too much credit… I'm not that good.
I hear someone coming. So be prepared
And soon your mission will achieve its goal.
(Enter CÉLISE and DURVAL.)
DUMONT. (*Giving his letter to CÉLISE.*)
Here, Madame, is a most important letter
Which Mister Germeuil…
CÉLISE. (*Interrupting him while taking the letter.*)
I've been expecting this for some time now.

DUMONT. They told me to deliver it today,
Madame; this haste is only meant to please you.
I'm very punctual.
CÉLISE. That's good. I need
To contemplate this enterprise in private.
Marton, you may retire… and take with you
This decent lad and take good care of him.
(*DUMONT thanks her and exits with MARTON. CÉLISE reads the letter apart and in a low voice; smiles and after a silence, DURVAL speaks.*)
DURVAL. I'll wager that it's from Damis.
CÉLISE. (*Showing him the portion of the letter she has read*)
Precisely.
From him and yet a thousand times more learned.
It's from his father, honorable Germeuil,
Who writes that for the longest time, Damis
Has longed to place himself beneath my rule
And wants to be allowed, so says his father,
To call me his adored and treasured mother
As soon as possible. The letter's charming:
For sure, Germeuil knows how to turn a phrase.
(*She puts the letter into her pocket.*)
DURVAL. He does and speaks at least as well in person.
CÉLISE. (*Interested.*) And what about the young man?
DURVAL. Sensitive and honest.
He's very likely to succeed and satisfy,
But he's caught up a little in the fashion:
The fad that makes a man prefer the sad
And useless pleasure of playing the field
To love, its tender charms, its divine flame.
And this is crazy, he'd rather pretend
Like he's engaged instead of really being
The happiest of lovers. What a fool!
CÉLISE. His vanity is but the fault of youth;
A happy marriage ought to set him straight.
In this respect, marriage is much less strict;
It lets you publicize its joys at will
And our young husband, settled down, I hope,

Will find there's nothing left to boast about.
For me, the main thing is that he has morals;
With morals, we recover from our errors
Which lead, in spite of us, to foolish youth.
Again we find them once the thrill is gone,
Their influence enflames our struggling hearts
And through their help we make our way to virtue.
In my opinion all the rest is chaff!
I'd rather such behavior a hundred times
Than the kind of prudishness that hardly
Suits a fellow well before he's twenty!
Love, in a word, is a young man's disguise…
It's just the matter of the proper choice.
DURVAL. And his prudent nature
Always made connections in good company.
All things considered, I must say in truth
That he has what it takes to satisfy
(*A little uncomfortable.*)
Either your daughter Adelaide or Julie.
CÉLISE. (*Happily.*) Yes, but at least, he must select the prettiest;
Yes, truly, he must choose. Our friend Germeuil
Is waiting, so he writes, for the outcome.
This nice dilemma will both entertain
Him and enchant him and like the boy,
I'm going to enjoy the merrymaking.
The final option must be left to him…
Do you hear me, Durval? (*With a little menace.*) Will you obey
The rules?
DURVAL. (*Uncomfortable.*) Yes, Madame, you're the one who calls
The shots.
(*Aside, with distress.*) Good God, the trouble this is causing!
CÉLISE. (*Still with menace.*) Why can't you simply give your full consent?
DURVAL. (*Still distressed.*) I do again and not to cause dismay,
I won't even express my heart's desire…
But let's suppose here, for a moment, Madame,
That Damis's choice might be unfortunate,

That he, in fact, might only bring regret
To her whose heart perhaps could never feel
The same affection fathered by his eyes.
Would you force her to love?
CÉLISE. (*Firmly.*) Certainly not!
In such a case to try to force a child,
Obliged by duty all her life to fake
Unhappy passion that she cannot feel…
To dare entrap the child against her will
Is like plunging a knife into her heart!
Why, it's the simplest way to open up
The door to every vice, to every sin,
To every manner of social injustice.
A mother, in a word, who'd do such things
Should terminate her life in deep remorse,
An outcast, far away at her last hour
From those she'd like beside her at her death.
DURVAL. (*With deep feeling.*)
How I respect in you these worthy principles!
How much you deserve the love of your children!
CÉLISE. (*Continuing happily.*)
Let Damis make his choice at his own pace.
He'll have to please one or the other fully…
And then the one who's more inclined toward you
Will make your triumph infinitely sweeter.
And when her preference for you is affirmed,
You'll feel the greatest and the liveliest joy
And talk about a rival here won't even
Waste time entering your head. Don't you think so?
DURVAL. Assuredly, Madame. Your tender words
Have moved my soul. I understand the rules.
CÉLISE. Let's finish all the preparations so that
Your rival can exhaust his intelligence. (*She rings; LAFLEUR, a servant enters.*)
CÉLISE. Lafleur, tell Marton that I need to see her.
LAFLEUR. I'm on my way, Madame, to tell her to come down. (*He exits.*)

DURVAL. (*Disturbed, calling back CÉLISE.*) Just to confuse the issue even more,
Would you mind telling me which of the twins
I've been in love with?
CÉLISE. (*Shrewdly*) Well… which one is it?
Let's see, could it be Adelaide?
DURVAL. (*Still a bit uneasy*) She'd be
Of no concern, except to cause confusion…
Perhaps I could choose her on purpose. Madame,
I'm simply looking out for the whole…
CÉLISE. (*The first two lines are jovial, the rest of the speech is serious.*)
Yes, I hear you! No, we must stay impartial
So Damis's choice is absolutely free.
For you to be in love would hinder us;
You must be cold, without a vested interest…
You're just a friend to keep me company,
Here by chance and without much ado.
Above all, when you're with him, you're his friend,
His confidant in love and not his rival.
(*Shrewdly*) Yes, that will be your role; you have to be
Impartial, unafraid of either choice.
DURVAL. (*Still uneasy*) I'm not afraid, Madame, and the resemblance
To my eyes is so strikingly the same
That for the last four months I've been unable
To figure out which of the two is prettier.
Now, faced with an insuperable choice,
The thing to do is put it in their lap
And make them choose between us… since my choice
Of either beauty will do me no good.
(*Enter MARTON.*)
MARTON. Madame, I'm here prepared to follow orders.
CÉLISE. Marton, go up and help the girls to dress,
Make everything the same… hairstyles and ribbons,
No difference in any of their clothes…
So that the sharpest eye can't tell the girls apart.
When everything is ready, send them down

And I'll take over caring for the girls.
I like the scene that we're about to play
And I want everything to be prepared.
Let's go. My dear Durval, you must excuse me,
But you've no idea how much these games amuse me. *(She exits with Marton.)*
DURVAL. *(Alone)* We'll soon see if Damis's a connoisseur.
The outside looks the same, yes, but alas
I see a subtle difference in their hearts.
I have to yield to this insanity
And hide, until the end, my secret love.
God, how could I have made a different choice?
Why, Adelaide's so sensitive and kind,
So full of sweetness, that it seems absurd
For someone not to love her at first sight.
I must pretend, however, since I'm bound
By friendship; and should I declare myself,
I'd aggravate and irritate Célise.
She found me out. Oh, what a stupid task
To try to hide your feelings when in love!
Your eyes betray your heart at every turn:
A look, a sigh, a gesture, a complaint,
A letter someone gives her, wishes, fears…
It all means something in love's dialect.
Oh, heavens, Adelaide, I'm just a lover!
Despite your promises, I'm insecure…
Deprived of your caresses, I could see
Myself dying of a broken heart.
I'll be unable to keep up appearances;
I'd give myself away by being nervous.
I'd rather not be here. Oh, God, it's she…
Before the silly make-believe begins,
I could perhaps assure her of my love.
(ADELAIDE appears, wearing a robe over her petticoat, nothing on her head, her hair in curlers, in the complete disarray of a young woman in the midst of dressing.)
ADELAIDE. I only have a moment.
DURVAL. Can I count on you?

ADELAIDE. My heart is yours.
DURVAL. How sweet is this assurance.
I must say I'm afraid of… and still dread
This cruel test. Alas, sweet Adelaide,
Everything's desire; all is pain
Or pleasure, joy or sorrow to the heart
Of him who loves you. Far away from you,
I start to worry; when you're in my arms,
Hope drives away my terror in an instant.
You see the powers of a beloved object;
Together, love and joy walk hand in hand
To reestablish peace where sadness ruled,
And change a moment's heartbreak into rapture.
In spite of everything you try to do,
The look of love is burning in your eyes,
You must admit it. I am terrified.
I'm frightened of the fire in your eyes…
As soon as Damis sees it, he'll be yours;
Don't move your eyes except in pleasant apathy.
ADELAIDE. (*Cleverly.*) But won't you be there?
DURVAL. Yes. Well, let's rehearse…
Imagine I'm Damis and listen to
The genuine expression of his passion.
ADELAIDE. No, no, the part's impossible to play…
I can no more pretend, looking at you,
Than I can show Damis the heat of passion.
Don't worry, Durval. I hear someone calling.
It has to be my mother. I must hurry!
Goodbye and cast aside your jealous doubts,
(*Looking at him tenderly.*)
My eyes will speak to no one else but you.
DURVAL. (*Running to kiss her hand.*)
Ah! But at least…
ADELAIDE. (*Tenderly, allowing him to kiss her hand.*)
Well! Do you still have doubts?
DURVAL. (*Enraptured.*) No, no, I promise you. A doubt would curse
A heart like yours. I'll never doubt again.

(*A noise is heard.*)
What's that I hear? I think someone is coming.
You'd better leave.
(*ADELAIDE exits.*)
Perhaps I'm going to be
Betrayed by all my tenderhearted senses.
I wonder if that was our man? Oh yes…
It's he… I heard someone announce his name.
I'll go and welcome him.
(*He takes a few steps toward DAMIS, who enters in disarray. Throughout the scene, DAMIS must play his role in such a way that his frivolous behavior at the start gives way to the frank and honest nature he truly possesses, obscured a bit by the manners of the day, taught to him by both the city and its clubs.*)
DAMIS. Heigh ho, Durval,
Leaving without a word? Ah, that's not nice.
When I dropped by your house, they told me that
You weren't at home. But how have you been able
To stay away from Paris for so long?
Are you in love? (*DURVAL nods "no."*)
Ah! Take a look at him:
So snooty-duty bound down to his toes,
Afraid to spill the beans about a lady,
Discretion to a fault, revering love,
Like people used to worship it in days
Of yore. A Cavalier of France.
DURVAL. (*Ironically.*) You don't agree?
DAMIS. No, not entirely. This outrageous mania
To take from love its most impassioned flame
Has not completely convinced me as yet.
I've never been deceitful in the least:
I never hide the "favors" I receive;
As soon as I get them, all Paris knows!
DURVAL. And Paris also knows the shameless rumors
You like to spread when you've got nothing left
To brag about.
DAMIS. Without a doubt. And in
So doing, doesn't it insure that women

Solely satisfy our heart's desires?
It's pride that rules, friend; just as much as love,
It wants to keep us under its control!
Believe me. The pleasures a person gets
From flaunting his own adventures are just
Run-down delights, the benefit of cares,
Of sighs, of melancholy feelings through which
A deadly boredom passes gracefully.
That is to say, in short, that people want
Intrigue; a love passed over bores us quickly;
You love out in the open, you're a hero!
And if you're not in love, you make it up
And very quietly spread it around.
DURVAL. The golden rule!
DAMIS. What? Yes, it's only credit…
In short, a debt without collateral
A person in the world contracts with Cupid;
Then pride co-signs the loan whenever love
Without delay decides to bless our rapture
And in the end, he pays back what he owes.
And if the person can't repay the loan,
Then pride permits him to get out of it
At least by puffing up his interest.
Or so it seems to me.
DURVAL. Ridiculous!
Why slander such an unsuspecting sex?
Betray it… punish it… just when a person
Ought to be trying to please it. Oh, no.
It's not the way I think things ought to be.
Damis, the love within my heart will never
Be depicted in that sordid shade.
(*Getting angry.*)
Insult the object of our tender passions,
Daring to divulge her sweetest errors
And so condemn her for loving too much
And make her repent for being weak,
Revealing faults for which we are to blame!
DAMIS. (*Interrupting him.*)

I see only too clearly that a woman,
Durval, is more than a god to you.
DURVAL. (*Continuing angrily.*)
Just put yourself in her place for a moment,
You wretched man, and be more flexible.
Close to that love in you, a useless longing
Day in and out is seeking satisfaction.
Be philosophical and guess the price
Of everything she has to sacrifice:
Look at her preferences, her education,
All that she must reject when you seduce
And master her; the awful barriers
Her duties rise against your reckless vows,
Which she can only overcome by feelings
Much stronger and more passionate than yours.
Since she is honorable, be just to her
And make up for her tender sacrifice
Through honesty, through unrelenting love,
Above all, through the secrecy that she
Respects in love. All sensual pleasure grows
Mysteriously; ah, good Lord, Damis,
It's so sweet to be pleasant, to be loved,
To be preferred without anyone knowing…
When sensitivity has tied the knot,
Its hand enshrouds it in a profound silence.
Any other way is just excessive.
A shameful fancy, a degrading taste,
That all together brands the man and mistress
And plunges both of them, despite your scheme,
Into public scorn, and what's worse, self-contempt.
DAMIS. If you want people to have so much truth,
At least deposit it among the women.
Make them share in this great sincerity
And let the falsehood that embodies them
No longer be for us their wit and art.
DURVAL. (*Quickly.*) Be truthful first, and shortly you will see
An end to that provoking artifice
You force upon them with your many crimes;

That art is your work; it's against their principles.
It's you who put those weapons in their hands;
In short, when you defy their tears, they need them.
Instead of being unfaithful to them,
Just love them without tricks or circumvention
And you'll soon see that frail and tender love
That's undefended in their graceful breast
Can only offer you a happy innocence,
The destiny of those who live in heaven,
Which you defile with your perverse behavior.
DAMIS. Though you might find excuses for those faults,
They're insupportable, even to hearts
Already predisposed in their favor.
These genuine crimes of society
Disintegrate the most sacred of spirits,
However that may be. The veil of love
Might hide them for a moment, but a calm
Intelligence will soon discover them
And if we should persist in our delusion,
Our vanity's the only reason why!
DURVAL. (*Gradually getting hotter until the thirty-sixth line; the last eight lines are spoken with the greatest passion.*)
Friend, be fair, and learn to understand
This object of seduction as you call her;
Examine her behavior and misfortunes…
Judge a woman fairly and you'll prize her.
See her condemned, alas, from infancy,
To rigid chains of male dependency;
Not leaving school except where, by and by,
Some money or ambition places her;
Always with a sweet and tender heart,
Escaping from the bosom of a family
When her bloom begins to fade, to die
Of boredom in the midst of rotting flesh
Should she by chance be married to an old man.
If she's young, well-made, with a pretty face,
It won't be long until lies and gossip,
Always looking out for sinful pleasures,

Betray and leave her to eternal sighs;
Consuming sadness, by which she is jaded.
See how the power is always against her!
How she'll forget it all if her oppressor,
Himself oppressed by fate, seeks consolation!
With what self-interest in these times of sadness,
Offering her husband the offspring of tenderness,
Does she awaken all at once within her battered senses,
The cry of nature and the tug of virtue!
Her self-respect, her woes, her recent fears,
Seeing that her hope fades with her beauty,
That in her old age, at the height of anguish,
Even her children will abandon her.
Forever, thus, a victim, and forever
Virtuous, forever tender and
Sensitive, and always unfortunate,
Beneath her footsteps having only seen
Misfortunes, cares, and disadvantages,
Adversity, or strife, and endless chains;
At last abandoned by parents and friends,
To spend her last days filled with apprehension
For want of ever having felt the joy
Of happiness a moment in her heart.
Yet you don't want us out of gratitude,
Or duty, even justice or amends,
To close our eyes to their few trifling faults.
We should erect a temple to their virtue,
A shrine, where every day in sincere homage,
A man adores their sacred ministry
Created by the kindness of the deity
To beg forgiveness for the sins of men!
DAMIS. Alas, I yield, my friend. Besides, the wedding,
I dare to say, will really do the trick.
To me, it's like a place of sanctuary
That just appeared to the navigator
In answer to the longing of his heart.
Captivated by this legal bond
(And happy to be bonded, I might add),

I want to draw the ties that bind more closely
With love and deep affection from the heart.
The bridles that we kid about while lovers
Are viewed by husbands in a different way;
Here, I assure you, I'll discover beauty
Where I finally set down my fickle nature.
They've given me the choice… Can't wait to see them…
Ah! Durval, strengthen my unsteady hope.
The choice is really free? No preference?
DURVAL. (*Interrupting him, disguising his concern.*)
That's what I hear and I've every assurance
That you, Damis, can choose the one you want.
DAMIS. I trust you, but before anything else,
I've got to wash the dust off from the trip,
Shampoo my "air" and scrub away my faults.
You won't make an impression, so they say,
Unless you're wearing all the proper clothes.

END OF ACT ONE

ACT TWO

(*The two sisters, ADELAIDE and JULIE, are both dressed exactly alike; it is impossible to see a difference between them either in their clothes or in their hairstyle. They wear clothing typical of the countryside adjacent to Paris, in the most exquisite taste, of the latest fashion, and in the brightest possible colors.*)

CÉLISE. No!
I never want to contradict your inclinations.
Since you were very young, my tenderness
For you, you know, has made you understand,
My children, that I never had the least desire
To be anything but your dearest friend.
I saw in your hearts the power of virtue;

My own has overcome its foolish fears…
I've proven it to you by more than words.
The choice with which we'll entertain ourselves today
Has two designs: to kindle and to test
The passion of the young husband destined for you
And to enable you, in turn, to say,
I guess, how much you're impressed by his suit.
Should he prefer the one of you whose heart
By any chance could not return his love,
The similarity between you will
Allow us to console him with the other.
We'll need to keep it in the strictest confidence.
And you can rest assured that if your hearts
Respond in equal measure to his love,
The one whom he prefers will be his bride.
If not, I promise you, he'll only wed
The one who's able to feel something for him.
ADELAIDE and JULIE. (*Together, kissing one of their mother's hands.*)
What kindness!
JULIE. Accept our gratitude at your knees…
CÉLISE. (*Interrupting her.*)
Dear daughters, I just want you to be happy.
At first, we'll offer only one of you
To our young suitor's amorous attentions;
As soon as we've presented Adelaide
For his delight, then Julie will arrive
Because the lad has got to make a choice;
And after that, at your convenience, each
Of you in turn can fascinate his eyes.
I think I hear him; Julie, go away…
You're the one who'll like the game the best,
For seeing you, he's bound to be amazed
At such an extraordinary trick of nature.
(*JULIE exits left. DAMIS enters right.*)
Here he is! (*ADELAIDE sighs.*)
I think I can read your heart,
My child, and it's not heaving sighs for him.

(*ADELAIDE nods "no."*)
DAMIS. (*All dressed up.*)
For more than an entire decade, Madame,
I've wanted to pay homage to your goodness…
But difficulties, troubles, certain duties,
Annoying situations have so long
Prevented me from carrying out my plans,
Which, regrettably, I have had to delay.
Madame, at last, I'm free and disentangled
From those obtrusive trifles that entrap a soul
Without allowing it the sweetness of enjoyment;
Today I can surrender to the pleasure
Of seeing and admiring your house,
A delightful abode, where, every moment,
Without effort, the soul is pleased to find
All the attractions of the city and
The peace and quiet of the countryside.
(*During the following lines, DAMIS looks closely at ADELAIDE. By the last lines, he is surprised by his interest in her. ADELAIDE blushes and lowers her eyes.*)
CÉLISE. We're certainly happy to have you here,
But these pleasures to which your soul aspires
Will hold little enjoyment for a man of fashion.
We all live here alone. We read, we talk,
We do our little jobs, we take long walks…
And I can't fathom why a person, of his own accord,
Would want to leave the pleasures of Paris
To come enjoy such bitter boredom here.
DAMIS. (*With a little consideration; the first five lines are directed to ADELAIDE; the picture varies slightly and, at the end of the lines directed to ADELAIDE, he says all that might be relative to CÉLISE with great respect.*)
Ah, don't speak to me of frivolous pleasures,
Those despicable symbols of caprice,
Where, in a terrifying emptiness,
The heart is dead forever to all comfort
And all affection. No!
These dreadful pastimes and coldblooded pleasures

Are not the destiny of today's man!
And I suspect one of the sweetest moments,
Madame, a man could have is spending time with you.
CÉLISE. The gallantry is dazzling in your words;
Be that as it may, sir, we are flattered.
(*Shrewdly.*) And if you enjoy our entertainment,
We might, then, believe your gallant speech.
Excuse me, I must leave you for a moment;
I have a dreary matter to attend to
And I am going to try and get it done.
Here, Adelaide will know how to take my place.
(*As she begins to leave, DAMIS offers her his hand.*)
No, no, sir, stay. No ceremony, please;
We left that dusty nuisance in Paris. (*She exits.*)
DAMIS. (*Drawing nearer to ADELAIDE.*)
Ah! How can she think that any time
I spend with you would not be fascinating?
You make the moments blossom with your presence;
Where beauty smiles, crowds gather just to see
Enjoyment being born, for beauty knows
How to attract it by her god-like charms
And all our pleasures are at her expense.
I can't imagine having any choice:
Who, more than you, deserves my tenderness?
Who, more than you, could captivate my heart and soul?
Who could seize it with a holier passion?
ADELAIDE. (*In a light and pleasant tone; throughout the scene, she cleverly disguises the small talk.*)
Such a hurried decision prevents
Me from believing anything you say.
How can you grant the victory to me,
Not even having seen the other girl?
Don't rush, sir; you can wait to flatter me.
Your eyes are much too easily persuaded;
I doubt such passion for me can continue.
Must you decide so soon?
DAMIS. Alas, I thought…
I was convinced that nature never made

So beautiful a being on the earth;
You are its masterpiece…
So perfect a creation can't be made
Again by nature's art… it's all used up
In you.
ADELAIDE. Could not this profound art, as you call it,
By virtue of its power reproduce
What it already made?
DAMIS. (*Quickly.*) What a difference it would make!
No… never… never… I'm so sure of this
That at this very moment, if the offer
Of my hand and heart…
ADELAIDE. (*Interrupting him.*) God, how impulsive!
I thought you were smarter than that. Your certainty
Is shortly going to turn into spite!
With wounded pride, I'm going to see you
Renounce those pretty ideas at the feet
Of my rival,
For, trust me, sir, we are alike in nothing.
Her eyes, her hair, her features… everything's
So different, as you're going to see
In a little while.
DAMIS. (*Impassioned throughout.*)
There's no one else I want to see; I'm so
Convinced that nothing is comparable
To such sweet female charms, my mind's made up,
You gorgeous mortal!
ADELAIDE. Your way, my victory would be incomplete.
They'll say it was just love at first sight;
That I took advantage of your smitten soul…
If I accepted your hand carelessly,
My heart would then be too unsure of yours.
Day in and day out, I would fear my sister;
You'd change your mind, you'd find yourself complaining…
It shouldn't be long before they'd find me dead,
Killed by your resentment.
Don't let yourself get excited so soon.
Still, I don't want to rob you of your hopes…

Make your choice after you've tested the alternatives.
Then if you feel a little love for me, still,
Perhaps you'll see me again and again.
My sister and I promised one another
That we would not say anything until
After the choice is made. That's our last word
On the subject. Consider it carefully.
DAMIS. That's cruelty like I've never seen before.
I thought that love was less severe in his
Domain since he permitted hearts the freedom
Of choice to serve him.
(Julie suddenly appears.)
JULIE. (*The first line is spoken quickly, the following lines are spoken artfully.*)
Sister… they're waiting for you… I'm coming to let you know.
(*She nods to DAMIS, who bows in return. He looks at her intently and with the greatest surprise.*) I'm inconsiderate and should be quiet
And stop chattering for the moment rather
Than breaking up so sweet a conversation.
I came in without thinking and I'm sorry!
DAMIS. (*Dumbfounded and continuing to look at JULIE with surprised disbelief. To ADELAIDE.*)
So that's your sister? She looks a lot like you!
ADELAIDE. By curious coincidence, we were born together;
Now and then, nature enjoys its little jokes.
Well, what's the matter? Didn't I tell you?
(*Mimicking him.*) There's no one else I want to see; I'm so
Convinced that nothing is comparable
To such sweet female charms, my mind's made up,
You gorgeous mortal!
(*Continuing with spite and jealousy.*)
You see, Damis, when a lover makes promises,
The mess in which he finds himself:
A facial resemblance, some pretty features,
The cruel man forswears himself
And conquering his former sighs,
Delivers his gullible mistress

To the bosom of sorrow.
DAMIS. (*Still intently focused on JULIE, but to ADELAIDE.*)
That sudden rapture that alarmed you so
Should only prove the triumph of your charms.
I like in her what most resembles you…
But it's the selfsame love, the selfsame bond…
That sweet surprise is only your own doing…
For duplicating you, I owe the gods
A double reverence.
Following their example, you are everywhere:
Entitled, just like them,
To people worshipping, at your feet,
A thousand different attributes creating
A single being. Thousands of qualities
Which, all at once, appear to glorify you.
Because of you, she's lovely; and if I
Adored her,
You would always be the one I'd idolize.
ADELAIDE. That's what they call an excuse for fickleness!
DAMIS. It was nothing like that at all.
(*To ADELAIDE.*)
Do not accuse my heart of being fickle;
No, no, it's not at all and like before,
This heart is only captivated by
Your beauty alone;
Alas, what fascinates me about her
Are the traces of those delightful charms,
So heavenly and oh, so soft, which from
The very first moment attracted me to you.
ADELAIDE. Ah! You're amazing!
DAMIS. It's excusable…
For what we see in you is so amazing, too!
(*Aside.*) That isn't true! Love is punishing me:
Its power is enslaving me beneath
A double yoke.
JULIE. (*Ironically and taking advantage of his discomfort.*)
We're going to give you a moment of silence
To reconsider your preference, sir.

At present, all there is to say has been said
And you're acquainted with the both of us…
So think about the two of us in peace.
When love is restless, rest is necessary
And quiet will better enable you
To make a choice, which, in our company,
Is hard to do politely.
(*She exits laughing and nodding to him.*)
ADELAIDE. (*Doing the same.*)
Henceforth, at least don't go making mistakes…
Learn to protect yourself from all delusions…
And if you want to make a judgment sanely,
Discreetly stop behaving like a lover.
(*She exits.*)
DAMIS. (*Alone.*) No, never have I been in such a mess!
I could have sworn it was impossible
To see another woman just as perfect…
Someone's playing a practical joke on me;
It isn't funny!
But still I persevere with my first choice;
A heart resists Adelaide's charms in vain…
What am I saying? God! What an illusion!
Can I shut my eyes to that image,
To that passion that fills my soul
And fans the fire when I think of Julie?
It's Julie I love forever and ever…
Alas, whatever happens, I see only regret.
As soon as I'm married to one of them,
Each day, I'll see the other in my mind;
I'll be the most unfortunate of men.
Why am I carrying on like this? Why?
To be linked with the most heavenly creature
Nature ever made?
The more her sister looks like her,
And the less it comes as a complete surprise,
Endlessly consoled by such sweet ecstasy,
My heart is bound to feel pointless remorse.
I'll have in one, at least, all the attractions

Of the other... But is it my choice?
No. No. It's yours, celestial beauties.
Your feelings must be taken into account.
That clarifies things for me quite a lot
And ties me to Adelaide's apron strings
Forever! (*Recalling her words.*)
"Then if you feel a little love for me, still,
Perhaps you'll see me again and again."
She just said that in the sweetest voice.
The choice is made, Adelaide, and my heart
Is going to pay you homage eternally,
Without change, and I guarantee it.
Worthless spirit... superfluous schemes!
Who knows if from now on I'll be able
To recognize them? The resemblance is so...
(*He sees DUMONT, who has entered quietly in uniform toward the end of the monologue and who was enjoying himself, making gestures that related to his master's turmoil behind his master's back.*)
DAMIS. (*Angrily.*) Oh, there you are, you villain!
You knew the trouble I'd be in here, but
You didn't warn me.
(*Calming down.*) You see how annoyed and anxious I am.
Nothing can solve my miserable dilemma...
We should have stayed in Paris.
(*Continuing passionately.*) You know how I react at times like this...
You got here first. Why didn't you tell me?
DUMONT. They told me not to say anything, sir,
They said it was to throw you off the scent...
And you know how discreet I am.
DAMIS. Scoundrel,
Your loathsome silence will cost me my life!
There's still time: I've got a sudden urge
To leave this place without anyone knowing.
(*After a moment's consideration.*)
Not now, I can't. Indomitable bonds,
Already you have tied me up in chains!
(*Continuing quickly.*) What do you suggest I do in this situation?
(*He strikes DUMONT on the shoulder.*)

DUMONT. (*Contrite.*) Alas, sir, I'm trying to find an angle
That, in a word, could put your mind at rest.
I'm pondering privately this sad affair.
(*Continuing triumphantly.*)
Sir, pay attention to me: this time nature,
Either through whim, or anger, or revenge,
Is making fun of us, in spite of love.
For God's sake, sir, let's beat it at its own game…
It's nature's fault. After all: comeuppance
Is fair play!
This is how I see the situation:
Those two sisters will always be two girls
Of equal dispositions, so alike
In beauty that no one can choose between them.
Above all, mind you, born at the same time…
They're not two girls, I tell you. What we've got here
Is just a being with two faces, sir.
Conclusion to be drawn: through nature's marvels,
You can marry both of them at once!
DAMIS. With all this talk, you're wearing out my patience.
Get out of here, you rascal, and be thankful
I'm not in the mood to punish you
For your insolence.
DUMONT. But if I'm in fact the cause of all
This commotion, my advice is…
DAMIS. (*Pushing DUMONT offstage, he sees JULIE enter and mistakes her for ADELAIDE.*) Go away! Oh, God, it's Adelaide.
At this moment, love governs my eyes
And I recognize her. Ah, the god
Living in my heart will not allow me
To make a mistake, I just know it.
(*Going to her and speaking quickly.*)
Oh, heavens, Adelaide, can I touch your soul?
Can I make it aware of all the love
That burns inside of me?
Too much eagerness displeases you,
I feel it.
In your opinion, a man should betray

His feelings at the feet of so much beauty…
He should be worthless and insensitive
And, in a word, appear in your eyes capable
Of only cool affection that does not
Excite him.
That's not the way my heart knows how to love.
For you, my love becomes idolatry…
Make your decision… speak my destiny…
Forever, I return to my first vows,
And, Adelaide, I swear to you, I long
For your attractions only, yours alone.
Yes, yes, my mind's made up, accept my love.
Don't keep me hanging in this horrid state
By hesitating. Yield and make me happy.
JULIE. (*Laughing*.) If all this tender love and lively rapture
You're expressing is for Adelaide,
I owe you nothing, sir. You should be
Thankful for that.
DAMIS. (*Still very quickly*.)
I'm not at all mistaken and this heart
Intoxicated with your striking beauty
Carries your image inside it.
No one deceives such sincere adoration.
Ah! You would have to pretend brilliantly
And I would have to give you up for lost.
Love is my only guide; it won't lead me
Astray. You are the one that I prefer;
You're the one that I adore; it's you,
Adelaide; alas, I'm begging you,
In the name of so much love,
Return my affection!
JULIE. (*Laughing, as before*.)
No, no, you're mistaken.
DAMIS. Whether or not I'm mistaken, I'm very
Unhappy. You're the only one I love…
From now on, you're the only one I need
To settle my eternal destiny.
JULIE. Me? No! I swear it. And you can be sure

It's true, sir. I'm the other one… I'm Julie;
You thought my sister was much prettier than I…
I know it. You love her. I don't want you.
But your emotion has its cross to bear.
I am afraid that Adelaide… ah, now
I'm going to confuse you… Adelaide
Is unable to return your love…
In short, she cannot make you happy.
DAMIS. Why do you want to plunge me into grief,
Cruel Adelaide? Ah, I hear your words…
Behind this mask, you shrink from my affection;
And you only use this clever trick
To spurn more easily my too faithful love!
JULIE. More than you think, sir, I am sympathetic,
But you can understand how hard it is
To prove it to you when I see your heart
Maintaining its delusions, when the truth
Is staring at you in the face.
What good would it do me to open up
My heart to you when here I see you burning
With another passion… and to my face
(To stir up my hostility more quickly),
You swear my sister is your chosen love?
DAMIS. (*Impatiently*.) It isn't her! God, I keep telling you,
You're the one who has my special fondness;
There's never a mistake where the heart leads us.
There's no point in becoming confused!
A lover's eyes can always tell the difference
In spite of all the similarities.
In other words, you're the one I love.
JULIE. Alas!
If I believed that you preferred my fragile
Features, I'd provide you with the means
To know which one your heart is courting now.
(*She takes a rose out of her pocket.*)
You see this flower? I will place it here.
(*She indicates her breast.*)
So that it can always point out Julie

To your impassioned heart.
(*Tenderly.*) Do you promise to love her all your life?
Tell me, Damis, at least tell me if it's
Julie after all to whom you pledge your faith?
DAMIS. You're not Julie… and you're the one I love.
JULIE. I'm Julie, believe me. Again, I swear it to you.
DAMIS. (*Aside.*) This time, I must be going crazy, but
I'll play along with her. What's in a name?
(*During this aside, JULIE cleverly exchanges places, and the rose, with ADELAIDE. DAMIS sees none of it happen.*)
DAMIS. Well, you're the one I love, seductive Julie,
And you're the one who'll bring me good fortune
In my life. Yes, place the rose among its sisters…
In that way… alas, even among the flowers
The resemblances are striking.
Too cruel beauty, that will be my revenge,
And the uncertain wind one day will be,
Like Damis, here, the victim of his passion.
ADELAIDE. As you wish…
See! there, I've placed the flower. Satisfied?
At least there's no more misinterpretation.
Now promise me, in all honesty, that
You won't yearn for my sister in the slightest.
DAMIS. I swear it to you.
ADELAIDE. In Adelaide's heart,
There is another secret in addition…
You can be sure my sister cannot love you.
DAMIS. (*So much the more peeved because he does not suspect the switch, because he is calling the girl Julie at her request, because he is not less convinced that he is speaking to ADELAIDE, and because he feels compelled to tell her this; the only time he is not mistaken is when he is being most deceived and as long as he is mistaken, he is not being deceived.*)
Who is the man who can fill her with passion?
ADELAIDE. Are you jealous?
DAMIS. No, I swear it. But
I want to understand where her deceit
Is leading…

To see through it to extinguish my flames.
ADELAIDE. Did she promise to return your love?
DAMIS. She didn't promise otherwise. I thought
I understood…I could expect her
To return my feelings… that I could
Lay claim to her. But a just
Anger has banished her from my heart.
I'll get over it. (*Aside, meant to be overheard.*)
What a false and deceitful sex!
(*Aloud, still in the same frame of mind.*)
She has great flaws; besides, she's much less pretty.
Comparing her to you is vain and foolish;
She doesn't have your features, or your eyes,
She doesn't have your bearing, or the color
Of your hair, so charming and so fresh…
That's a difference…
ADELAIDE. An enormous one,
I'm sure. Alas, sir, you appear unhappy;
You're upset.
DAMIS. No, I swear to you, I'm not.
Humbled pride brings me back to my senses.
I think I hate her.
ADELAIDE. (*Quickly.*) You're losing your mind.
God, what is my destiny? Must he
Lament my rival with so much passion
Before my very eyes?
Well, sir, very well, enjoy your passion.
No one will impede your faithful love.
Happy Adelaide! Go ahead.
Tie the knots around your faithful slave
And never charm that ingrate who today
Has scorned my kindness!
(*Spitefully, she removes the rose.*)
You've won. Look at her. Look at my rival.
But my contempt is uttered here in vain.
I'm going… so that this will occupy
My heart no longer.
DAMIS. (*Aside.*) Good Lord, it's really Julie. I was wrong.
See how a person can get so confused!

ADELAIDE. (*Overtly switching places with JULIE.*)
Hurry, Adelaide!
Come receive the faith, that liar's vows…
Nothing can outweigh his choice, nor his love.
I leave him to you, in a word, forever. (*She exits quickly.*)
DAMIS. (*Full of rapture, throwing himself at JULIE's feet in the belief that he will no longer be the object of abuse and that he, at last, possesses ADELAIDE; he speaks quite rapidly.*) Adelaide, at last
your victory is complete.
She called me unfaithful and forsworn in vain.
See, I always knew how to recognize you…
Nothing could confuse me about your features.
Nothing, no, nothing could make me forget
The one who reigns victorious in my heart.
Let's hurry. Let's hurry. Let's go right now,
To get Célise's satisfied consent.
It's time, at long last, for the marriage knot
To reward the most ardent adoration.
What can I hope for?
JULIE. (*Getting up.*) Everything. But just on one condition:
That if you find you've been deceived,
You won't change your mind.
DAMIS. I promise you that.
And let's not separate… no more tricks. (*He offers her his hand.*)
JULIE. (*Giving him her hand.*) No more distance between us,
Damis.
DAMIS. (*Enthusiastically kissing her hand.*) Love, at last, you have rewarded me
For all my trials and tribulations!
(*He leads JULIE by the hand to CÉLISE, who enters with everyone else.*)
DAMIS. (*To CÉLISE.*) Madame, it's time. Crown my fidelity.
Confused in my choice by so many similarities,
I was deceived by Julie for a moment;
But, today, at last, it's Adelaide
I dare implore you to bestow upon me
As a wife.
She, alone, will always share the raptures
Of my heart. Madame, do not object

To my desires.
CÉLISE. My wish, dear Damis, is to make you happy;
But you don't want, I hope, to force the girl
To do anything she might regret;
Would you want her if it broke her heart?
DAMIS. I anticipate my happiness
Only from her consent.
CÉLISE. Adelaide, come answer for yourself.
ADELAIDE. Since my mother allows me to choose
A husband, thanks to her great tenderness,
Here's my hand, Durval. I give myself to you.
DURVAL. (*Ecstatic.*) Nothing can express what I'm feeling right now!
JULIE. (*To DAMIS, who is confused at being duped again.*)
In exchange for a breach of promise,
If your heart demands them in return,
Take, without remorse, your oaths forever
And keep them without regret.
CÉLISE. We're through with playing practical jokes!
(*Indicating JULIE.*) If that one there, sir, cannot captivate you,
You must be deprived of what belongs to us.
Soon, a thousand beauties, attracted
By your glances, will be consolation
To you for these two unimpressive losses.
DAMIS. Ah!
You couldn't offer me compensation
More suited to the desires of a lover!
(*To JULIE.*) In marrying you...
(*Indicating ADELAIDE.*) My heart will cherish her;
I'm going to adore her in her more
Beautiful likeness.
CÉLISE. (*To DAMIS.*) Your frivolity, sir, for a long while
Deserved, without exception, to be punished.
The best way to take care of the situation
Was to take advantage of love and your
Personality. Will you forgive us?
DAMIS. Is there any doubt? Who wouldn't want
To provoke you for such a reward?
CÉLISE. Ah! the lesson, sir, when you provoke us

Might not be so sweet another time.
DUMONT. (*Very seriously, to his MASTER.*)
Tonight, at least, sir, don't be mistaken.
MARTON. Someone will make it her business
To set him straight.
CÉLISE. (*With feeling.*) Here we are, all full of joy:
Only my friend Germeuil is missing at
The celebration; since he's ready to leave,
Let's all go invite him without delay. (*Everybody exits.*)
DUMONT. That means another trip for me. I think
I'll get married first.
(*Dragging back MARTON, who was trying to exit with everyone else.*)
Marton, what does your heart say? Could so rare
An example make you behave nicer
To me?
MARTON. Good Lord, I don't think so. Weddings scare me!
You know how rarely they turn out happily?
What's more, I only feel lukewarm about you.
DUMONT. Nothing hotter than lukewarm, Marton?
Blame it on my state in life.
MARTON. If you want to,
Let's get married. I consent…
But I don't promise anything.
DUMONT. Will there be two of you, at least?
That's the way you can get your revenge…
MARTON. (*Interrupting him.*)
You shouldn't think, dear Dumont,
That any of this is strange.
How many husbands,
To relieve their boredom,
Would like their daytime wives
To be different at night!

THE END

The Freak

Introduction

Two manuscript copies exist of the five-act comedy in alexandrines that Sade called *The Metamist, or The Changeable Man* in *The Descriptive Catalogue of 1788*. The first manuscript bears the words 10 *The Capricious Man*, five-act comedy in verse, on its dark green cardboard cover. On the last page, in Sade's hand, is written: "This piece was begun on 24 December 1780. The sketch was completed the 8th of January 1781 and the play was finished the evening of the 24 of the same month. It was revised and corrected between 24 January and 8 April of the same year; and from April 5th through the 19th inclusive, it was copied out. That constitutes 16 weeks of work in all. It contains 1824 lines." Notes on the inside cover indicate that the play was revised in August 1807 and again on 6 and 7 June 1811. On the same page, Sade suggests that this copy of the play might be better than the one copied by Thierri at Charenton. (This note has led the editors of Sade's *Théâtre* to believe that Thierri is the name of the inmate at Charenton who copied *Oxtiern* and *The Shyster* as well.) Thierri's copy, bound in pink cardboard, includes a lengthy foreword to the play; the green copy does not have Sade's introduction, but does have a number of alterations and corrections in Sade's hand.

When the play was finished, Sade sent a copy to his old mentor, the Abbé Amblet, with questions indicating the author's concerns about the moral of the play, the dialogue, the plot, and the development of the main character. Although Amblet's reply is lost, in a letter dated 6 July 1782, Madame de Sade[25] suggests the Abbé's response:

---

25 In an earlier letter dated 18 May 1781, the Marquise de Sade expressed her own opinion of the play: "Your piece is excellent.... The characters are well made: that of the valet does not at all resemble an ordinary valet; he is original. The character of the indecisive man is quite outstanding, well developed, well done. The baroness, a good friend, but a little fishy in her motives, just enough not to give away the ending which she clearly makes us understand at the beginning of the second act.... Fermeuil seems to me to be an ordinary lover in the style considered good. [Célénie], charming especially at the end, is noble and full of tenderness. This piece is certain to be applauded and if the French actors make any adjustments to it, they will be small—I don't even know where they would be."

Amblet's reaction to your comedy: after reading it, he didn't want to write down his feelings because he says, frankly, there's nothing good to say about it; that if his work entertains you, you can continue it as entertainment, but as for appearing in public, he says that's impossible. You want him to be honest with you and that's what he honestly told me.

Undaunted, the Marquis began to send the play out to theatres for possible production. In a letter dated 28 October 1791, Miramond, the administrator of the Théâtre de la rue Feydeau, refused the play on the grounds that his theatre was "especially intended for musical works" and even to consider a five-act comedy would be useless. Another document, dated the same day from Dorfeuille, representing the Théâtre de la rue Richelieu, is somewhat more aggressive in its refusal of the play:

> As I promised you, I've read your comedy, *The Changeable Man*. I should not and cannot deceive you. The work is too weak to produce. You have yielded too much to the abundance of your ideas than to the rules of drama. You wanted to write verses and you wrote them, but in actuality, this is in no way a comedy. Everywhere the color is pale and you have neglected to make the play dramatically interesting, the thing that sustains the framework of these kinds of structures.

After the negative reception in 1791, Sade must have welcomed the response from Dubuisson at the Théâtre de Louvois, whose encouraging reply, dated 2 May 1792, held out the promise of production:

> It is with great pleasure that I have the honor of announcing to you the reception of your comedy entitled *The Changeable Man*. I beg you to come to the theatre at 11am next Friday, the 4th of this month, with your manuscript to agree upon the actors you're choosing and certain slight changes that seemed necessary and afterwards to copy out the roles.

Unfortunately, nothing came of Dubuisson's interest and Gilbert Lély reports that Sade was still peddling the play in 1795 when he sent out a circular to the theatre directors in Bordeaux, Toulouse, Lyon, Besançon, Rouen, Caen, and Rennes, advertising the play as a "character comedy... accepted with corrections by the Théâtre Français." No communication exists between Sade and the Théâtre Français to prove his claim. All we know is that the play was never performed.

The Freak
Preface

It's been almost a century since Piron[26] wrote that the most difficult thing in the world was finding new characters to put on stage. How difficult then should it be today after so many harvests in the same fields? It seems that everything has been completely investigated and taken and although the human heart might be a labyrinth, each winding road of which offers it alone an indefinite number of different shades, people think that everything's been said even before they think they've seen everything. Don't pity our posterity. Certainly, we've done a lot, but there will still remain a lot for them to do. Will there be nothing for them besides having so many old characters to redo and rewrite in the vernacular of their age? The root of behavior doesn't change, people know that. But the absurdities and vices that are the result of behavior and of the kind of government where a person lives undoubtedly vary because of the general impulse of the state or of its constitution. As a result, these attendant manners are not only different in a peaceful monarchy than in a turbulent nation, they are even very different in a republic than in a monarchy. The pretentiousness of the reign of Augustus was a bit like the pretentiousness of the reign of Louis XIV, but the pretentiousness of Louis XIV's reign is certainly not the same as that of the League[27] and that pretentiousness is certainly no longer the same as that of the old republic of Venice. The heart of a man is a kind of soil appropriate for all kinds of plants. It must produce them out of necessity, but those plants will hold the ground that gives them their existence: they will be more or less fragrant in one climate rather than in another, more or less juicy in the hands of a calm farmer rather than drenched with the tears of a nervous

---

[26] Alexis Piron (1689–1773), a witty, often coarse playwright whose election to the Académie-Française in 1753 was vetoed by King Louis XV because of an obscene "Ode to Priapus" Piron had written in his youth.

[27] The League of Augsburg, a coalition between the Holy Roman Emperor Leopold I, the kings of Spain and Sweden, and the electors of Saxony, Bavaria, and the Palatinate against Louis XIV. In 1689, when William of Orange became King of England, that country also joined the league.

worker who, at the sight of a plundering soldier, is ready to melt over the frail consolation of his pains.

The character offered here was among the kind forgotten, or neglected certainly, by artists much more famous than we, who, after one or two character plays, have given the dearth of subjects as an excuse for their laziness. Yet wouldn't he have offered an enormous scope for the delicate brushes of the past century.

The comedy was barely outlined when we began to feel how the French language lacks words to express certain characters; for it is extremely necessary that the word *capricieux*[28] unite all the different characteristics that create the individual here in question. But, all the same, how is it accomplished? I thought of resorting to compounds in Greek—but how to construct them? What do you call in this language *one who wants and no longer wants, one who desires so much and cares about nothing*. It is impossible to create any collective term regarding two contrary things because it would no longer be understood distinctly. One of the first lessons of logic is that in the compound, the meaningful parts must present only one idea—one fixed and determined sense; and in a word made up of two compounds, one will always determine the other. Having recognized these difficulties, it was then necessary to return to the term in the French language most suitable to that diversity of opinions found at every moment in our hero and no other word than CAPRICIEUX could be found.

At the beginning of the last century, Destouches wrote a comedy called *The Indecisive Man*.[29] So that no one thinks that we have only touched up that model, or rather, that we have mutilated his work in order to write a new one, we're going to set up an exact parallel here to show the essential difference between the two characters. We encourage our readers to take a glance at this because from the same parallel, they will derive a more precise idea of the character that's being portrayed here and they will imagine him in a more definite way than they would be able to do by referring to the title which we have been obliged to use for lack of anything else.

---

[28] Literally, "capricious" or "freakish."

[29] A verse comedy in five acts, produced 15 January 1713 at the Théâtre Français. Destouches was the professional name of Phlippe Néricault (1680–1754), an actor and playwright who sought to infuse the drama with a heavy dose of morality and sentimentality.

The indecisive man is one who can't decide on anything. The freakish (or capricious) man is one who cannot stick to what he's decided. The one wants and doesn't want; the other wants and no longer wants. The one wavers for a long time over the course of action that suits him; if he doesn't take it, it's because a different option seems better to him. The other takes his course of action very quickly; a single obstacle disturbs it; that alone is enough to make him decide and if he changes his mind, it's because the object is drawing nearer and there's no longer an obstacle. The one, always guided by reasons, only hesitates in the fear of choosing poorly. The choice is completely equal to the other so long as a hard-to-attain pleasure is involved and, above all, so long as thorns maintain the illusion; for it disappears as soon as the tips become dull. Capriciousness might be the odd habit of both of them, but Destouches's Dorante is only capricious incidentally. That's because indecisiveness is the daughter of capriciousness—whereas the Marquis de Fonrose is capricious by inclination, by habit. What is to us the most important point is only incidental to Destouches. Forced to return at length to the original meaning of the words that name them in our language, one changes through irresolution, the other through capriciousness. The need to change one's mind is essential to both of them, but what a difference in the motives that lead to the alteration. The effects or necessary complications for one or the other of these characters will serve as evidence. The most indecisive man can and even should be a very intelligent man since that's why he's indecisive. The capricious man, at least the way he's portrayed here, the man marked by this kind of vice, will certainly be nothing but a fool. But if one proves to be a very wise man and the other a fool, how could the two characters ever be the same? The difference between the two characters is still better established in the causes that determine their variations. The proof that the indecisive man only changes his mind through reason is that, when Nérine happens to tell him that Julie loves him, that settles him on Julie. It would have simply taken that fact alone to disgust the Marquis de Fonrose: he breaks away from Célénie and the Baroness at the very moment he thinks they're in love with him. In another situation, Dorante changes his mind because he's afraid of loving his wife too much and because he recognizes that affection alone is enough for a married couple. Indeed, that's a pretty bizarre reason, but it is a reason after all and still very different than the motives that make our character change, for, once again, it's the fear of loving too much that alters Dorante. As for Fonrose, he only changes from the fear of being loved and from the certainty of the sharp disgust that comes over him immediately in return.

Destouches has ridiculed a weakness more to be pitied than censured. Instead, the absurdity much more marked that we're portraying here is enough not only to cause the misfortune of the one who possesses it, but even to wreak havoc on all those around him. The first is only a very unfortunate infirmity; the second is really a rather certifiable illness of the brain. Destouches managed to make his own character theatrical only by overdoing it, by ridiculing a man who's only unfortunate, by setting him against other absurdities that force him to be ridiculous and creating (in spite of nature) a vice, which is only an excess of reason. Our own creation, inviting absurdity on its own and supporting the entire weight of that absurdity without needing any contrast, took less trouble to write and as a result, we are worth less in that regard. But it is not less certain that when one wishes to run such a course, one would be better to use characters naturally weighed down by themselves such as ours than characters that need to be blackened by the stroke of a paintbrush! The one gets its substance from nature, the other has to derive it from artifice. If the indecisive man makes up his mind only with a lot of effort or quickly deserts the course of action he has just adopted, it is in the perpetual fear of losing happiness or that he won't find it in the option he's taking. But that happiness is an entity very much in existence in his eyes; he is only hampered with knowing where to put it. On the contrary, the capricious man sees happiness only as an imaginary thing that eludes the person who seeks it and that leaves a few feeble flowers of its false or deceitful existence only to the one who skims over everything without ever going into anything deeply because his eyes, in such a case, by going deeper into the void, would destroy the illusion and instead of pleasure, only the despair of having been deceived would remain. The indecisive man is a serious, ponderous man; the capricious man is a giddy, frivolous man who never thought about his life. A thought would ruin his pleasure, it would chill him, it would analyze what for him only needs to be superficially experienced. Note carefully that the indecisive man always has excellent reasons for changing his mind. He is therefore not ridiculous since the most complex reason is always the motive for his variations. His character is purely passive. That of the capricious man is always active. He only ever changes and varies on a whim without reason even being the smallest part of his motives. It is vice all by itself: the force of vice alone that is operating. What a difference for the theatre! The character of the indecisive man isn't his own, it belongs to everything that surrounds him. The character of the capricious man belongs to him. It becomes the prime mover of his variations and all the motives that determine the first would be almost always the ones that would cause the second to change. Finally, at the resolution, Destouches was so well aware that his Dorante was anything but reprehensible that he didn't dare punish him, whereas one would inevitably fall into a rage against us if we dared not crush our Marquis de Fonrose with all the thunderbolts that hover over his head. Yes, undoubtedly, he had to be punished. We were excused from correcting him because it is hardly probable that those characters deeply marked with a vice, who appear to have had it since childhood, and who, after having done in twenty-four hours more than they would have in six months, would end up contradicting themselves in the resolution if one wasn't obliged to condense their characteristics. But Fonrose needed to be taught a lesson and we taught it to him.

It's enough to stress the parallel and what has just been said is more than sufficient to establish the specific difference between Destouches's character and our own. With regard to the arrangement of either work, the two are so dissimilar that I'll never be afraid of the slightest accusation of plagiarism on that account: we submit it to the examination of our most severe critics. It would narrow the course tremendously not to think that we are allowed to work in a style somewhat similar to that of an author who has preceded us. And without including plays that are completely rewritten, would we have ever had the excellent comedy *The Wicked Man*[30] if Gresset had been afraid of *The Scandalmonger*?[31] Would we have had the priceless

---

[30] A verse comedy in five acts produced at the Théâtre Français on 27 April 1747.
[31] By Destouches (1715).

drama *Beverly*[32] if Saurin had dreaded Regnard's *The Gamester*?[33] Finally, would we have *The Two Sons-in-Law* without Piron's *The Ungrateful Son*[34] and the comedy of Conaxa? The same is true in all the arts. Would La Tour[35] or Van Loo[36] have created such beautiful heads if they had been afraid of Albani's paint brushes?[37] Would Saxe and Voltaire breathe under the learned hand of Pigalle[38] if that famous artist had been terrified by the pure and delicate style of Praxiteles? If he had been discouraged by the virile and vigorous chisel of Michaelangelo? It's not imitating, but embellishing; it's not copying, but correcting. And anyone working in a style entirely like that of another artist who will carry it over to his model will always have the quality of originality since he will have found the perfection that had eluded his predecessor. But let us leave this topic, which we have no right to sustain since we claim to be offering here a character that is absolutely new, and let us conclude with some purely analytical thoughts about our subject.

It would take much more time than the twenty-four hours prescribed by the rule to develop a character as wide-ranging as this one. It has to be tightened, shortened, and brought into closer perspective. Such is the story of all the characters presented by a dramatic author: they lose something and are a great deal less striking than they could be through the extended nuances of the novelist. Everything hampers the one; everything serves the other. How different is the work! Let someone try a *Lovelace* on the stage. All he'll ever come up with is *Milord Clarendon*, a charming sketch unquestionably; but would the pen of Beaumarchais, in spite of all his magic, ever have been able in twenty-four hours to make *Eugénie* as interesting as *Clarissa* and *Milord Clarendon* as wicked

---

[32] A *bourgeois* tragedy staged on 7 May 1768. In *The French Stage in the Eighteenth Century*, Frederick Hawkins calls it the first example "in Paris of the domestic tragedy so firmly implanted in England" (II, 153).

[33] A verse comedy in five acts produced in 1696.

[34] A verse comedy in five acts, also called *The School for Fathers*, produced at the Théâtre Français on 10 October 1728.

[35] Georges de La Tour (1593–1652), noted painter of candlelight scenes based on Biblical or Christian iconography.

[36] Charles-André Van Loo (1705–1765), noted Rococo portrait painter.

[37] Francesco Albani (1578–1660), a seventeenth-century Bolognese master noted for frescoes based on mythological subjects.

[38] Jean-Baptiste Pigalle (1714–1785), noted as a forerunner of Neoclassicism with a highly personal, realistic style.

as *Lovelace*? This twenty-four hour rule is a terrible obstacle! And in general, rules are ridiculous when one only wants to be entertained. It's forcing an acrobat to walk the tightrope in heavy boots and, no matter what anyone can say about it, a minor tyranny that will never result in anything but lessening pleasure.

It was very difficult to make a person like this interesting; there's something so revolting about him that he often annoys rather than entertains. It's with good reason that Marmontel said *that an uneven and grating character could never stick*. It was therefore necessary to set aside any interest in either the individuals he deceives or those who unveil him. Generally, the play was mildly susceptible to passion. High comedy allows very little of it. Thalia restricts herself to scenes depicting the ridiculous and leaves the sharpening of swords to Melpomene. The one only seeks to entertain and correct through the depiction of vice; the other should terrify by portraying the danger of crime. Every intermediate genre will only ever be at the expense of one or the other. We are certainly far from wanting to rob it of continual merit, but we will venture to assert at least that this mixture will create a genre that, except for La Chaussée and Destouches (who elevated the style in his *The Spendthrift* and other plays) and some *dramas*, would not easily exist.

The principal aim of this play was to conceal the plans of the Baroness from one end of the play to the other, but all the same, allowing her to be discovered to some degree could not be avoided. She wasn't plausible without that and the pleasure of being completely surprised at the resolution did not compensate for the tediousness of her inconsistency. It appeared then absolutely essential to us to allow her to be a little predictable.

One will find the character of Saint-Fard too serious, perhaps. But what better contrast is there to Fonrose's frivolity? It's only through the use of opposites that one can succeed in creating nuances; that was Molière's great secret. Unfortunately, he did not pass it on to us. Saint-Fard's ill humor must necessarily increase when he discovers his niece's passion since he understands all the misfortunes that can come of it. It seems very natural that from that moment on, his scenes should become gloomy. The description he gives her of a capricious man's life is very serious. "Yes," our *supporters* will say, "fathers of a family will not think that way" and it's for that reason, even more than for frivolity, that we're creating these characters.

One will undoubtedly be very surprised that we are not submitting the very mediocre play *The Fickle Man* to the same analysis. To demonstrate the vast difference between the capricious man and the indecisive man is enough to demonstrate the most certain difference between our play and that of Colin d'Harleville. Is a word nevertheless necessary? Here it is: the fickle man takes a dislike to something only because he possesses it—the capricious man only because he's afraid of possessing it. But all pride aside, if one still wants a stronger proof of the great difference that exists between these two plays, let one compare them and read them side by side. If the advantage rests with us, we will conceal an anecdote as certain as it is disagreeable about our competitor. If not, we'll tell all—but not without the fear that revealing the secret will not tremendously diminish in Colin the tiny moment of glory the bias of the reader would have given him.

END OF THE PREFACE

The Freak
Verse Comedy in Five Acts

CHARACTERS

The Marquis de Fonrose, the man who can't make up his mind
Célénie, Mr. Saint-Fard's niece
Mr. Saint-Fard
The Baroness Florange, widow and friend to Célénie and Verneuil
Verneuil, in love with Célénie
Deschamps, Fonrose's manservant
Servants of the Marquis, several non-speaking roles

The action takes place in Paris in the living room of a house belonging to Fonrose and where Saint-Fard, his niece, and the baroness live as tenants.

ACT ONE

It is between eight and nine o'clock in the morning.

FONROSE. (*Alone, in a very elegant dressing gown.*)
No one ever gets up in this house!
No worries, no problems, and free from cares,
These are the tenants of this happy home;
How heavenly it is to be like them:
Always undisturbed, to want for nothing,
And always satisfied with everything...
To have nothing but the selfsame taste
For centuries! Hey there!
Germon, Lafleur, bring in my dressing table.
Hurry up. Let's go. I want it done
Before these people see the light of day.
(*Two servants carry on a dressing table and attempt to set it down stage right.*)
Hmm. Good! Yes... put it there. No! over here.

(*They set it down stage left.*)
Call my servants.
(*One of the servants exits; the other remains. The marquis takes a seat upstage and looks at himself in the mirror.*)
I look awfully pale!
I think I'm losing weight. Ah! when your soul
Can constantly be moved with so much passion…
Oh! it's a heavy burden having both
A head and a heart!
(*Two hairdressers appear wearing aprons over their morning coats; FONROSE's hair is in rollers; one of the hairdressers comes forward to comb it out. The two servants remain upstage.*)
(*He has his hair done during the following two lines, the delivery of which is intermingled with all the business of getting dressed.*)
That Mr. Saint-Fard… what a happy nature!
What he likes once pleases him forever.
(*Unhappy with the servant who is doing his hair, he gently pushes him away and signals for the other to replace him, which he does, and the speech continues.*)
Oh! For myself, I willingly admit
I love pleasures, only to vary them.
Ah! I've no complaints. This sweet existence
Is, I think, preferable to his
Stability. I'm seeking happiness;
He, he says, has found it. Consequently,
He's less happy. It's a proven fact:
(*He gets up; the servants remove the dressing table. A single servant remains upstage.*)
Happiness is a god our mind creates.
To the man who thinks he's captured it,
It offers nothing but an illusion.
Only to the man of indecision
Who, alone, knows how to pamper it
Belongs the secret of true happiness.
DESCHAMPS. (*Carrying in tea, lemons, butter, etc.*)
What will you take your English tea, sir?
FONROSE. Tea, you good-for-nothing… tea?
DESCHAMPS. With your permission, sir…

FONROSE. I said chocolate.
DESCHAMPS. Sir, on my honor,
You ordered tea. I am incapable
Of making such a great mistake. Perhaps
You had a change of heart while it was brewing?
FONROSE. Scoundrel! Don't go trying to convince me
That I'm responsible for your mistakes.
Go. You can keep your English tea;
I don't want to drink it anymore.
Next time, try to listen to me better.
DESCHAMPS. (*To the servant to whom he gives what he is carrying and who takes it out.*)
Or learn how to read your mind!
FONROSE. (*Overhearing what his servant has just said.*)
Amen! Read my mind.
Just because nature has chosen to give you
Stupid and foolish desires… always unchangeable…
Logical inclinations… ever steadfast…
You think people ought to be as definite
As you? And not see that ideas give way
To dissatisfaction?
DESCHAMPS. Your way of thinking's a deep mystery,
Sir, which my stupid intellect can scarcely
Comprehend. Myself, like a poor fool,
I believe that to enjoy something,
The basic point is, first of all, to have it.
For you, it's just the opposite.
FONROSE. Come on, dress me
And while so doing, babble if you like.
This creature's funny; he knows how to make me
Laugh!
DESCHAMPS. (*Still busy with getting everything ready. From this asterisk (*) to the next, the scene should be occupied with the simple washing of the neck and shoulders, which must take up as much time as possible.*)
Oh! You're so very kind to condescend
To put up with me. It really is
A great indulgence. But I can improve!

FONROSE. With a little diligence. I want
To go to Célénie's immediately
To find out if, eventually, some happy
Inclination will make her respond
Less harshly to my last proposals.
DESCHAMPS. To marry her?
FONROSE. Not a word.
DESCHAMPS. (*Surprised.*) And what are you going to do about it?
FONROSE. Give her to Verneuil, whose pining love
On her behalf annoys me at the moment.
Célénie is the very image of
Verneuil. They both have very prudent minds
And tender souls. The one, just like a Roman,
Believes in the bond between two hearts.
The other thinks, at twenty years of age,
She has to have old morals.
They suit each other perfectly.
DESCHAMPS. And you, sir?
FONROSE. Florange! What do you think of that, Deschamps?
DESCHAMPS. Heavens! she's an angel. Truly, Cupid
Created her especially for you;
But I think she's a flirt… and just between us,
Those crooked feathers, in a word, that wardrobe,
Which, although careless, seems to be so sure
Of attracting notice with its simple
Affectations… in a word, that wardrobe
Makes a man suspicious of her heart's
Languishing designs.
Either I'm very much mistaken or
Under this exterior, without
Much skill, the lovely baroness is hiding
A cheating heart!
FONROSE. That's what bothers me; and for the past two
Long and drawn out days, against my will,
I've been a slave to love.
DESCHAMPS. For the past two days?
FONROSE. You have my word.

Will you ever finish scrubbing me?
DESCHAMPS. Look! All done!* What do you want to wear?
The short green velvet coat?
FONROSE. Gladly! But I wore it yesterday.
Give me the lilac one. Why not the yellow?
Or the red one and the chenille vest…
No, I'd rather have the orange brocade.
(*Seeing that DESCHAMPS isn't moving.*)
What the devil are you waiting for?
DESCHAMPS. (*Arms crossed.*) To see you make up your mind.
FONROSE. I'm getting there… I'm getting there. Go. Quickly
Find me the one for which, the other night,
While dining at Mélite's, someone gave me
The pattern. It's for the dance tomorrow.
DESCHAMPS. It won't be ready. It was only yesterday morning…
FONROSE. Ready or not… what does it matter? Oh!
Everything's difficult.
DESCHAMPS. But if it's still
In pieces?
FONROSE. Go, I tell you. Imbecile! *(DESCHAMPS exits.)*
(*Alone*) Good. Setting up Verneuil with Célénie
Will win me a less hostile reception
From Florange. For it annoys me greatly
The baroness is flighty. Deschamps knows her
All too well! Good heavens! What a conquest!
A prude… a widow… oh, it's delicious!
But let's be careful. Let's give this some thought.
Am I really in love? Me, who has never
Been in love for three days in my life…
Is it really serious or is it
Only a desire to try my hand
At someone new? I really cannot tell.
And if her torch of love does not shed light
Upon my heart with more security,
I'll long remain in error through my passions.
What does it matter after all? Let's never
Analyze, but let our feelings yield

To success.
If, toward me, Florange is always gloomy,
Well, quite simply, I'll love Célénie.
Young and made to please, attractive features:
Big eyes, wild and dark, which you unlock
In kissing them… the innocence of youth
And the age when nature's whisper follows
Childish games. They're definite attractions.
But that Mr. Saint-Fard, who believes,
Seeing he's her uncle… and especially
Long-winded… that he has the inane right
Of lecturing his niece. With his convincing
Arguments, he'll disrupt my affection.
He's a tough one. Ah! May heaven never
Grant me other miseries than being
Without plans. I have the delightful pleasure
Of making them, of breaking them, of getting
Sensual delight out of all my schemes.
Oh, yes! Saint-Fard, I can assure you,
I don't get the least bit tired of wishing
For things!
(DESCHAMPS enters, following the servants who are carrying FONROSE's clothes.)
FONROSE. *(About to leave, no longer aware that he is in a dressing-gown.)*
Is my hair combed? Did you tell someone
To comb it?
DESCHAMPS. You're changing your mind again. Let's finish
Getting dressed.
And besides, sir, try to recollect
That you have to go to Célénie's.
Abandon for a moment your sublime
Affairs
And consider that she and her uncle
Are tenants here in your house… which you're sharing
With them.

FONROSE. (*Without paying attention to what is being said to him, but noticing the servants.*) Why aren't those servants changed? It seems to me
I said…
DESCHAMPS. Oh, yes, they're the same ones.
FONROSE. But why?
DESCHAMPS. Oh, good Lord! What a way of doing things!
Alas! Give it up, sir, give it up.
Acting like that, you'll have hooligans
Who, only considering your house
A temporary place of employment,
Will scatter through the neighborhood a thousand
Wicked rumors just to play a prank
On you. But let's take a look at your clothes.
FONROSE. (*Looking at them.*) Oh, they look stupid.
DESCHAMPS. Ah! I told you so.
Even so, they spent the whole night making
Them for you.
FONROSE. (*Grabbing them to look at them.*)
They're a sorry mess. It makes me mad…
Here, take them away.
(*He gives him the clothes.*) Did I not hear
Something? Could it be someone calling? Go on,
Get me another suit. (*DESCHAMPS exits.*)
SERVANT. (*Announces.*) Mr. Verneuil.
FONROSE. I think he's crazy, coming
So early in the morning. It's irrational.
DESCHAMPS. (*Carrying in another suit of clothes.*)
He's outside. Let's hurry.
FONROSE. (*Dressing in haste.*) It could not
Be at a more inopportune time.
Farewell to all my plans. All right, go. Leave us.
Let him approach the bench! Oh well,
To punish him, let's catch him in a trap! (*All the servants exit.*)
(*VERNEUIL enters.*)
FONROSE. (*Walking towards VERNEUIL*) Hello, my delightful…
VERNEUIL. Oh! Hello,

My dear Marquis.
FONROSE. What brings you here so early in the morning?
Well? Are you getting married?
VERNEUIL. To whom, my dear? Célénie?
FONROSE. No, really, the baroness… and for life.
You know very well the other has
My hand and my heart.
VERNEUIL. So you tell me… and that's today's news?
Last night at the opera, in a strange way,
You swore to adore Madame de Florange…
But I should have known the morning never
Finds you with the intentions of the night.
FONROSE. There you go, every one of you,
Measuring my mind by your fragile
Heads. You think, my respectable fools,
That at every moment of the day,
I change my mind like you.
That opinion offends and annoys me.
I never change my mind… and especially
Where the fair sex are concerned. This morning
I had that inclination which you claim
To have seen last night…
But who could have anticipated it?
You change your tune out of stability,
Out of excessive caution. In a word,
I pay my lone respects to Célénie
And you can be certain, they're the ripest
Fruit of my ideas.
VERNEUIL. (*Ironically.*) How long will this
Decision last?
FONROSE. (*Quickly.*) My lifetime. What? Can I
Be inconstant loving Célénie?
If I thought one day I'd have to dread it
To return to her chains, I'd go and face her.
VERNEUIL. (*Pretending through the rest of the scene.*)
My friend, by virtue of this glad exchange,
Can I speak to Florange from now on?
All right!

Do I need to say it and to tell you
Openly? I only let you have her
Yesterday out of respect. Not very
Sure of her affection… and noticing
Your own,
I thought that she was conquered… and that never
Could I win back a heart that you seduced.
But, look at me, I'm calm and now I see
That certain gestures, certain words of praise
From the sweet nothings whispered to Florange
Had no other goal than to encourage
Me to paint a love for her, a love
She'd like to share. All right! I'm going to see her.
(*Acting as if he's leaving.*)
FONROSE. (*Nervous, restraining him.*)
What? Then she loves you? And she said that to you?
There… really said it, herself?
VERNEUIL. No. But one understands such things. They are
Words spoken very softly, loving sighs
That people don't recall. Wide, open-eyed
Glances at the lover
Without pretending anything that he
Wards off as soon as he can intercept them!
You know that, regarding love, a trifle
Is expressive and frequently a no
Is awfully affirmative.
FONROSE. (*Still even more uncomfortable and disguising his discomfort with irony.*)
Oh! Yes,
I know that. Tell me about all the rest…
As passionate as you are, eager, fiery,
And clever, you ought to be better off
Than you say.
(*VERNEUIL is about to speak, but stops himself.*)
Discreet even among his friends; should you
Hide from them? Are you afraid of something?
(*With a firm tone.*)
By revealing everything to me,

You expose yourself to nothing. Fickle
In my pleasures, but steadfast in friendship,
I know the value of a confidence.
VERNEUIL. The point is, it's no longer a secret
Since she's free.
You alone held me in this wretched balance;
Having you as my rival, I was afraid
Of failing. But since you yield your place
To me, I can acknowledge everything.
Well, my dear Fonrose, she loves with tenderness;
Few hearts, I think, are as exquisite
As hers. Cupid, who created her
For pleasure and for love,
Heaped upon her all the gifts she needs
To set a heart on fire.
If you only knew how sensitive
She is! People might say that her heart,
Having so logical a right to rule,
Desires to be bound to you because
Of the deep feeling called for by her eyes.
FONROSE. (*Still between nervousness and irony.*)
I see that you're quite taken with her! I thought
She was a flirt… the counterfeit confusion
That governs her attire looks a lot
Like sleight of hand.
VERNEUIL. Oh, no, it isn't that.
Trickery in such a one upon whom
Nature liberally lavished gifts?
What good would it do?
FONROSE. (*Firmly and taking VERNEUIL's hand.*)
It's the mask that women
Wear.
Artifice, by nature, is imprinted
In their souls; the stroke that tortures us
Is delivered by deception. Hatred,
Love, and jealousy… it has its hand
In everything. All right. Do not destroy
Your clay-footed idol. As soon as it

Disappears, emotion vanishes.
Love her like she is… or like you see her.
VERNEUIL. I see her without flaw, the way I should.
And I sympathize with your mistake
About the fair sex. You cannot love it
If it seems reprehensible to you.
Spurn the efforts of whoever can
Hurt you and think about her virtues when you
Assume that she's at fault.
Your superficiality, I see,
Excuses your behavior.
FONROSE. Oh, let's get back to a subject that I like:
That sacred object of your tender love,
Whom you promise to worship forever.
Are you aware that she's thirty years old,
Ten years of which were spent in married life?
VERNEUIL. Ah! When a woman looks like her, she has
Only one age and that's the age of consent!
FONROSE. Oh, how gallant! You portray your passions
Like a man in love.
VERNEUIL. I'm taking you into my confidence
Out of friendship.
For when a man no longer is afraid
Of any competition, willingly
His heart appears without protection.
FONROSE. Well done! I commend you! And so tell me,
Dearest, did you come to this conclusion
Without misgivings? I, in no way, want to
Trouble such a touching enterprise.
A business matter, at this very moment,
Forces me to leave. Goodbye. (*He exits quickly.*)
VERNEUIL. (*Alone.*) He's worried.
By faking an affection for Florange,
Which his unpredictability
So handsomely sets up for me,
I was sure to create a distraction
In his heart. Indeed, it's there, I think,
In his acceptance of the love I'm faking

To get Célénie back. Yes. But that's not all…
For my own peace of mind, it is important,
At the moment, to consult that heart
Upon which my only happiness
Will depend forever. I must see
Florange again. She's fond of Célénie;
She's the one who came up with this joke
And she recommended it to me
As a very certain means of driving
The Marquis away from someone who
Can in no way suit him. But perhaps
She loves him! Alas!
I'm very much afraid. I see her coming…
I'm seized with anxiety…
Since you have conquered me, love, strengthen me!
And when I see her, either make me more
Charming or make her more sympathetic!
(Enter CÉLÉNIE.)
CÉLÉNIE. (*Merrily.*) Really, sir, you are invisible;
My uncle's very mad. For almost a week,
Surely busy with new love affairs,
You haven't once come by to play music
And you've left him gloomy and melancholy,
All alone, with no desire to blow
On his bassoon. He grumbles about you
A lot and with good reason. People just don't
Act that way!
VERNEUIL. What, miss? Can he mistrust
My dedication for a single moment?
In that case, his mistakes are worse than mine.
CÉLÉNIE. Well, then, how will you apologize?
For I'll tell you in advance, he'll scold you.
VERNEUIL. (*Timidly.*) Will you condescend, at least, to take up
My defense?
CÉLÉNIE. No. Really and truly,
I'm handing you over to his rightful
Anger.
Tell me, how will you defend yourself?

VERNEUIL. By saying that someone is afraid
Of you as much as he desires you…
That a wretched lover who is sighing,
Without hope…
When you deliver him to the harsh tortures
Of uncertainty and greater evils,
Whose deadly appearance he sees only
Too well… that a wretched lover ought
To see, from experience at least,
If absence could return him to the state
From which you removed him.
CÉLÉNIE. (*Wildly.*) Well, have you experienced that peace
Of mind?
VERNEUIL. Can I, cruel one? While I'm in love with you,
Can I see, desire, know anything
But you yourself?
CÉLÉNIE. So there you are, just like you were! Well then,
You did not have to abandon us;
It wasn't worth the trouble.
VERNEUIL. Still sarcastic!
Is that the way to talk, kind Célénie?
CÉLÉNIE. (*Resuming a more serious expression.*)
But is there some bond between us other
Than that which friendship ordinarily
Allows?
VERNEUIL. No, no, there's not (to my extreme bad luck!)
And when I try to complain to you
About it, it's a horrible mistake
Which you do not excuse. How happy Fonrose
Must be. (*CÉLÉNIE blushes.*)
Why are you embarrassed?
CÉLÉNIE. (*A little disconcerted.*)
Well, what are you looking at?
VERNEUIL. His fate…
And my pain…
Alas! May a sweet marriage soon unite you;
May he learn how to love you as I do…
If he can; then I'll regret it less.

Ah! May he make you happy and as soon
As he possesses you,
May he know the value of the treasure
That I'm surrendering to him. Unable
To obtain it, I'll go far away
From both of you
To spin out my wretched life and die
In misery.
CÉLÉNIE. (*Sighing.*) If only he had your heart!
VERNEUIL. Or if only I had his appeal?
But his mistakes will cease, stop worrying,
And, without a doubt, the greatest… cast
Aside forever, as soon as he has
Your heart… is infidelity.
CÉLÉNIE. You're making me sad. All right, now, no more
Melancholy. Did you bring those airs
From *Iphigenia*?[39]
You know my uncle wants to play along
With them. Ah! Luckily, here comes Florange.
FLORANGE. (*Entering; to VERNEUIL.*)
Go, get everything prepared for our
Recital. We will join you when it's time.
I have to stay here with her for a moment.
VERNEUIL. (*Going out; softly to the Baroness.*)
Madame, I was a great success with Fonrose.
He really believes that we're a couple,
As I said, but here… much worse than ever.
FLORANGE. (*Softly to VERNEUIL.*)
Let's continue to pretend so nothing
Can go wrong. (*VERNEUIL exits and the Baroness comes forward.*)
CÉLÉNIE. (*In a sarcastic tone of voice.*)
Well, lovely Florange, still whispering
Little nothings to that nice Verneuil?
At least he adores you.
FLORANGE. (*Trying to make it believable.*)
No, but without
Being too presumptuous, I think
He likes me a little.

---

[39] *Iphigenia in Tauris,* composed by Chistoph Willibald Gluck in 1778 with a libretto by Nicholas-François Guillard. This opera marked Gluck's final triumph at the Paris Opera.

CÉLÉNIE. A little?
A lot!
FLORANGE. That's a likely story! Are men
Able to love? Judge that by your own!
CÉLÉNIE. Mine is excellent.
FLORANGE. No more than that?
CÉLÉNIE. Concerning love, my heart will never change.
But him?
FLORANGE. Really. Without a doubt, given
His personality, a woman, I agree,
Cannot be very sure of what he's up to.
Would you like to test him?
CÉLÉNIE. To what advantage?
FLORANGE. Let me have him under my control
Just for a day.
CÉLÉNIE. So?
FLORANGE. So if he resists
And puts up a fine defense, you will
Count on him with greater certainty.
CÉLÉNIE. And if he succumbs to you?
FLORANGE. In that case,
Why regret him?
CÉLÉNIE. (*Quickly.*) Why? Because I love him
And I cannot overcome my feelings.
FLORANGE. But if he's unfaithful?
CÉLÉNIE. Does that make him less
Likeable?
That would make me capable of loving
Him a hundred times more. Oh! You always
Have wonderful methods... and besides,
Who answers to me?
FLORANGE. What? For my feelings?
CÉLÉNIE. Why certainly. Myself, do I know where
You want to go with this charming speech?
FLORANGE. All right, all right. You're joking. Don't I have
Verneuil? Look. I'll deliver him to you
In the very same predicament.
Let's test both of them... undoubtedly,
I've drawn the weaker hand!

CÉLÉNIE. Why's that?
FLORANGE. (*With a look of suspicion.*) Verneuil...
CÉLÉNIE. (*Smiling.*) Well?
FLORANGE. (*Same as before.*) I'm afraid of you.
CÉLÉNIE. Ah! I'm afraid
Of you a lot more next to the object
Of my desires!
FLORANGE. Well, let's risk it.
CÉLÉNIE. If he becomes romantic?
You won't fail to do your utmost...
FLORANGE. Verneuil
Will avenge you.
CÉLÉNIE. I am hardly apt to
Show love when I don't feel it.
(*Peevishly.*) In short, why put ourselves through all this trouble?
FLORANGE. To know them thoroughly and to no longer
Be deceived by them. Your love must concern
You deeply to fear a game like this.
CÉLÉNIE. And if it managed to succeed? Alas!
A horrible regret's in store for me.
(*Shrewdly.*) Fonrose adores you.
FLORANGE. (*Delighted that she fears the possibility.*)
Indeed! What foolishness!
CÉLÉNIE. (*Arrogantly.*) I don't believe a word of it.
FLORANGE. Delighted with it. Since you're wavering,
You haven't any pride at all!
CÉLÉNIE. (*Laughing half-heartedly.*)
Oh, you really look to me like you'd part
With Verneuil!
FLORANGE. I'll risk it.
CÉLÉNIE. Ah! But that's
What devastates me. You've nothing to lose;
Whereas I'm sacrificing myself...
FLORANGE. Nothing to lose? Why not?
CÉLÉNIE. Indeed! You don't
Love him.
FLORANGE. (*Somewhere between sarcasm and truth.*)
Who, Verneuil? Why, I adore him.
CÉLÉNIE. (*Entirely sarcastic.*)

What about him? Is he completely taken
With your feminine charms?
FLORANGE. The question's touching!
CÉLÉNIE. Answer me.
FLORANGE. My answer is that you're
Delightful... trying to chain both of them
To your carriage!
CÉLÉNIE. (*Bursting with laughter.*)
Oh, my God! Far from it!
(*Continuing persistently.*) Is Verneuil very affectionate?
Very passionate when he describes
His love? Does he entirely express
The raptures of his soul?
FLORANGE. I'll punish you
For this.
CÉLÉNIE. (*Still laughing.*)
We haven't come to an agreement.
FLORANGE. You wouldn't risk it.
CÉLÉNIE. (*Out of patience.*)
Oh, nice little scheme:
To drive me to despair to see me yield!
I must certainly agree to it...
I can't defend myself!
FLORANGE. (*Energetically.*)
Listen, let's admit the things we do
Between ourselves to guarantee success
Without open discussion. But Fonrose
Will have to openly announce his choice
In front of both of us!
CÉLÉNIE. All right. Agreed.
FLORANGE. Let's go back inside; they're waiting for us.
Most of all, be brave.
Everything depends on that alone.
Oh, in this day and age in which we live,
Shouldn't we try everything that can
Make men accountable to us?

END OF ACT ONE

ACT TWO

FLORANGE. (*Alone.*) Yes, I must make an effort to unite
The two of them.
They're both my friends… I've got to make them happy.
Fonrose would never get along with Saint-Fard.
While the same house, coincidentally,
Brings them here together, they cannot
Live together. For the one, there always
Must be some new objects of affection;
He must have high spirits and good times,
All the experiences of life;
On the other hand, Célénie's uncle
Is an admirer of rest, peace, and quiet.
(*Pause.*) With much ado, Célénie has agreed
To my plans. When I think about it, men
Are clearly right to make their little jokes
About our inconsistency. Quite often,
Just as foolish as they are, we're seen
Liking a lover only for his faults.
(*Enter FONROSE, dressed for the outdoors.*)
FONROSE. (*With the greatest passion.*)
You see me, Madame, in traveling clothes…
I'm leaving at this very moment.
FLORANGE. (*Putting up a front for the entire scene.*)
Where does that dark cloud come from?
FONROSE. Oh, no! I will not give up this trait…
The victory was certain. Conquered by
Your charms, I set all my happiness
In having you for a wife. I didn't
Imagine that I'd find in you a heart
So cruel and so false. Finally, I'm
Controlling my emotions. For I feel
That I'll always be within your snare…
Despite all my attempts to break the bonds,
Treacherous woman, a frenzied love
Carries me away and leads me on.
And when I come here to give it up,

The only thing I remember is that
I adore you.
FLORANGE. (*With the greatest composure.*)
My God, what have I done?
FONROSE. What have you done, you ungrateful bitch?
Yesterday, when your lips called me back
And flattered me, elated with my fate,
I went to you, on my knees, to swear
Never to cherish anyone but you;
Not to look at, not to like, in all
Of nature, anything
But what amuses and what pleases you.
In short, when I invest in you my pride
And reputation,
You sacrifice me to Mr. Verneuil.
Madam, he told me. Unsuccessfully
Does your deception try to mask that horrid
Injury? No longer will you take
Advantage of my heart or of my trust!
FLORANGE. (*Pretending to be cold.*)
I'm not trying at all.
FONROSE. I believe it.
Really. Put an end to your inhuman
Work and let the insult be succeeded
By contempt. Have you no other blows
To strike?
Here I am, Madam, prepared to bear
Them all.
I deserve my fate; I must bow to it.
But don't treat me so unfairly. You don't
Part company without an explanation.
You tell people what they did wrong.
FLORANGE. (*With a fake sensitivity.*)
An indiscreet remark from a young birdbrain,
Who hardly should be listened to! Should it,
Sir, attract this scandal to me? Heavens!
Have you deteriorated to the point
Of suspecting that somebody else

Has the skill to dominate my heart?
That's thinking very little of yourself!
FONROSE. (*Eagerly.*) I could hardly believe it! That betrayal
Tarnished your halo every bit as much
As mine. In the end, there's nothing to it…
Say it to me, Madam, yes, indeed,
Swear it to me…
FLORANGE. (*Annoyed.*)
No. Since you have so poor a grasp of me,
Since you have passed so bad a verdict on me,
To punish you, I want to keep you guessing.
FONROSE. (*Furious.*) Very well, I'll believe everything!
FLORANGE. (*Pretending to be tender.*)
And you would be right. I certainly
Acknowledge, in that case, your superior
Wisdom. (*She pretends to hide a few tears.*)
FONROSE. (*Noticing them.*)
Ah! Forever I relinquish any
Suspicion that harms you. But be a little
Lenient on your part. I would have been
Less afraid if I had less affection.
FLORANGE. Yes, there's your excuse and there's your influence!
Men, so very dangerous, your skill
Is to seduce. And relishing the sight
Of our pride annihilating itself,
You confront the tears that you make flow.
But you don't know that tenderness is never
Offended unless by your affection
(In proportion to the insult, a few
Tears escape) and that the heart, at last,
Torn to pieces by your arrows, soon
Giving up its frailty for outrage,
Hampered by its chains, breaks them and gets away.
FONROSE. Never anticipate
That moment filled with horror! Occupied
Like me with that moment of happiness,
She most certainly has left behind

The memory of my reprehensible
Offense. Speak a single word, a word
To reassure me...
Pardon the most ardent penitent.
FLORANGE. (*Pretending to be tender with a great deal of skill.*)
Well then, I agree... but to hold you back,
With my love longing to be put to use
Completely, sir, allow me to ask for a
Guarantee, which surely won't be any
Trouble to you now.
FONROSE. (*Passionately.*) Command, command, and to be worthy of you,
Whether you needed my blood, my fortune,
Or my life, I'd deliver everything
And willingly, according to your wishes,
Thinking, alas, I've done nothing yet.
FLORANGE. No, I do not demand so rare a favor:
I want your heart; it alone concerns me.
I only want a simple document
From you, sir, for the price of my affection...
A document in which you'll swear to me
That in the dire event you should betray me,
You grant me the rights to you, which revenge
Allows our sex when someone offends it.
Will you not consent to this?
FONROSE. Oh, I am so very touched by this.
(*On this expression of consent, the Baroness exits offstage to gather everything necessary for writing. During that time, the Marquis speaks, aside.*)
Look at me, already almost totally
Detached! If Verneuil was here...
(*To the Baroness who re-enters.*)
Speaking in such a way nevertheless
Offends me...
(*Looking around on all sides, expecting to see VERNEUIL enter; aside.*)
The devil take him! Never
Is that idiot here when you need him!

(*Returning to the Baroness, tenderly.*)
I'm really distressed to see you have such
Suspicions right away. You mistake me.
FLORANGE. Oh, I understand you very well.
But at my desire for a document
Which makes you accountable to me,
You're creating so great a fuss, so much
Amusement, that between us...
FONROSE. (*Stuttering and interrupting.*) Not at all.
(*While the servants set up the writing table downstage, FONROSE goes upstage and calls to VERNEUIL in a low voice. Returning to the Baroness.*)
When my hand's about to write,
You'll see my heart direct it instantly!
(*He goes back upstage to call VERNEUIL. He sits beside the table.*)
All right, Madam, are you going to dictate
To me?
FLORANGE. (*Sarcastically.*) I thought that your heart should settle this.
(*FONROSE becomes gradually more uneasy as he sees fewer ways of putting it off. Trying out all the pens, never finding a good one, and interspersing his writing with everything that can prolong it, he continues looking, from time to time, behind him to see if he in any way can catch sight of VERNEUIL.*)
FONROSE. It's a matter of blending your words
With mine. The result of this would be
That never, in no other...
No, not in any pledge would there be so much
Love! All right! I'm writing, Madam. "Today,
On this day, I swear and make a solemn
Declaration of sincerity
And love. Even of marriage... to Gertrude
Amelise...
(*Continuing.*) Baroness de Florange, to whom
All rights are, by said document, surrendered
Every time she can accuse my heart
Of negligence, in short, when she'll have caught me
Being unfaithful."

(*Very happy to have gotten through it.*)
That's pretty good, I think.
FLORANGE. (*Mockingly.*) The document is chivalrous.
It's obvious it comes from the heart
Of a real lover. The style's exquisite!
FONROSE. (*Still looking to see if VERNEUIL has made an appearance.*)
Oh, my heart spares no pains. The moment it speaks,
I write in letters filled with passion. Read it
Carefully.
(*While the Baroness is reading the document, FONROSE again returns upstage to catch sight of VERNEUIL. Finally, he sees him, signals him to come forward, and speaks to him.*)
Come on. I'm working for you.
(*He drags him in and places him behind the Baroness in such a way that she sees VERNEUIL instead of him as soon as she is about to stop reading. He says while escaping.*)
Finish it, if you can. I've had enough!
FLORANGE. (*Surprised.*) What! It's you. Has he run off?
VERNEUIL. And quickly,
Too!
FLORANGE. (*Annoyed.*) You joke in vain, you're not his mistress…
You don't hate him; I do. What a man!
Read the solemn promise of his love.
(*VERNEUIL looks over the document and gives it back to her. The Baroness continues.*)
This is an important document
For our plans.
If he asks Saint-Fard to give him his niece,
We can…
VERNEUIL. (*Interrupting.*)
No. That way would be committing
An evil deed, which I'd resort to only
Very reluctantly. We have to make things
Clear and to do that, we have to fake
Everything, but so that nothing seems
To be compelling her. I want to earn her

More than win her.
FLORANGE. Well, leave it to me!
He's stopped impressing our stuffy uncle
And I'm very certain the old man
Would never want a bond like that. Saint-Fard
Sees him clearly now for what he is.
VERNEUIL. Does he know?
FLORANGE. I'm afraid not. It's a secret.
Without knowing anything about it,
I saw that, before speaking to him,
Célénie would have very great desires
Which someone was warning her against.
And this afternoon, if I had agreed
To listen, I strongly believe that soon
She would have chosen me as her envoy.
But I changed her course by playing fickle
And faking this test in which I've the right
To chain the object of her love to me
For the entire day.
The same rights apply to you and her.
Take advantage of this situation.
VERNEUIL. For me, she'll be the image of a lovely
Dream; I see the end of it already;
She's listening, laughing. She sees you
And she is silent.
Need I go any further? To portray
With passion my excessive love for her?
A solemn way of speaking, in that case,
Resourcefully, returns me to respect.
FLORANGE. Don't despair. My plan is leading her
To your intentions step by step.
VERNEUIL. (*Kissing her hand.*) Ah! You're delightful.
SAINT-FARD. (*Entering with CÉLÉNIE, discovering the situation, and upstage, indicating VERNEUIL.*)
Ah! divine Baroness,
His somber look, now, has no more surprises
For me and I begin to see why I have
Suffered so much from his discordant notes

At the concert this afternoon.
(*Drawing closer.*) What's more, it's a good idea!
I approve of both of you.
Happiness is so rarely found in marriage,
That with a learned friend, whom you know well,
It's never too soon to tie the knot.
FLORANGE. (*Emphasizing what follows.*)
When the heart is still filled with one's first loves,
To forget them so soon would be madness.
CÉLÉNIE. (*Sarcastically.*) She's not thinking about them. And that
Expression intercepted by our eyes
Is only absent-mindedness. I'll bet
On it!
FLORANGE. (*In a playful tone of voice.*)
Whatever you may say about it,
Whatever Saint-Fard may think about it,
Lovely Célénie, someone will soon
Reply to your unreasonable behavior.
And maybe you'll be humbled with a single
Word. I really need a moment to postpone
My anger.
CÉLÉNIE. You'll have to do better than that
To convince me.
VERNEUIL. (*Softly to CÉLÉNIE.*)
Ah! How far we were
From what you're thinking!
CÉLÉNIE. (*To VERNEUIL.*) I don't see why you're
Apologizing for it.
SAINT-FARD. Incidentally,
Madam, have you heard the story about
Our dear Fonrose? It's very funny stuff.
Did you know about his lawsuit for that
Country property a few miles from here?
It was his one concern. We watched him lose his
Mind because of it for three days…
The land is magnificent and the house
Is very beautiful…

There were no more obstructions to his claims;
Somebody was going to pass a verdict
And without any disagreement,
Everything was going to go to him.
The course was sure. So what does our man do?
"Oh, no, no," he says, "it's on flat land…
I want a picturesque location, either
Woods or mountains."
He leaves and goes looking for the Marquis
De Saint-Fonds.
"For crying out loud, let's not litigate
Any longer," he says to him cheerfully.
"I'll give you the whole thing. It's enough
For me to see, sir, that that property
Gives you some pleasure…
I'm no longer interested in it.
Off with you. Take it quickly. And come autumn,
I'll go there to visit you and hunt."
FLORANGE. Ah! The story's very good. It's great!
SAINT-FARD. What an idiot!
CÉLÉNIE. It shows he has
A kind heart and in actuality,
The whole thing's very much to his credit.
SAINT-FARD. Are you out of your mind? A kind heart? What?
To surrender his inheritance
To somebody he's never met. All by
Himself, to rob his children of what's due them…
A good deed of that kind's a great mistake.
Don't think his heart has anything to do
With it.
He's a man who can't make up his mind,
A freak who can't be rehabilitated;
Who, as soon as he thinks he possesses
Whatever he's been seen to prize,
Takes a dislike to it immediately
And would like it to go to hell!
In his fickleness, you see his only
Motivation. To my eyes, such a man

Is quite unbearable. A person only
Experiences pleasure from enjoyment;
And enjoyment offers consolation
From the purgatory of desire.
VERNEUIL. Everyone has his way of doing things,
And his…
SAINT-FARD. (*Hastily interrupting him.*)
To listen to you, it seems you would also
Like to defend his behavior?
(*To FLORANGE.*) Madam,
That tone of voice should really charm you!
FLORANGE. He's making excuses for a friend.
Should I blame him for it?
SAINT-FARD. But if he copies
His defects when you're his wife, your heart
Won't have too good a reason to rejoice!
FLORANGE. We're not there yet.
SAINT-FARD. (*To the Baroness.*) No, but you're on your way.
(*To VERNEUIL, shoving him impatiently.*)
Look! Madam, you'll defend yourself for nothing.
(*Irritated.*) Oh, good Lord! What lovers! What composure!
What a way of speaking! People didn't
Used to love like this when I was their age.
But emotion has become extinct
Along with morality.
(*Pointing to VERNEUIL.*)
For gentlemen like this, there's neither charm
Nor chivalry.
FLORANGE. What causes all of this?
SAINT-FARD. (*Continuing heatedly.*)
You, dear ladies, you cause it yourselves!
Have other ways of dealing with a love affair:
The better you're acquainted with your rights,
The harder you'll protect them and more sacred
Will they become in a lover's eyes.
When you get him used to winning easily,
You make the art of smashing his restraints
Much easier for him;

And weary of a conquest free from sighs,
He ventures to awaken his desires
With other ties. Do you want to maintain
Control for an even longer time?
Make him earn the favors he desires
And let the happy hopes of those divine
Rewards be only in proportion to
His morals and abilities.
To be worthy of them, he must have
A noble heart, he must have both the love
And respect of his family, and he must
Be the pride and joy of his country
Or the fearless conqueror of its enemies.
Then crown these glorious brows with myrtle leaves
And without shame be the fruit of their victory.
Undoubtedly, it would be better, hearing
Only the voice of honor, to resist
The desires inspired by your heart.
This very significant endeavor
Would truly be the best…
But if your defeat inspires the same,
If our forgiveness, after all, is due
To your mistakes, that's the time when virtues are
Created or repaid. Let's go back inside.
While preaching to you, I forgot that Fonrose
Promised that a famous virtuoso
Would perform for us tonight. At least,
Let's hope that for once in his life, he won't
Have changed his mind at a moment's notice.
The man is singing a piece from *Armide*[40]…
Let's all go in to hear him.
(*To VERNEUIL, jokingly.*)
Come on, come on,
You bashful lover, I ruined the moment
Of your cozy little chat. I'll be

---

[40] Gluck's opera with a text by Quinault, based on Tasso's *Gerusalemme* libretto, produced at the Paris Opera on 23 September 1777. Before Gluck, the story had been set to music several times by various composers, among them Lully (1686), Graun (1751), Traetta (1763), Jommelli (1770), Salieri (1771), Sacchini (1772), and Gazzaniga (1773).

More discreet when you advise me better.
(*He exits with VERNEUIL.*)
CÉLÉNIE. (*Delaying the Baroness, who is also about to go inside.*)
And what about our arrangement? If I
Can make myself quite clear, you have the skill
At best to capture both of them?
FLORANGE. (*Laughing.*) Let's follow your uncle. Come on.
Really!
You'll find out about everything. Only
Keep up the role until the very end.

END OF ACT TWO

ACT THREE

(*Enter DESCHAMPS and FONROSE, magnificently dressed in clothes different from those in the first act.*)
FONROSE. (*After looking at DESCHAMPS for a moment.*)
You're going to lecture me. Oh! I'm trembling
Already! But I'll listen to you patiently
Provided that you're touching, eloquent,
And please my ear at least while you're annoying
Me.
DESCHAMPS. You shut me up, sir, with that tone of voice;
Your cool and joking manner turns me cold;
It frightens me. Saint-Fard is furious.
FONROSE. Furious?
Why?
DESCHAMPS. A certain virtuoso...
FONROSE. He's got
His nerve! If he thinks his pleasures are my
Only concern. Something more important
Came up and distracted me.
DESCHAMPS. (*Smiling.*) Did Arsinoe
Keep you busy at her apartment?
FONROSE. No. She combines too well the arts of pleasing

And deceiving. And besides, what right
Does she have to deserve to be loved?
We're lovers for three days and on the fourth,
Overcome by bliss, and also a bit
Tender, we deliver the impression
That the general public thinks we ought
To have!
DESCHAMPS. In that case, then, what is the charming object
That just forced you to lay down your arms?
FONROSE. Ah! She's a beauty. Heavens! If you saw her…
Her features were drawn by Cupid's hand;
Those eyes (you surely know), those eyes in which
You can read the secret impulses
That nature inspires. A ravishing figure…
A brunette… with a rosy complexion,
Fresh as all outdoors…
This playful liveliness of tender youth,
So heavenly, changing into a sweet
Intoxication, seems to guarantee
To the one who might succeed,
An entrancing ecstasy that words
Could not express.
DESCHAMPS. As much as I can see of the picture
You're painting, what you've said here is the goal
Of all your love affairs. And here you are,
Determined never to go back to them
Again?
FONROSE. I've no desires but to unite
Myself with her.
DESCHAMPS. Are you prepared to see
Your expectations carried out?
FONROSE. I hardly
Know her.
DESCHAMPS. Ah! perhaps your burning passion
Only has a picture for its food.
FONROSE. I have met, my dear, that marvelous object
Whose charm and grace I worship at the moment.
(*Striking his heart.*) And her image is in there!

DESCHAMPS. Have you been
Trailing her from the time that you met?
FONROSE. No, I found out what I had to do
From one of her people and you, my dear
Deschamps, you alone can consummate
This delectable scheme.
DESCHAMPS. And what does it
Involve?
FONROSE. A trifle, a mere nothing.
DESCHAMPS. Damn it!
With you, mere nothings are occasionally
Very dangerous.
FONROSE. Often, but they're quite appealing this time.
DESCHAMPS. Anyway, explain yourself.
FONROSE. (*Taking him aside.*) My beauty
Has for a companion an old lady,
Seventy years old, and formerly
Her governess, they say, to whom a jealous
Guardian bequeathed all the sweetest rights
Regarding the child. Our duenna
Has been widowed four or five times…
You might have to marry her.
DESCHAMPS. (*Astonished, looking at his master.*)
Oh, well,
It's something different. You were right not to
Frighten me. So I have to get married
To the widow!
FONROSE. Precisely. Already your illustrious
Intellect sees through this mystery
And understands the trade: some love letters,
Then with nothing to worry about,
A private meeting safely arranged by you
And the old lady. You'll see. The jealous
Fool will be completely taken in.
And you'll see how much in all of this
Your happiness concerns me, because I
Will pay the dowry.
DESCHAMPS. Thanks for all your trouble!

It's only up to you, sir, to control
The needs of a miserable valet
Who, for the past three years, while sacrificing
The best years of his life for you, despite
Your great ability to change your mind
Daily, wanted to attach himself
To your destiny forever.
No longer knowing what you have to do
To get rid of me,
You put me in the hands of an old shrew
Who's already been bereaved of four
Husbands. That's sending me straight to the bottom
Of the coffin!
Really, no one is concerned about you
More than I, but if you do not have
Another means entirely to take
Possession of your lovely mistress, well,
You would be wise to think of her no more!
I will not get married.
FONROSE. Imbecile!
DESCHAMPS. Oh, without a doubt! I know quite well
That I'm wrong, but I've no desire at all
To go off on that solemn road that I
Must follow, marrying your silly watchdog![41]
FONROSE. Who's telling you…
DESCHAMPS. Enough! No, let's talk about
Something else…
Do you know that everybody here
Is upset with your behavior?
FONROSE. And who's
Still sulking? Now then, tell me this, what is
My latest fault? Coming from these people,
Nothing ever amazes me!
DESCHAMPS. I don't know, but this afternoon I heard
The Baroness muttering rather softly
A certain, hardly flattering remark
Which was not, really, very strongly in your
Favor.

---

[41] Literally, Argus, the herdsman sent to watch Io in Greek mythology. He was called Pano.

FONROSE. She's crazy!
DESCHAMPS. And how! But as
Far as I could see, you were so happy
Together this morning.
(*As if a little surprised by such a change in so short a time.*)
It's true that since…
FONROSE. She wants to get married…
DESCHAMPS. But this morning, sir, without the slightest
Hesitation, you said…
FONROSE. Me? No!… Maybe
On a whim. But if I'm going to tie
Myself to the bond of holy matrimony
Forever, I want a brand new heart.
DESCHAMPS. Then you had a falling out?
FONROSE. I'm giving
Her to Verneuil.
DESCHAMPS. Do you think he'll be happy
About it?
FONROSE. Without a doubt.
DESCHAMPS. Sir. Look, I bet he's after someone else.
FONROSE. (*Interrupting nervously.*)
Who is it, Célénie?
(*Grabbing him by the collar.*)
Out with it, wretch!
DESCHAMPS. (*Howling.*) Ah! Don't strangle me. Let the old lady
Be in charge of my death!
FONROSE. (*Greatly disturbed.*) What? Célénie?
Ah! God! The woman I adore!
DESCHAMPS. (*Aside.*) Ah! At least in this case, there are no more
Widows to fight off!
FONROSE. Then finish. Finish
Breaking my heart.
DESCHAMPS. Well, to put it simply,
You were mistaken. And Verneuil adores
Célénie. I'm certain of it.
FONROSE. (*Eagerly.*) Does she

Love him?
DESCHAMPS. Oh, that…
FONROSE. (*Still more eagerly.*) What?
DESCHAMPS. But it's insanity
To try to pull a secret out of a girl…
You told me often, I recall the line:
Strictly speaking, a woman is always
Fickle by necessity
And deceitful out of habit.
FONROSE. (*With heated excitement.*)
That rule doesn't apply to her. No! In her,
Nature created its perfect design.
Ah! Ah! I understand you, Madam Baroness!
You were laughing at me this afternoon.
All of this is nothing but a joke
And Verneuil's the one who benefits.
It's a solid plan. I'm beginning
To see clearly. We will disrupt you!
I have the most burning desire for this
Marriage; if ever I get engaged,
It will only be with her. Good heavens!
My friend, you see me a hundred times more
In love than I was before!
DESCHAMPS. An obstacle to your tender desires
Is enough to convert you in an instant
Into the most submissive slave. But if
Nothing offers opposition… goodbye
Sentiment.
Sir, you are the image of a flood:
While it's behind the barrier, it bubbles,
It gurgles; but if the barrier is broken,
Immediately, upon a bed of grass,
Its stream begins to wander without noise
Or violent passion, softening the sand
And caressing the flowers.
FONROSE. (*Still highly agitated.*)
Really, this afternoon, I did a silly
Thing. I'll make the most of it. It was

A surprise. What artistry! But that
Verneuil! He loves her! He's loved in return!
Everything here can't help but validate
My misfortune. I'm going to find Saint-Fard;
I'm going to see Célénie. The happiness
Of my life depends on her alone.
(*He is about to exit. DESCHAMPS stops him, giving him his letters which a servant brings in.*)
DESCHAMPS. Your letters, yes, sir.
(*He gives him the bundle of letters.*)
There they are. It's Flemish.
Calm down for a moment so you can read them
In peace. Perhaps there's something important
Inside.
(*FONROSE takes the bundle, opens a letter initially, then spends the rest of the scene reading them while speaking, careful, nevertheless, to stop reading when the line requires it. One by one, he puts them into his pocket.*)
FONROSE. Demised. Defunct. Ah! it's from court.
DESCHAMPS. (*Very eager.*) To fulfill your expectation about
Getting that regiment…
FONROSE. What? Oh, yes,
I got it. Thought as much… it seems that
Today, fate outdoes itself, heaping honors
On me. No. No. I no longer want to hold
That position. They made me have it
Just to make me hate it. Oh, that's settled!
I cannot accept that privilege.
DESCHAMPS. (*Astounded.*)
Ah, God! You wanted it for so long.
(*To his master.*) What, seriously?
(*To himself.*) Oh, he's cracked in the head!
FONROSE. (*Emphatically.*) When I wanted it, I didn't have it.
My imagination made it attractive;
But as soon as I possess it, the veil
Of mystery disappears. Go, swiftly,
Take this letter to Fonfrède, to whom
I owe this important commission. Tell him

That, at the moment, I cannot accept
This favor from the prince. Yes. Go, quickly!
DESCHAMPS. Oh, sir!
FONROSE. Off with you!
DESCHAMPS. Oh, what odd behavior! *(He exits.)*
FONROSE. *(Alone and very disturbed.)*
This time, I can't make heads or tails of it.
What pretense did that crafty woman use?
Oh, too cruel result of a deadly
Egotism! Alas, you disguise
Our mistakes and stupidity with your
Illusions.
And when we think we're following good sense,
Your skill is capable of forcing us
To follow only you. But if she thought
She was taking Célénie away
From me with that phony document,
We were both mistaken.
(A pause.) The tender grace of that beloved child
Would soon sort out the truth. I should express
Surprise and, in the end, her innocent heart
Would follow in the way of my impressions.
But I see Florange. I must pretend
And try, at last, to find out what she's
Hiding from me. Above all, let me guard
Against her fiendish cleverness. A woman
Is to be feared when she's caressing you.
Let me try to avoid her.
(Here the motivation of the two characters should be as follows: FONROSE's motivation is to try to uncover the truth of what he has just been told; and FLORANGE's is to prevent him from doing so and not to satisfy him until she can find the means to provoke him more relentlessly than she has already. It is therefore essential to color this scene with all the shrewdness possible on both sides in their line readings.)
FLORANGE. *(Aside.)* He's walking right into my hands. Good. This time,
I'd like to chain him up forever.

(*To FONROSE.*) What?
It's you?
FONROSE. (*Pretending to be embarrassed and uneasy.*)
When one suffers, one prefers
To come where one thinks he'll encounter
The object who, alone, can ease the pain.
FLORANGE. (*Sarcastically.*)
Can one know the name of the object of the
Moment?
FONROSE. (*As before.*) Ah! But to hear you, Madam, it would seem
That one's heart could be inclined to love you!
Undoubtedly, a suspicion like that,
Is meant to offend me.
FLORANGE. (*As before.*) You make me think of that sublime affection…
I had forgotten all about it, even
It's faintest expression. Don't you think
A person has her fickle moments? Do you
Think she'd want to tie herself to the same
Desires and waste the lucky talent
For multiplying them?
FONROSE. (*A bit surprised at her tone.*)
I'm not presenting you with an absurdity
Like that…
If you ever believed in such a thing,
I wouldn't be so proud to think I was
The object of it.
FLORANGE. (*Laughing, with a little bitterness.*)
Really that tone suits you entirely…
But you would grumble at me if I did
Nothing to you.
(*Seriously and a little peevish.*)
Anyhow, this afternoon, didn't
You go off in such a way to convince
My angry heart that you were lacking, sir,
In integrity?
FONROSE. Don't ever think

That I would lay myself open to that.
Verneuil was the reason for so hasty
A departure. By your command, no doubt,
He caught me in the act of passion. And that
Certain document, in which my tender
Heart depicted the most ardent raptures
Of my soul for you. Your alleged love
Only needed it as a sacrifice,
Madam, to my lucky rival.
FLORANGE. (*Bursting with laughter.*)
Ah! Nothing's funnier, nor more peculiar!
What! Has Verneuil heard about this?
FONROSE. Continue, Madam, continue to pretend…
And who then, who encourages him, who
Brings him back here every day,
If it wasn't you… if he wasn't looking
For you? As for myself, I only see
That you're here to please him.
FLORANGE. That pretty arrangement's just a myth, though.
FONROSE. What do you mean?
FLORANGE. It was never Verneuil…
FONROSE. You're joking. No other love could live
Inside him. I know his heart too well.
FLORANGE. Then what about Célénie?
FONROSE. A witless child? That's slander. I would swear
To it.
FLORANGE. Ah? You'd be making a big mistake.
FONROSE. How could that little doll captivate him?
He could…
FLORANGE. He adores her!
FONROSE. Oh! A likely
Story! If you hadn't said it, I would
Not have believed it.
(*Disguising himself as best he can.*)
Well then, is he getting
Married?
FLORANGE. Saint-Fard is completely against it
And nothing, no! Nothing can change his mind.

FONROSE. (*Revealing himself, in spite of himself.*)
Was she very much in love with him?
FLORANGE. More than I can say. It's just exactly
What people call obsession…
But having lost the hope of being his wife,
She has sworn never to see him again.
FONROSE. Why does Saint-Fard…
FLORANGE. Having reached a certain
Age, even becoming a bit senile,
He's terrified a marriage might proceed,
In the long run, to alienate
That child from him, that child who makes his final
Days an unparalleled pleasure.
FONROSE. He's talking
Drivel. And Verneuil?
FLORANGE. He wants to travel.
FONROSE. Youth!
FLORANGE. To heal his heart.
FONROSE. It can be healed
In France. The surest way of getting over
Something lost is finding something else.
FLORANGE. But I didn't say Verneuil is leaving
The country.
FONROSE. I didn't understand that odd behavior.
FLORANGE. No. I'm leaving for my estate. He will
Go along with me.
FONROSE. (*Without wanting to, he reveals, through a bit of jealousy, his sudden change of heart.*) Another unbelievable story!
FLORANGE. And why is that? The same fate unites us here;
Misfortune brings a hopeless pair together.
He has to give up the marriage that he's
Looking forward to,
(*Stuttering on the following line and blushing.*)
And me, I love
A faithless man, impossible to please.
And with no other ties between us than a
Quiet sentiment, we'll go together
Into that troubled sanctuary

To philosophically forget the world.
FONROSE. (*Disguising his distress under the appearance of the utmost composure and objectivity.*) Now there's what they call a fine how-do-you-do!
And what about your Célénie? Really,
Madam, you have to devote yourself
More to the needs of the heart. You're her friend…
And I should think, after all, that it would
Be more proper to soften her grief.
Will you accomplish that by going away
From her?
And if you want to show her a few signs
Of your goodwill, is it a wise choice
To go travelling? Moreover, can't you
See the danger in this scheme? People
Will start to gossip.
FLORANGE. (*Adopting the Marquis's tone.*)
What does it matter?
To anyone who has for a motto
Only to rely upon his own
Reputation, to anyone who thinks
That living unattached is living happily,
The words of fools are nothing, really.
FONROSE. (*Confused and as if forced to change his tone.*)
And the
Public, Madam?
FLORANGE. Well, we stand up to it.
Must we become slaves to its relentless
Animosity? Today,
A blissful stoicism puts me at ease…
Unable to take part in it, a person
Suits the world to himself.
FONROSE. (*More engaged in his personal interests than in the truth.*)
And bitter regrets…
FLORANGE. (*Quickly interrupting and still using the Marquis's tone.*)
Good Lord! what madness!

Ah! Merriment releases us from grief
To drown our sorrows in its ecstasies;
A person has the good fortune of changing,
Which wipes out his regrets.
FONROSE. (*Confused and very disturbed.*)
Then you're leaving
All of us for pleasure? At the point
When he starts criticizing you in your
Sanctuary, are you determined, Madam,
To put up with it?
(*With all the uneasiness of jealousy.*)
Will your friends, at least,
Be able to visit you there?
FLORANGE. I have no
Friends!
FONROSE. (*With the most emphatic zeal.*) Ah! What a terrible mistake!
I know one of them, who perhaps loves you
More tenderly than you know.
FLORANGE. (*Aside.*) I've got
Him in irons!
(*She goes through the motions of leaving.*)
Excuse me.
FONROSE. (*With all the impulsiveness of his emotions.*)
You're leaving…
Either swear you'll stay or I will follow
You.
(*Enter SAINT-FARD.*)
SAINT-FARD. (*To FONROSE.*)
I come to thank you, sir, for all your trouble.
FONROSE. (*Aside.*) The devil take the old bore!
(*Aloud.*) I have faults,
I know. There you are, severely angry
At me. But when you know everything…
(*Pointing to the Baroness.*)
Sir, she's leaving us. It seems to me
You ought to prevent her going.

SAINT-FARD. You're leaving us, Madam? Where are your plans
Taking you? So that was it. Verneuil
Should not be deceived about this.
FONROSE. (*Quickly.*) But she's
Going with him!
(*The Baroness signals to SAINT-FARD to put on an act, but he does not understand her.*)
SAINT-FARD. Good! Good! What a display!
FLORANGE. What he's telling you, sir, is not without
Probability.
SAINT-FARD. What? Would you marry
Him? My niece is right, then?
FONROSE. (*To SAINT-FARD.*) Since your refusal…
SAINT-FARD. (*Still surprised.*)
What refusal? He's mistaken. You're all
Talking nonsense, raving, ranting! If I
Stay much longer on these premises,
Even though it would be against my will,
I'll be liable to be just like you.
FLORANGE. (*Softly to FONROSE.*)
Don't say another word. No doubt he wants
To put on an act.
FONROSE. (*Softly to the Baroness.*)
I'll keep quiet,
But bear in mind…
SAINT-FARD. What a strange surprise!
He'll be trouble for you, too, lovely
Florange. If you'd rather have him, take him
At his word because he doesn't have the
Deficiency of loving very long.
FONROSE. With her, that's a defect that's convenient
To have.
SAINT-FARD. Good. Good. Lovers' talk.
FLORANGE. That people are a very long way from
Understanding…
SAINT-FARD. But that people like
Nevertheless. Oh! That's for sure.

FLORANGE. They laugh
About it, make fun of it…
SAINT-FARD. And keep on
Doing it anyway.
(*To FLORANGE.*) Praise pleases you;
That's your stumbling block in everything.
Whoever knows how to travel the path
Of that profound art, whoever can
Gratify your tastes and celebrate you
Soon has the secret of how to tame you.
(*To FONROSE.*) Come, sir, let's spend a moment with my niece.
If it's possible, clear away all
Her little distresses concerning your
Regrettable oversight, which continues
To offend her and upset her. Women
Don't like it when you make false promises
To them. Come apologize.
FLORANGE. (*Going out with them.*) Ah! That's
His greatest skill. His habitual faults have
Developed them into a way of life.

END OF ACT THREE

ACT FOUR

CÉLÉNIE. (*Irritably.*) What I had anticipated has happened
In spades! Fonrose is finally enthralled
By you alone. How you took advantage
Of me! I am no longer deceived.
I see only too well that he attends
To you exclusively. But why all this
Pretending?
Tell me what the purpose of it is.
FLORANGE. Where did you get that idea, if you please?
CÉLÉNIE. I came up with that scrupulous assumption
Strictly based on everything that's happened.

FLORANGE. Your anger is released needlessly
Because of that. I've done nothing wrong.
CÉLÉNIE. All the same, you love him... and you're stealing
Him from me, laughing all the while, no doubt.
FLORANGE. I'm in no way taking him from you.
If he loves me, am I the cause of it?
To imagine that I love him, oh!
That's another thing entirely.
CÉLÉNIE. (*Offended.*) Is he devoid of charm in your opinion?
In that case, we see him with very different
Eyes!
FLORANGE. Good! Delighted when you see him causes me
Great displeasure; now you're going to scold me
From the opposite side.
CÉLÉNIE. You're making me
Lose my patience! Well, then, tell me who
You plan to choose today.
FLORANGE. Oh! That's my secret!
CÉLÉNIE. (*Coaxing her.*) At least out of kindness... Tell me.
Does
Fonrose love you?
FLORANGE. Oh, I'm certain of it...
If, however, his heart is capable
Of loving for a moment.
CÉLÉNIE. (*Quickly with the bitterest sarcasm.*)
I have doubts, but for you, a lover
Cannot, I know quite well, permit uncertainty.
Loving you and pleasing you must be
His concentration; and the means he uses,
Free from all suspicion, cannot have the
Appearance of any infidelity
Whatsoever.
FLORANGE. Then again, he used them
So as to be convincing.
CÉLÉNIE. (*Continuing to mock, shrewdly.*) Who is not
Convinced of your ability in conquering
Men? But can't you let us in on those
Delightful means?

FLORANGE. I'm going to annoy you,
Showing them to you.
CÉLÉNIE. (*Her bitterness increasing in proportion to her fear of the evidence.*)
No, no, don't hesitate for any reason…
I give myself too much credit. I see
The effects of capriciousness around you…
And by what right, moreover, would I want to
Take him away? Would I be able to fight
For him without being afraid? My only
Weapons are my innocence and my heart.
You have experience, a great talent,
And sex appeal. You see,
Between us, everything is too unequal.
(*With the faint resentment of youth.*)
Well, to avenge myself, I'll tell his rival!
FLORANGE. Do better than that… fall in love with him!
CÉLÉNIE. You're reassuring… really, madam, you are
Delightful!
In compensation for a love I'm losing,
Your tender friendship offers me new bondage!
That warmhearted kindness which is so concerned
About me would certainly like to give me
The one I gave it. But that's being heroic!
Anyway, let's see them now. Show me
All at once the horrors of my fate.
FLORANGE. (*Giving her the Marquis's document.*)
Since you desire proof of his affection,
See the most definite expression of it
In these strokes of the pen.
CÉLÉNIE. (*Rapidly skimming the document and only stopping at the following words, at which she sighs, smiling maliciously.*)
What tenderness! "To whom all rights are by
Said document surrendered every time
She can accuse my heart of negligence."
There's a clause missing here: the penalty clause!
(*Aside.*) The villain!
(*Aloud.*) Really,

He never used so much sincerity.
(*Furtively, she puts the document in her bosom while rummaging around in order to have the letter which is about to be in question. The Baroness does not appear to notice.*)
Wait. I must repay your confidence…
I had your complete power over Verneuil;
See how I made use of the authority
And of his feelings, which are expressed here.
(*She gives the Baroness a letter.*)
But, at least, have some respect, I beg you.
(*With a lot of sarcasm.*) I'm the one who's the object of the joke!
Since the document was not written
Underneath such charming eyes, ecstasies
As touching will not dominate them.
Read. Read it all. You must…
FLORANGE. (*Reading.*)
"Oh, sweet object who rouses and arouses me,
Do you thus allow my burning sighs
To venture to express to you at last
The feelings and the longings of my soul?
Loving you… saying it and proving it
Unceasingly… is the holy commitment
Of my heart. At your knees I promise it.
But bear in mind, alas, that such a vow,
When it obtains the mistress' endorsement,
Is a wish which she grants to her lover."
I'm not at all jealous.
(*Giving her back the letter.*)
Believe me, Célénie… ah, God! If he
Marries you, your happiness will be
My every comfort.
CÉLÉNIE. Then you don't love him anymore? Oh, I don't
Understand any of this!
FLORANGE. Soon you'll understand everything. Let's leave
The action to Fonrose; the right to make
The decision belongs to him alone.
If he insists in giving me his heart,
Must you persist in standing in the way

Of my happiness? No. You wouldn't do
Anything. You're generous! You'd be
Overjoyed to know that I was happy!
I'll leave you to think this over without
Being afraid or suspicious. Good-bye. (*She exits.*)
CÉLÉNIE. (*Alone.*) That makes a lot of sense to me! Does she
Love Fonrose? Ah! I can't believe it.
Then why enslave him? Is it whim or vanity?
Verneuil's note had no effect on her…
Then who's she after? Honestly, I'm lost.
That Verneuil!
How he loves me and how sensitive he is!
(*Sighing.*) If only it was the other, alas!
No, never able to adore me enough
To forsake everything, he charmed my heart
Just to control it! What does it matter!
Ah! Every day I'll make such a sweet study
Of how to please him meticulously…
I'll anticipate so well his slightest
Wishes that undoubtedly he'll yield
To my fervent sighs. Going about it
In such a way, could it be possible, then,
That a wife might become dear to her husband?
Are they monsters rather than husbands
Today? Ah! We often have faults in turn!
But my uncle… Oh! there's the huge snag
In this affair. Fonrose has hardly found
The talent of pleasing him. He'd never
Agree to these bonds. Of my cruel concerns,
That's one of the most horrible! I see
Fonrose. All right, let me try to control
Myself.
(*Enter FONROSE.*)
FONROSE. (*With subtlety, for this is only an explanation of convenience; he still loves the Baroness at this point.*)
Well, miss, there's no more time for pretending;
Everything I was afraid of has
Succeeded only too well! My awful

Fate is finally made clear.
CÉLÉNIE. (*With irony.*) Tell me, where does this gloomy sadness come from?
Don't hide it from me... your fate interests me...
A sorrow vanishes when it's confided
In the calm and pure breast of gentle friendship.
FONROSE. (*Getting hotter because of the coolness he's being shown.*)
Of gentle friendship?
CÉLÉNIE. Why doesn't that word
So tender paint what you should be expecting
From my heart?
FONROSE. (*As before.*) It's for the best, most certainly...
And I'm entirely aware of my error,
Expecting to see a more burning passion
In your heart. I judged it by my own.
See how a person can make a mistake...
CÉLÉNIE. I object to that inconsistent judge, sir.
It's not permitted.
FONROSE. (*With feeling.*) Despite this refusal,
Very little from your lips should be
Heard more enjoyably. The temple where
Your image is worshipped should accept only
Your word alone.
CÉLÉNIE. It will be very difficult for you
To convince me that what I say will guide you
In absolutely everything. But you're
Making me concerned... we dread a scandal...
The baroness could certainly be close by
Listening to us.
(*Stressing the following lines as if to remind him of the document.*)
If caught, you'd lose, for an eternity,
The delicious hope of happiness
Offered by her tenderness to your
Passionate love. Would I compensate you,
Alas, for that loss? Think about it
Carefully. Caution, they say, should go
Along with sound judgment.

FONROSE. (*Heatedly.*) Ah! I recognize her in this cruel insult…
I easily perceive her loathsome work…
Her sole intention is to separate us.
We must both of us oppose this scheme.
CÉLÉNIE. Who, me?
I should go disturb that perfect union?
She would hate me for stealing her catch…
I'd lose a friend and wouldn't have a lover.
FONROSE. (*As before.*) Do you question my heart?
CÉLÉNIE. Oh, Lord! By no means!
(*She takes out the Marquis's document, crumples it, and rolls it up ostentatiously between her fingers.*)
I know too well, when it speaks, with what spirit
It apologizes for the raptures
It feels. Somewhere, I've seen its touching style.
FONROSE. (*Disturbed by the paper she's holding.*)
What's that piece of paper?
CÉLÉNIE. It's my lover's.
FONROSE. (*Asking for it.*)
Without being indiscreet?
CÉLÉNIE. Very indiscreet!
(*Letting him take the document.*)
But, even so, I want to submit to your
Request. Read it clearly and without
Misunderstanding.
FONROSE. (*Tearing up the document with incredible speed as soon as he has glanced at it; speaking what follows with a nervousness and uneasiness that cannot be described.*)
Well, as I was saying, it's an illusion…
A joke… a nothing… a figment of the
Imagination. See what should be done
With this glorious moment…
You have to destroy it and, above all,
Disregard it. You mustn't think about
It a moment longer or you'd be
Doing yourself a great injustice. In this,
You see deceit and foul play.
CÉLÉNIE. (*In tears.*) I see,

I see a faithless and a fickle heart,
Whose sole pleasure is changing its mind!
(*She turns away and hides her tears.*)
FONROSE. (*With all the speed and energy of passion that is felt very deeply, but also very gradually.*)
The desire to be happy shows us
How to change our minds. We imagine
We'll find happiness in everything.
But as soon as anyone loves you,
He no longer looks for happiness…
Because it put its sacred attributes
In you, or rather, from you it derives
Its essence. You're the one who creates
Its blessed existence. That holy feeling
That makes us godlike is nothing other
Than the gleam radiating from your eyes.
I feel it. Through it, my enflamed soul
Soars in bolts of fire into your thoughts…
Leave it there to purify itself
In bonds so sweet… to sparkle… to expand…
Uniting with you… it can compel you
To share my passion. For a moment, then,
We have only one soul; don't separate them
Or be frightened by the strain which could
Shatter the moving forces of your soul.
(*Drawing near to her.*)
Be so good as to look at me. Calm
Your anger. I'm punished enough to have
Been able to offend you. Turn your eyes
In my direction without fear or dread
And, at least, with pity, look at me
For a moment. When I dare to beg
Forgiveness for my mistake, regret
Erases it with tears of blood.
(*He throws himself at her feet.*)
Forgive, forgive a lover most sincere!
(*CÉLÉNIE is touched; she gives him looks enflamed with love and tenderness. He seizes the moment fervently.*)

Great God almighty! Look! Look at the magic!
Look at the powerful bonds that keep me close
To you. Look at the sacred chains that bind me
Forever! Without ceasing, show me as much
Love in those eyes and your happy reign
Is irrevocably established.
CÉLÉNIE. (*With feeling and helping him back to his feet.*)
God, how weak I am! At least when I
Forgive you, swear to me that you'll forget
The baroness.
FONROSE. (*From here, his machinery begins to fall apart gradually and imperceptibly until the end of the scene so that it might be absolutely no more than his lips that speak the last line; but he still disguises himself well enough, however, for the woman to be deceived by it.*)
At your feet I swear to worship you alone.
I would like something to be sorted out
Between us. Is it true about Verneuil?
CÉLÉNIE. No. Not on your life!
FONROSE. Your uncle, she said,
Had little desire for it, but that you…
You adored him and no longer having
Any hope of success, you had promised
One another
Never to see each other again!
CÉLÉNIE. Verneuil loves me, it's true, but in vain.
Ah! It's not hard to see that woman's
Ingenuity and hatred.
FONROSE. How her revenge cries out in all of this!
Do you know all the rest?
CÉLÉNIE. What do you mean?
FONROSE. She was leaving. She was taking Verneuil
With her.
CÉLÉNIE. It was set up for you to see!
That's really an unbelievable trick!
FONROSE. I'm so gullible!
CÉLÉNIE. (*Sarcastically for the first few lines, with concern during the rest of the speech.*) Yes, it's your fault!

But didn't you know her plans this afternoon?
We were to exchange our lovers so that she,
With confidence, could more successfully
Ply her skill and power over you;
Then you were to make up your mind in front of
Both of us and that final decision
Was supposed to make you happy. She'll tell
You the same thing. Let's keep the wager going
In front of her tonight. Ah! I implore you,
Come ask my uncle for me earnestly.
I'm going to warn him myself while waiting.
Don't make him angry anymore and let him
Have his ways of doing things. Stop trying
To find inconsistencies in them.
You know that he likes to see them admired.
FONROSE. Oh, I'll do everything just like you want!
CÉLÉNIE. I love him and at least out of kindness,
You might show a bit of tolerance
For his pleasures.
FONROSE. I'll finally take music lessons if you
Like and without complaint. Say the word.
Speak! Yes, on my honor! For the little
That might please you,
Three months from now, I'll be playing the bass.
CÉLÉNIE. (*Smiling warmly.*)
No, I want only a little more kindness
From you. Don't make him angry by being rude.
Remember, he's Célénie's uncle.
(*Looking at him with all the tenderness possible.*)
The uncle
Of the woman who makes loving you
The joy of her life!
FONROSE. (*All of a sudden, thrown by that last glance.*)
How that touching
Admission can invigorate my heart!
CÉLÉNIE. To avoid Florange's anger
And everything else that she might do,
Seeing her hope disappear forever,

We ought to hurry and immediately
End the conversation that keeps us here.
When you see her, use a little pretense.
The wise man pits restraint against misfortune.
FONROSE. (*Frigidly.*) What, already tearing yourself away?
CÉLÉNIE. I have to. Love me. And take these tokens
Of my sincerity: my hand and my
Word of honor.
(*She gives him her hand; FONROSE kisses it.*)
Ah! Adieu. Goodbye.
FONROSE. (*Alone.*)
The poor child! She's attractive. If I were
A little more inclined toward marriage,
I really believe that I would take
A chance on her. But to tie myself down!
Who, me? No. Good heavens! No, never!
The dear baroness is an incredible
Creature. There's a great deal of passion there!
Oh, I forgive her for that secret plan
She thought up and that, in a word, naïve
Employment of that document I wrote!
That amusing exchange of lovers… all that
Describes her soul and makes me see to what
Extent her passion was burning for me.
This one loves me well, but too naively…
With her, a person doesn't have the pleasure
Of complaining for an instant! The other
Is more titillating. Ah! It's the custom:
Nothing is like a little apprenticeship
In love! But as soon as that stupid uncle
With the bassoon finds out that I just sold
His house, what is he going to say (*Mockingly.*) to his
Niece's plan? But it appears to me
It's time to go in and be resourceful!
I'll have to find him. Well, here he is!
You could say that he suspects because
Of his cloudy expression.
(*Saint-Fard enters.*)

FONROSE. I was going to see you, sir, to talk
To you about business. By chance, might you
Have seen my lawyer this afternoon?
SAINT-FARD. No.
What's going on?
FONROSE. I sold my house.
SAINT-FARD. That conduct
Doesn't make a hint of sense! What! Without
Giving us notice? Are you unaware
Of the way that things are carried out?
FONROSE. No, sir, I know the way that things are done…
But when my profit is so definite
In such a sale, by no means am I afraid
Of seeing you displeased about it.
It's a bargain and I'm sure it would
Upset you to see it fall through.
SAINT-FARD. You're making a lot of money then.
FONROSE. Yes. I'm only losing a third of my
Investment.
SAINT-FARD. (*Aside.*) This guy's really a nut!
(*Aloud.*) And that's making a profit? Good Heavens!
What a way to run a business!
FORNOSE. But, sir, consider the time I've lived in it…
It's been almost six months! The improvements…
SAINT-FARD. (*Interrupting him.*)
Should have given you very strong motives
To want to enjoy them for the rest
Of your life. They cost you at least… oh, yes!
I bet more than a hundred thousand francs.
FONROSE. And that's the point, really. A wife, sir, and a
House! As soon as one possesses them
And spends a lot of money on them, they
Rapidly stop looking beautiful
To us. Simple possession weakens desire;
You know quite well it is the death of pleasure!
The more zealous the passion at the idol's
Altar, the more enlightened pride deserts
It or destroys it. Ashamed of having

Squandered incense on the god, man treats it
With contempt to make up for his senses!
SAINT-FARD. Your arguments are full of incongruities.
By detaching yourself from the blessings
Of existence,
You're on your way to madness and disgust,
Without ever waking up… and without
Enjoying anything, you're bored with everything!
FONROSE. To be happy, do you always have to
Become duller? This way, people don't live
Long enough to fulfill every pleasure.
According to the way you feel about it,
A man in his declining years, upon
Reflection, would have tasted, at the most,
Only a third of nature's delights…
All of which he can cultivate by yielding
To his whims and doing nothing but
Touching them lightly and drawing from them.
Since everything's provided, why then have a
Preference?
SAINT-FARD. This impulsiveness cannot
Be appealing. You think you're attending
To your tastes; you're feeding your dismay;
You're hurrying the saturation point
You thought you could prevent by acting fickle.
The too common habit of indulging
Our senses enfeebles us in our old age…
And one could still enjoy real pleasures when there's
Nothing left but horrible regrets.
FONROSE. They're a lot more certain with the sad thoughts
Of slighted desires and discarded passions.
They take from us the means for making amends
For our offenses when nature enslaved
Our endeavors.
You cast a longing eye upon your reckless
Youth; the bewitching scenes from your life
Which create, in such a case, that piercing
Rage for not having scratched the surface of all

Tastes, like you did when you were a boy.
Between the aging hypochondriac
And the rational old man, that is
The difference, notable in every case.
The one, savoring the pleasures that he
Feels, still delights his mind with their divine
Appearance. The other, disheartened to have
Limited his being, dies regretting
What he wasn't able to experience.
SAINT-FARD. What! Can a person enjoy all things equally?
No! Whoever wants to experience
Everything feels nothing deeply. Sensual
Delight is ruined when you try to stretch
It out. The man who can discover it
And spread it over fewer objects should have
The best experience, of this you can be sure.
It must submit to his interests alone…
With all its features joined together in the
Object that delights us, let us yield
To its sensations without fear…
But let virtue moderate its fires;
The art of being happy is created
Out of the harmony between virtue
And sensual delight. Real pleasure is not
A departure into insanity.
Those effects are noted when they spread and
Multiply. And then what happens? Sinning
Dazzles us…
And we mistake the eccentricities
Of the mind for happiness. That dangerous
State leads to independence…
And often leads us farther than we think.
Everything gets easier when we're
No longer ashamed of anything;
One trivial excess leads to another.
First, it's just a trifle we conceal
From ourselves;
Then a slight shortcoming, a mistake,

An absurdity. And without even
Being aware of it, we're living a life
Of vice. It attracts us. We try it…
We go to excess; and soon, little by
Little, without even thinking about it,
We're swept away by crime into the depths
Of the abyss.
FONROSE. That's painting everything
In a bad light!
SAINT-FARD. It's seeing the truth!
FONROSE. Man was born to enjoy life.
SAINT-FARD. Prudently.
That's the rule and measure of true happiness.
It makes it strong and sweet, keeps it alive
And purifies it.
FONROSE. Let me adapt that kind
Of happiness to the splendors of a
Long stream. Let me be less truly happy,
But let me be happy every day.
SAINT-FARD. Useless rationalizations, sir!
FONROSE. (*With warmth and good nature.*)
Look at nature. Does it reveal itself
To you under the auspices of an
Infallible rule, the boring picture
Of uniformity? Everything in it
Is changing; everything's variety.
In none of its amusements is its hand
Alike. That's the way it pleases us…
That's the way it delights us. Look at the
Nimble animation of the breeze;
Do you ever see it prolong its favors?
Hovering indiscriminately over
Flora's daughters, its delicate breath
Seeks only to make them bloom. It finds them…
It runs through them and freshens their senses…
And in one day, they all take part in its
Designs. The tender deities to whom
Our raptures are directed are the same

Objects, alas! of its caresses.
A woman, a beautiful lily,
A rose, a carnation… are gifts created
By the hand of nature. And believe it!
They have no other difference between them
Than a little more or less of artifice
In their fragile existence. Without fear, then,
Let's be breezes in turn and let's adore
Pleasure and despise love.
SAINT-FARD. (*Peevishly.*)
Yes, let's despise love… friendship… and nature.
Let's defile its blessings to insult it
More effectively! Let its people,
And its gifts… let everything be turned
Upside down and finally, just on
Principle, let's have no more virtue!
FONROSE. (*Continuing heatedly.*)
It's frivolity which incessantly
Leads us to virtue by its rapid flight.
Ah! How much better you appreciate
Its sublime value when you've lived a while
In sin! Variety alone is the spice
Of life. Once it disappears, everything's
Boring and regularity leads us
To the grave, of which it's both the image
And the horrible reflection.
SAINT-FARD. (*Eagerly to VERNEUIL, whom he sees entering.*)
Ah! My
Friend Verneuil.
(*Indicating FONROSE.*) Try, if you can, to make
That nincompoop less of a lunatic.
As for me, I'm like a chicken with its
Head cut off!
(*To FONROSE.*) I'm going to think, sir,
About providing for myself elsewhere
Since you're throwing me out into the street!
Your company has become too annoying
For me; I intend to live where nothing
Will disturb me and to end my days

Peacefully, at least. A mind so fickle
Suits me not in the least! (*He exits.*)
VERNEUIL. He's quite upset!
FONROSE. Good! He's a fool, I tell you, who's always
Distressed and moaning about nothing at all.
But you, what devil possessed you, my dear,
To keep me in suspense, to deceive me,
To toy with me, even to frustrate me?
I knew all your secrets; why this precious
Mystery? When a person's a friend,
Should he be mysterious all the time?
VERNEUIL. Love, sometimes, does friendship a disservice.
I'm afraid of you.
FONROSE. Mistakenly.
You know that I'm tied, by religion,
To romantic love. That kind of love,
In my opinion, is so ugly that it
Manages to get complete control
Over me out of holy respect!
(*After a moment of thought, he takes VERNEUIL's hand and leads him away.*)
Come, and for once and for all, stop being
Suspicious of my fidelity!

END OF ACT FOUR

ACT FIVE

(*Enter Saint-Fard and Célénie, following her uncle with the gait of a person distressed.*)
SAINT-FARD. Don't think that I'll ever give in to you
On this point. Your affection pleads with me
Terribly in vain. I see farther
Than you into the dark future; think about
The cruel misfortunes that nothing can end…
They expose themselves indifferently
To my calmer mind, but when a foolish

Love misrepresents them in your eyes,
At least, still listen to the voice of reason.
CÉLÉNIE. Ah! Forgive me, uncle, the voice of reason
No longer speaks to me; I have allowed
That deadly love to take too much control.
I told myself a hundred times everything
You're supposed to say to yourself and you can
Clearly see I haven't been successful.
(*With resentment.*) He must have used a spell to captivate me
In this way.
SAINT-FARD. That spell and your vulnerability…
And his detestable ability
To charm a woman with that pleasant manner,
With that false exterior of sincerity,
When his heart is filled only with corruption!
CÉLÉNIE. Can't he change?
SAINT-FARD. Yes, but maybe for the worst!
He can control himself for a month, at most.
Even at that, I have no idea.
And soon, without any consideration,
He'll dive right back into the gravest sins.
(*Seeing CÉLÉNIE's distress, he approaches her tenderly.*)
If you could know how much that bothers me!
Why did you hide that wretched fever from me?
Did you have doubts about my feelings?
I would have consoled you. From the start,
Alas, that burning desire would not have had
The horrifying power that it has
Today. The baroness should have confided
In me.
CÉLÉNIE. Her behavior's hard to understand.
It's inexplicable. It's useless to try
And figure her out. Nothing comes to light.
SAINT-FARD. You really ought to know her, after all.
CÉLÉNIE. Oh, I don't know her very well right now,
For nothing gets through her exterior.
She used to be my friend and ever since
I was a child,

Next to you, she had my most tender feelings.
You know that, uncle; and now I don't know
(*With resentment and pride.*)
If she even has the right to my
Affection.
SAINT-FARD. Is she your rival? Ah!
Let her have the honor of arousing
A man like that and capturing his heart.
But tell me, do you know about his newest
Blunder? Oh, no, because with you, undoubtedly
He misrepresents himself. It's not
Only the house; there's that regiment which he
Was anxiously applying for, you know.
He gets it, he refuses it. Oh! What a
Scatterbrain! In three years, I expect him
Not to have a dime. His father
Inherited over a million dollars
And that fine human being left it all
To him…
I think he's on the verge of bankruptcy.
That's the dreary fate that heaven has
In store for him.
CÉLÉNIE. Marriage will surely restore
Him to his senses. Can any man
Withstand, dear uncle, the tender attachment,
The promises… such sweet attentions from a
Darling wife?
(*As emotionally as possible.*)
I'd devote everything at my disposal
To make him happy. Could he be ungrateful?
No, no, he'd love me and respect me, uncle,
And he would change!
SAINT-FARD. He'd love you? A week! Come on,
Come on, you can believe me about this.
I know too well the story of these charming
Gentlemen in bonds like these; for them,
The issue is the dowry. When it's settled,
That's all that they need. Quickly, you'll see

Him disappear from the house. He'll say
He's never in control of his time:
Today, it's something he's concerned about,
Tomorrow, it's something he has to do,
A case to plead, a minister to see.
Do you believe any of it? Not a word!
Our butterfly is fluttering around
Those deities that pleasure manufactures;
Not those that you pay for. Oh, I'd prefer it…
The less holy the worship, the less dangerous
It is! No, our poor fool is with attractive
Women,
With women, quite foolishly, respected,
Who, hiding under their high-sounding names,
Think they can defy honor without risking
Contempt. Caught in the clever traps of these
Tender sirens, his fervent passions
Will leave yours behind. After all, in their
Care, his heart will breathe in that aversion
To virtue, which he sees them abandon;
He's ruined at last. Those women of importance
Don't take any money, but indulge
In what you spend on them.
There are teas… dances…. concerts… bouquets…
And since he wants to change things every day,
Out of the depths come an untimely gang
Of creditors to sweep through the rest of the
Fortune. He sells. Temper interferes.
And those sad children of abandoned ecstasies,
Those innocent assurances…
Far from fastening life's sweetest knots
Become a new topic of aversion.
No more peace of mind, no more affection,
No more friends, no more possessions. The excess
Of misfortune provides the bonds with a sword
And the monster, unlawful, unbridled,
Unobstructed, proceeds by suicide
To shorten his career.

(*Seeing CÉLÉNIE in tears.*)
You're crying, child.
Come into my arms. Ah! Come. Feel the beating
Of my heart for having troubled yours.
CÉLÉNIE. (*Throwing herself into her uncle's arms with all the frankness and affability of youth.*)
Don't add to my suffering and my pain
And, good heavens! Save me from the fate
That's sweeping me away.
I'm awfully unhappy having it
And yet, a thousand times more so, not having
It. In this case, which way should I lean
And what should I do?
SAINT-FARD. (*Very tenderly.*)
God almighty, for only one day,
Return her noble father to her. Let him
Come and soothe her! Seeing that on his deathbed,
He commended your fortune and your fate
To me, I have neglected nothing in your
Upbringing.
Everything I have will soon be yours
Because I'm leaving all of it to you.
Look at me, I'm old. At least before
I die, I want to see you married…
Happily married. Despite the difference
In our ages, I feel that if ever
A husband, saying it's the common practice,
Dared not to have your happiness as his
Only objective, I'd still be ready
To point out his mistake. Should he kill me,
What does it matter? What does my life matter?
A few days more or less…
(*In tears, squeezing her in his arms.*)
My dear Célénie,
When you're so close to port, you start to see
That no longer do you put your hopes
In anything down here.
(*Indicating heaven.*) You put your hopes

Up there.
CÉLÉNIE. (*The first word with a bloodcurdling cry, the rest in tears.*)
No! For pity's sake don't torment me.
I'm only asking here for your advice.
Live, both to love me and advise me.
SAINT-FARD. (*With the utmost intensity of feeling and taking her again in his arms.*) Ah! I
Want never, never to leave you.
(*Pulling himself together and both of them very poignantly for the rest of the scene.*) You say
He's going to come to present his request?
CÉLÉNIE. He promised me, uncle!
SAINT-FARD. (*Indicating the door.*) Do you want me
To prevent his coming in?
CÉLÉNIE. (*Self-conscious.*) No, if you
Were to say to him…
SAINT-FARD. Why entertain him?
What will that accomplish? Why mince words?
I know he'll make promises…
CÉLÉNIE. But if he
Kept them?
SAINT-FARD. No, don't believe any of it,
Do not believe a thing, poor foolish girl.
Another horrid principle these gentlemen
Create for themselves… another dreadful
Custom which they use systematically…
Honor, that holy restraint that fascinates
Their souls and links them all together,
Is worthless with women.
(*Enter FLORANGE and VERNEUIL.*)
FLORANGE. (*Laughing.*) Well, what do you
Think about this latest bolt from the blue?
He's throwing you out of the house?
SAINT-FARD. You, too,
Madam. My congratulations! Oh! Our
Trust in that kind of a fool was madness!
I can give you a friend to stay with–

One of my best friends, in fact–while you're
Making arrangements elsewhere.
VERNEUIL. Right. Right.
He'll change his mind; the day's not over yet.
SAINT-FARD. He must have changed it twenty times! But I've
Made up my mind completely: I want nothing
More to do with that man. Everything
Will be worked out by our usual lawyers;
I couldn't be far away enough
From here where the air is saturated
With his insanity.
(*To MADAME FLORANGE.*)
But even more than us,
All of this upsets you, for tonight,
Didn't you say you were going to
Exchange the name of Florange for Verneuil?
FLORANGE. It's something I made up. Oh, I've got much more
Pride than that!
CÉLÉNIE. (*To her uncle.*) Didn't I tell you? It's
Mr. Fonrose.
SAINT-FARD. That certainly serves her
Right.
FLORANGE. Now then, I suppose that both of you
Were very sure of yourselves?
SAINT-FARD. (*To the Baroness.*) Come on, I
Didn't believe a word of it. You're making
Fun of me.
CÉLÉNIE. Ah! Believe it, uncle.
That's where the mystery is.
SAINT-FARD. (*To his niece.*) Why then were you
Trying to disrupt this situation?
And didn't you say that I was going to see him
Come here asking for your hand and really
Want to win it?
CÉLÉNIE. He swore it to me.
FLORANGE. Of course, in jest! Haven't you gotten used
To his gallant behavior?

SAINT-FARD. Yes, wantonly
To seduce the mind of a young child,
To plunge it into sin, and to laugh while
Humiliating it;
That's what's now called gallant behavior!
It's lucky if it stops at that and the
Poor unfortunate girl preserves her honor
By pitting her strength against her heart's
Control! If she's more weak than wise, she succumbs
To the fever. For her deadly master,
It's something new to laugh about. A triumph,
Then, prepared by Cupid, whose cruel pride
Is shamefully gratified. What customs!
Célénie, ah! I congratulate you…
And if, madam, there's really a proposal
Of marriage, may heaven, shedding light
Upon it, make you happy once again.
CÉLÉNIE. (*Aside.*) Deep down in my heart, there's always hope.
(*Enter FONROSE.*)
FONROSE. (*To CÉLÉNIE.*) Please forgive me, lovely Célénie,
But, seeing that I have to make a choice
For life and since you want my genuine
Admission…
(*To the Baroness.*) With you alone, alas!
I want to tie the knots. Madam, every
Excuse for your uncertainty is thus
Taken away by my meticulous
Attention. Must I renew an eternal
Vow? To forget, to renounce all other
Feelings?
Take it, Florange, and let your affection
Finally condescend to crown my vows
And my ecstasy. No longer be
Afraid of my unpredictability;
Your charms guarantee my fidelity.
CÉLÉNIE. (*In the utmost despondency.*)
Good heavens! That's the price of my affection!
I'm dying, ah! Good heavens!

(*In tears, she falls into a chair. Indignantly, SAINT-FARD goes to her, returns, and looks at FONROSE with rage, all the while listening to FLORANGE.*)
FLORANGE. (*To FONROSE, resolutely, with dignity.*) It is time
For me to stop both taking advantage
Of you, sir, and deceiving
(*Indicating CÉLÉNIE.*) This sincere friend!
I have to exonerate myself.
I've suffered too long concealing my soul
From her; it's appropriate at last
For my friendship to regain her heart,
Her tender heart. It still owes me a great deal;
I wanted to be of service to it…
Service is rendered. *(To FONROSE.)* To enslave you,
I took advantage of my weapons: pretense,
Guile, and a few wanton charms. These are
The gifts that nature lavished on our sex
For us to take revenge on yours. I used them
All. And because of my stamina
And a few other tricks, I'm the chosen one.
(*Indicating CÉLÉNIE.*)
But I only wanted to rescue her
From a man as vain as he is fickle
And empty-headed! *(To FONROSE.)* Without a doubt,
All this seems ridiculous to you.
Men, I know, unscrupulously assume
The despotic right of betraying us;
But, at least, we have the right to punish
Them! Observe that I'm making good use
Of it and while you might have been correct
Calling my behavior strange, I tell you,
Sir, I have to give you up forever.
Go console yourself with new affections;
But if you want my opinion, find refuge
Somewhere else: you should not bring sorrow
And trouble into the midst of an honest
Family. Your behavior toward us
(Excuse the advice) is charming in a

World ruled by indecency; compared
To wisdom,
(*Indicating CÉLÉNIE.*) It's just an obscenity!
(*CÉLÉNIE is still in tears and seated in a chair.*)
See the awful state to which you hurl
This valued object whom you wantonly
Betrayed.
(*Rushing to her, lifting her up, and holding her in her arms.*)
Come, come, embrace me, my beloved Célénie,
And finally recognize your truest friend.
(*She goes to take VERNEUIL's hand and presents him to SAINT-FARD.*)
Sir, here's the only one to whom you ought
To give her. In him, you'll find whatever
Happiness requires:
Money, honesty, integrity,
Affection, good breeding–he has it all!
(*To CÉLÉNIE.*) My child, become his reward.
SAINT-FARD. (*To CÉLÉNIE.*)
I join with both of them to ask this of you.
VERNEUIL. (*At CÉLÉNIE's feet.*)
In a day, could you give up everything
For me? To entreat you, I have only
My passionate respect for you. Compared
To your virtues, what good are titles
And inheritance! But if I have to
Earn them to deserve you, I will learn
The skill to acquire them from love.
CÉLÉNIE. (*Helping VERNEUIL back to his feet and addressing FONROSE with all the determination and bitterness that her situation inspires.*)
Cruel man! You lied to me. I was your victim!
Friendship kept me from falling off the edge
Of the abyss; I owe it to friendship
To submit to its wishes. Here's my hand,
Verneuil, let's turn our thoughts to marriage…
The only delay is what tact requires
To heal my extreme frailty. I must

Make you certain of all my emotions:
Only too well do you deserve a heart
That's innocent and pure. You will have it.
(*She gives her hand to VERNEUIL, who kisses it ecstatically.*)
SAINT-FARD. (*To FONROSE.*)
From now on, sir, the house will be available…
We won't be sleeping here.
(*More sarcastically.*) When the desire
To whisper sweet nothings, by chance, comes back
To you, recall the lesson…
(*Squeezing his hand tightly.*) And the virtue.
(Enter DESCHAMPS.)
FONROSE. (*With a light enough attitude.*)
You know all about my misfortunes?
DESCHAMPS. Yes, sir, and perhaps I'm coming to increase
Them by letting you know the sad truth:
They always follow one another.
FONROSE. (*Disturbed.*) What then?
DESCHAMPS. They're not trivial misfortunes of love…
These are more substantial.
FONROSE. (*Getting up, with a great deal of concern.*)
Explain yourself,
Quickly!
DESCHAMPS. (*With a slow and serious delivery.*)
To begin with, everybody's
Leaving you. Your servants, hearing what you
Said this morning, have bolted unexpectedly
To save themselves. I'm all you have left.
It's said you no longer want to sell
Such a beautiful house. People remember
That you change your mind twenty times a day;
They're scared about their cash; they want a full
Accounting, here and now… for what you sold.
It's the same old fear. Uselessly, I try
To reassure them. They paid the money,
You promised them, they're moving in, in next to
No time at all, in return for which, sir,
You're without a place to go. Moreover,

That creditor, that chubby Mr. Dorsille,
Whom you so liked to manhandle, aware
Of what's happening, he's stopped everything:
Conflicts encumber all the real estate,
Sheriff's officers and bailiff's men
Have just taken the furniture, and if
The hand of fate does not stop striking us,
Neither you nor I will have a thing
To eat tonight! Oh, God, what misfortunes!
I beseech you, sir, take it upon
Yourself in this situation to do
Something. You're losing all your most valuable
Properties at the same time. Oppose
Such great misfortunes with your courage.
FONROSE. (*After a pause, with determination.*)
All right, I know the strange injustice of fate;
It wants to punish me for being fickle…
(*Taking DESCHAMPS's hand.*)
But just when you might think its wrath is draining
Me, it offers me great pleasure.
I'm going to change my profession! (*He exits.*)
DESCHAMPS. (*Watching him with amazement.*)
Oh! Really! Once a fool, always a fool!
(*Alone.*) Imitating his odd habit, that would
Certainly be the case. No… no… my heart
Is reluctant to follow that horrid
Example. Seeing that he's unhappy,
I want to love him, always.

THE END

Henrietta and Saint-Clair
or
The Power of Blood

Introduction

In a letter written on 26 April 1781 to his wife, the Marquis de Sade indicated that he had a number of completed plays in his portfolio. These were *Henrietta and Saint-Clair*, *The Freak (The Inconstant One)*, *The Madness of Misfortune*, and *The Twins*, all products of the Marquis's incarceration at Vincennes Prison between 1778 and 1784 because of his mother-in-law's "lettre de cachet."

The prison was the perfect setting for Gothic melodrama with its sixteen-foot walls and arched ceilings over thirty feet high. The only illumination for this dank, gray environment came from high, narrow windows which were protected by thick iron bars. Two moats, forty feet deep and twenty feet wide, guarded the exterior of the building. In his first year at the prison, Sade was assigned to Cell No. 6, a very dark, very cold, damp room overrun by rats and mice and containing no furniture but a bed. He was allowed only the bare necessities: a green overcoat, a white waistcoat, a pair of serge breeches, a pair of black stockings, two nightcaps, a pair of slippers, two shirts, two handkerchiefs, and two towels. Except when food was pushed through a small hole in the large iron-lined door to his room, he had no contact with another human being and all books and writing materials were forbidden.

After three months of solitary confinement, Sade was allowed to use paper and pens and to take exercise. At least by 24 December 1780, the date given for the composition of *The Inconstant Man*, the Marquis was writing plays in his cell. In addition, during his exercise periods, Sade was fond of trying to stir up the other inmates by suggesting, among other things, that the food in the prison might be poisoned. Such undisciplined behavior usually earned him a curtailment of exercise privileges that, in turn, prompted him to cause even more trouble.

However, the most celebrated disturbance arose from the Marquis's dislike of his distant cousin, Mirabeau, imprisoned because of some romantic adventure and who enjoyed the use of a private garden at the prison. Calling him the "Commandant's catamite," Sade publicly insulted Mirabeau, accused him of being personally responsible for the cancellation of his exercise privileges, and threatened to "lop his ears off" as soon as he was released from prison. Without losing his composure, Mirabeau replied, "My name is that of a man of honor who has never dissected or poisoned any women, a man who will be only too pleased to write his name on your shoulders with a razor, if only you're not broken on the wheel before I have a chance to do so." In addition, upon leaving Vincennes, Mirabeau wrote out his official discharge on the reverse side of the record of Sade's arrival at the prison. As a result of the incident, Sade was deprived of physical exercise for nearly nine months, during which he suffered extreme delusions of persecution, engaged in epistolary quarrels with his wife and friends, and wrote plays.

There is no evidence that the Marquis de Sade ever sought to have *Henrietta and Saint-Clair* produced. Certainly the subject of an incestuous relationship between a brother and sister ignorant of their parentage would not have rendered the play unproduceable; the precedent for theatrical incest had been established with *Oedipus* nearly two thousand years earlier. And though Gilbert Lély dismisses the drama as having been written in "the cloying sentimental vein of the worst of Diderot… far removed from the powerful boldness of Sade's novels," a letter from Sade's wife in June 1789 indicates that, in its own day, the play's honest emotional appeal might have been esteemed:

> I've read *Henrietta* and I recognized the author of *The Madness of Misfortune*. I think it is fundamentally good and made to create the greatest effect on those who have a soul. It will disgust those faint-hearted souls who will not appreciate the situation and the problem. It is different enough from [Diderot's] *The Father of the Family* not to be considered an imitation. In general, it has many beautiful passages that will not be appreciated by everybody.

That's my opinion based on a first reading. I will read it again more than once because I love to distraction all that you've written and am too prejudiced to give an opinion with confidence.

Though there is perhaps a greater similarity between Sade's play and Diderot's *The Father of the Family*[42] than the Marquise de Sade is willing to admit, the fact remains that the Marquis's dramatic creations were perfectly in line with the theatrical climate of his day. It comes as no surprise that twentieth-century critics prefer his novels to these middle-class dramas espousing traditional values in highly effusive, sentimental language. Yet plays like *Henrietta and Saint-Clair* compare quite favorably with the bulk of La Chaussée's tearful comedies and Diderot's domestic dramas.

---

[42] The plot of *Henrietta and Saint-Clair* is actually more similar to Diderot's *The Natural Son*.

Henrietta and Saint-Clair
or
The Power of Blood

Prose Drama in Five Acts

"He falls into the trap trying to avoid it." *Oedipus*, Act 5, scene 4.

CHARACTERS

Mr. Volsange
Saint-Clair, *a young officer, Mr. Volsange's son, in love with Henrietta*
Valville, *Saint-Clair's friend*
A Traveler, *a retired officer in the Spanish army*
Pauline and Henrietta, *two strangers*
Madame de Lormeuil, *Mr. Volsange's sister*
Lapineau, *game-keeper at Volsange's estate*
Lucette, *a young country girl in the service of Madame de Lormeuil*

COSTUMES

Mr. Volsange, *dressed as a prosperous landowner*
Saint-Clair, *dressed first as a young man returning from the hunt, later, as a military officer*
Valville, *dressed in simple country clothes*
The Traveler, *dressed in clothes that are threadbare, but not rags*
Pauline, *dressed in a simple middle-class outfit*
Henrietta, *dressed in a modest negligee*
Madame de Lormeuil, *dressed like a woman who is at home in the country, without ostentation*
Lapineau, *dressed as a game-keeper*
Lucette, *dressed in peasant clothes*

ACT ONE

(A room in the castle. Stage right stands a frame for embroidering tapestries. When the curtain rises, MADAME DE LORMEUIL and VALVILLE are already in the room. MADAME DE LORMEUIL is at work on the tapestry. VALVILLE is reading pamphlets placed on a small table located a little behind the frame on the opposite side of the stage. Consequently, MADAME DE LORMEUIL does not see him. She works, sighs, and ponders.)

LORMEUIL. This is bothering me too much. I haven't been able to sleep a wink. Oh! I've got to stop working on this. I don't know what I'm doing. (*She lifts her head and notices VALVILLE.*) Ah! There you are, Valville. I didn't know you were in the room.

VALVILLE. (*Getting up and walking toward MADAME DE LORMEUIL.*) You were deep in thought. I didn't want to interrupt you. All this disturbs you, Madame, I can certainly see that.

LORMEUIL. Well, Valville, can you make anything out of your friend's behavior? To invite you to come all the way out to the country and visit him… to persuade you to give up your youthful enjoyments in favor of those we are able to provide for you here… and then to leave you alone here every day. Those hunts he runs off to without you… that look of distress he always wears on his return. Really, it would be a great favor to his father and me, and maybe even to him, if you could figure all of this out. Saint-Clair is young and impetuous. Love usually takes the color of the soul it conquers. If ever Saint-Clair falls in love, he would be the most unfortunate man of the decade and from the way he's acting, sir, I'd bet you he's in love.

VALVILLE. I agree with you, but how do we clean up the mess? Saint-Clair is avoiding me as if I were his enemy. I excuse his behavior because I like him. His affection makes up for all the little faults in his character.

LORMEUIL. Saint-Clair was born with that special energy which makes us capable of performing great deeds as well as making great mistakes. When he chooses to be virtuous, it's because he's squeamish. When he acts like a fool, it's because he's sensitive. Still, his upbringing will not allow him to stray from the path of honor, but I tremble at the thought of him in love. That

will be a terrible disaster. And without a doubt, the best luck he can hope for would be to become a husband before falling in love. That way, the woman destined to be his lifetime companion could ignite the fire of love and the nuptial torch both at the same time.
VALVILLE. Ah! Certainly. But Saint-Clair will only marry a woman he loves. His heart will make up its mind, perhaps, only with a great deal of trouble… but he will be in a great deal of stress when he pays attention to its impulses. According to him, no woman has yet had the slightest effect upon him, but his gloomy behavior betrays him. A kind of melancholy extends over everything he says and I think he has already been wounded by the arrows he pretends not to fear.
LORMEUIL. (*Quickly.*) Ah! You're right and my nephew is wrong when he told you that he's not in love. Heavens! Here I am, only strengthened in my fears. But you don't know the half of it, Valville. You don't know the half of it. I wish I could tell you what I know.
VALVILLE. (*Starting to leave.*) Here comes Mr. Volsange, Madame. Maybe he will be better informed. I'm leaving.
LORMEUIL. No, no, you won't be in the way. We have to work together for the happiness of your friend. I know that he greatly needs our advice. (*Enter VOLSANGE.*)
VOLSANGE. (*Agitated.*) Well, sister! (*To VALVILLE.*) Good day, my friend. (*To both.*) Well, have you found out anything? Will that unfortunate child keep us in suspense until it kills me?
LORMEUIL. I had hoped to be enlightened by Valville, but he hardly knows as much as I do. Saint-Clair distrusts him like he distrusts us… like he distrusts everybody.
VOLSANGE. (*With spirit.*) Ah! That affection of his is dishonest since it makes him blush. The shame drawn on the forehead of a libertine is the obligatory respect he pays to virtue. And the first steps a person takes toward vice are always at the expense of his self-esteem. That's the moment of fear we have to use to bring him back to his senses. Valville, you'll help us. We're counting on your honesty and affection for us.
VALVILLE. You can be sure that I will use all the spirit I can muster. And if my friend listens to me, he will never behave

according to the whims of his heart, but according to the guidance of so respectable a family.

VOLSANGE. Let's join forces. We must work for his happiness; let no other motive hold us back. Let's see, now. Sister, what do you know about this? My heart is heavy. What do you know, sister?

LORMEUIL. I would tell you willingly, but I'm afraid of increasing your distress rather than relieving it.

VOLSANGE. No. It would relieve me just to settle on something in this business.

LORMEUIL. You remember the walk I took the day before yesterday. Your son, who had cleverly made me take Nérac Street, pretended to be out of breath when we reached the city walls and argued that it would be impossible to return to the estate without stopping for awhile. "Let's go rest at the home of a widow I know. I can see her house from here," he tells me. "She's a foreigner who's lived on Nérac Street for about a year. I think she has fallen on hard times... she has a very beautiful daughter!" Saint-Clair, who noticed that I was looking at him, quickly stopped his passionate oration and changed the conversation to how injustice humbles the people who most deserve praise while it elevates those who only merit degradation. His passion sufficiently calmed by that paradox, Saint-Clair stopped talking and we moved on.

VOLSANGE. You have no idea, sister, how well I'm following these interesting details.

LORMEUIL. I allowed myself to be led. We entered a very small house, where a poor woman, around forty years old, greeted us with well-bred politeness much superior to the environment that surrounded her. Soon, an eighteen-year-old young lady appeared. And so busy was I watching the impression she made on my nephew that I had to stop myself from being struck by her face, her delicate body, and above all, her sensitive manner, which showed the mark of innocence written all over her features. She joined her mother in providing us with the best they could offer in such a sad hovel. Saint-Clair was very impressed. He hid it well. But, in spite of himself, his eyes showed me the state his heart was in. From beginning to end, a careful modesty and a great shyness characterized every gesture, every look, every word of the young lady. And, brother, I swear to you that I left as convinced that my nephew is in love with that girl as I am that she is honest and virtuous.

VALVILLE. (*Full of interest.*) What was the conversation like, Madame?

LORMEUIL. Simple and vague. The mother did not conceal the fact that, treated poorly by fate, she had resolved to retreat to the country, where, having fewer expenses than in Paris, she could sustain an existence all the more painful since heaven had not prepared her by birth for such cruel reversals. Tears fell from her eyes with this admission. The young lady rose to conceal hers. Your son was very disturbed and, as all of this happened when we were about to finish a visit which was supposed to be a momentary rest stop, Saint-Clair gave me his hand and we left.

VOLSANGE. (*Coming out of a deep reverie caused by the narrative up to this point.*) What feelings you have made blossom all at once in my heart! I can express neither what I feel nor what I fear. Continue, sister, continue. That child was born to make my life miserable. You'll see that this passion…

VALVILLE. I found nothing offensive about it up to now. I think it's just a little out of proportion.

VOLSANGE. Eh! My dear Valville, you don't know all that I am going through. Please, sister, continue.

LORMEUIL. As you can well imagine, Saint-Clair was eager to ask me on our return if the mother hadn't a face that betrayed the misfortune in which we perceived her… if the daughter wasn't lovelier than the dawn… and wouldn't whoever could win her heart be the happiest of men? "Saint-Clair," I told him, looking at him, "you want to be that man. You're the one who idolizes that girl." At this point, your son's heart was dashed to pieces. It became impossible for him to lie and the admission he made to me about his love was accompanied by vows never to belong to another woman.

VOLSANGE. Wretched boy!

LORMEUIL. (*Continuing quickly.*) "I met them by accident," he told me. "A drunk attacked them in the woods. I drove away the scoundrel and walked them home. Since then, I never stopped seeing them and love… what am I saying? A sentiment unknown to all mortal men, which could have been placed in my heart only by Cupid himself, love made me offer to this young lady all the most tender and submissive duties of the soul. I passed myself off to them as the son of one of my father's tenant farmers. The girl trusts me because she has my word that I will never marry anyone but her. But I don't want to fool her or pretend any longer. You have certainly seen through my disguise, auntie. I am still your little boy. In persuading you to pay them a visit, I have obligated these two respectable ladies to visit you in return. My father will receive them and when he sees the woman I love… ah! That's all I want. He's my father. He's sensitive. He won't refuse me." (*Pause.*) I've explained yesterday's walk. They're poor. They're virtuous. That's all that I know. You alone, dear brother, can now decide what remedy to use on a patient who I believe has swallowed a deadly poison.

VALVILLE. I'd bet that today will not go by without a visit from those two women.

VOLSANGE. (*After a little thought.*) It is impossible that such a thing could please me. I was reserving Saint-Clair for someone who could bring him happiness and a fortune at the same time. He would only destroy my plans… overwhelming me with sorrows.

VALVILLE. Alas! Sir, in a young heart, the desire to love is rarely ruled by propriety. Love, the most active of all feelings, cannot be bridled and the parents' consent, necessary to make it legal, is the formality that troubles love the least.

VOLSANGE. I know that, my dear Valville. But you will also admit that true happiness is only found when passion can join forces with duty. It's fortunate when a well-directed choice presents no problem to the parents nor forces them to raise any objections in the best interests of their children.

VALVILLE. Yes, but is that what always determines their decisions?

VOLSANGE. It ought to be.

VALVILLE. But is it?

VOLSANGE. (*Continuing quickly.*) No. Very often, I grant you. But Saint-Clair doesn't have to worry about that with us. I certainly will not allow him to contract an alliance which, like in this case, could only result in regret. But if the person I want him to marry doesn't attract him, I tell you that I won't force him. It's time for him to return from the hunt. I want to see him with no other witness but his aunt. If you run into him, Valville, don't say a word about what has just happened. Keep an eye on everything for the moment. If these strangers appear, I beg of you to entertain them just until I've had enough time to probe your friend about these most unbelievable developments.

VALVILLE. (*Going out.*) You can count on my discretion.

VOLSANGE. How is it, sister, that you couldn't even find out the names of those two women?

LORMEUIL. Brother, forgive me. One of them is called Pauline, I think.

VOLSANGE. (*Very agitated.*) Pauline? Good God!

LORMEUIL. Indeed, the figment of your imagination… I didn't think that it would make such an impression on you… but for the fact that you're certain that the person you know of that name is dead. Really, there isn't even the slightest probability.

VOLSANGE. (*Very troubled.*) Oh! I know it. I know it. But the name of someone who was dear to us always reawakens feelings over which we have no control. If in the meantime… Ah! Heaven would never allow me to be so happy. Do you know the name of the other one?

LORMEUIL. They promised to tell me today. I didn't dare ask your son too many questions. I didn't want to appear too interested. As for the rest, you'll certainly be enlightened in a short time, for I'm certain that Saint-Clair is anxious for the meeting. He seems to have put all his hopes in the good impression he expects her to make on you.

VOLSANGE. I cannot express to you the uneasiness with which I anticipate this interview. The strangest things in the world are coming into my head. Could my father have died with that deadly secret? Here comes Saint-Clair. Sister, go to your loom. I'm going to get a book and ignore him. I know how sensitive he is. By manipulating his affection, I'll get what I want from him.

(*MADAME DE LORMEUIL goes to the loom. VOLSANGE sits next to the table. He takes a pamphlet and reads it, facing away from the side of the stage where SAINT-CLAIR enters.*

SAINT-CLAIR enters in hunting clothes. He goes to kiss his father's hand. VOLSANGE lets him do so without giving him the least bit of attention.)

SAINT-CLAIR. You have nothing to say to me, Father? *(Approaching his aunt, he kisses her on the forehead. He is met with the same indifference.)* Dear Auntie, what's the matter with my father?

LORMEUIL. I can't imagine… but he's depressed. You know very well, Saint-Clair, that he has reason to be.

SAINT-CLAIR. *(Quickly.)* You didn't tell him anything?

LORMEUIL. *(In a low voice.)* Everybody knows. *(Aloud.)* Your behavior does not give your father the satisfaction he should expect from you.

(She stays at her loom, where she works throughout the rest of the scene. She does not participate in the conversation except by sighing and shedding tears every now and then. MR. VOLSANGE throws down his book peevishly, gets up, and starts to leave. SAINT-CLAIR, deeply affected, flies to him and stops him.)

SAINT-CLAIR. What's this? Is my presence annoying you? Why are you running away from me, Father?

VOLSANGE. *(Firm.)* I thought I was your friend, sir… but I see that I was mistaken.

SAINT-CLAIR. *(Throwing himself into VOLSANGE's arms.)* Oh, honored creator of my life, you are everything to me: my friend, my comforter, my father. And if nature had even more sacred titles, they would all be collected in my heart and I would declare them all to prove my love for you.

VOLSANGE. *(Somewhat affected.)* Nevertheless, you keep secrets from me.

SAINT-CLAIR. *(Confused.)* Secrets? I have secrets? Ah! I haven't a single one. Out of respect for you, I could have delayed admitting something…

VOLSANGE. *(Interrupting him quickly.)* Which you know would displease me.

SAINT-CLAIR. *(With firmness and passion.)* That's not what I'm afraid of. You are just. You don't want your son to be unhappy. And when you're convinced of the complete strength of his emotion… when you see the object of his passion… when you're persuaded that both his love and his life now have the same source and that you'd be depriving him of life rather than extinguishing the extraordinary flames that burn inside him, you would remember that you're a father. You would remember that you called me your friend and you won't want me to give up any right to those titles so dear to me.

VOLSANGE. Ingrate. Never lay claim to them as an excuse for your vices!

SAINT-CLAIR. Vices? Ah, father, how far my heart is from vice. My love is the purest incense I can offer virtue. She whom I adore is its image. Through her features, virtue shows itself to mankind. Through her features, the universe worships virtue… and alas, her mother! If you only knew her…

VOLSANGE. (*Interrupting him.*) Yes… yes, I know all about that. See how the imagination always deifies its mistakes. This pretended regard is only one of the illusions of pride. A person wants to embellish the god he serves and he imagines himself to be so much less foolish when he has succeeded in making a fool out of himself.

SAINT-CLAIR. (*With the greatest passion.*) Don't be offensive to them, father. They're poor, virtuous, and sensitive. Don't insult them, I implore you.

VOLSANGE. We must help them if they're poor; respect them if they're honest; and it's an insult to their misery and their virtue to seduce them with a vain hope or to abuse them by your tricks.

SAINT-CLAIR. (*Boldly.*) Love made the tricks necessary and I never considered the hope in vain… so long as I had the same father and the same heart.

VOLSANGE. Don't think, however, that I will take part in your mistakes.

SAINT-CLAIR. (*As above.*) An honest feeling doesn't know how to make mistakes!

VOLSANGE. Unfortunately, it has already led you to be disrespectful to me! (*He starts to leave.*)

SAINT-CLAIR. (*Throwing himself at his father's feet, stopping him.*) Have pity on me. I'm not myself, father! (*SAINT-CLAIR begins to cry while holding on to his father's knees.*)

VOLSANGE. My son, my friend. I certainly want to call you by that name again because I expect that you deserve it. Like you, I know this delirium of the senses that people call love. Like you, I've known its delights. Don't learn how to weep for its sorrows like I did. Your birth was the most important event of my life. It is time, son, that I tell you about it. May this distressing story teach you to fear the reefs where all the happiness of my life ran aground. (*They sit.*) I was only twenty years old. Your mother was sixteen. That was our misfortune, that inequality from which obstacles are born, with which reasonable parents must oppose the desires of their children. Pauline and I were too young.
SAINT-CLAIR. (*Trembling.*) Pauline… Pauline, father?
VOLSANGE. (*Equally affected, but returning to the story.*) Yes, Pauline. Her name was Pauline. Too young to listen to good advice, we heard nothing but our love. Pauline and I eloped and soon I had the joy of reaping the fruits of our secret marriage. You were born in Madrid where we were hiding, content with a mediocre existence, thinking all we needed was love to survive. Your mother, pregnant a second time, was again about to crown my affection for her when the most hideous of nightmares came to disturb our happiness. One day—its horror will never leave my memory—I had just left your mother. I was only ten feet away from the house. Someone attacked me; someone threw me into a coach. Four days later, I found myself unmercifully imprisoned in a fortress at the French border. There was no news about my family… no news about your mother… or you. Twenty times I thought about succumbing to despair. Two years later, my father finally appeared, overwhelming me with accusations. "The woman who gave birth to you was dead," he told me. "Having that knowledge, you should find less harsh the conditions that I place on your freedom. Here is a marriage contract that must be signed or you must resign yourself to spending the rest of your life here." You imagine my problem. Only one consolation was left for me. I was told that you were alive, that I would see you. I believed everything. I signed. We left.
SAINT-CLAIR. (*In astonishment.*) Father… perhaps they were lying to you!
VOLSANGE. I don't know. We arrived. A month later, I was married. At the end of ten months, I was a widower. A short time

after that, I lost my father. Completely free, I decided to live only for you. My sister, widowed as well, consented to come and share my retirement and to act as your mother. I had no children from my second marriage and you are my only heir. I am on the verge of merging the property I'm leaving you with the richest land in the province. And it's under circumstances like these, my son, that you want my heart to remember all the sadness of my past mistakes. And you want to imitate them and maybe set yourself up for the cruelest of life's misfortunes by marrying a girl you know nothing about? (*Here he rises spiritedly. His sister leaves the loom and all three come together on stage. SAINT-CLAIR stands in the middle.*) My friend, I will never allow it.

SAINT-CLAIR. Very well, Father, you will rob me of my life. You will treat me with the same harshness of which you had been the victim… because nothing in the world will make me give up my darling Henrietta!

VOLSANGE. (*With the greatest distress.*) Henrietta… that was one of your mother's names. Sister… son, I want you to bring those two women to me immediately.

SAINT-CLAIR. (*Frenzied, going out quickly.*) Father. (*He takes VOLSANGE's hands passionately.*) Ah, father.

VOLSANGE. Well, sister, do you still have doubts? Pauline… Henrietta… Do you still have doubts, sister? She was pregnant when I left her.

LORMEUIL. God, I'm trembling. Ah, poor Saint-Clair!

VOLSANGE. (*In the greatest agitation.*) Go, sister, go keep Mr. Valville company. While you're having dinner, I'm going to sort out my thoughts. A thousand conflicting ideas are crowding my head. I need a moment by myself to clear up the mess. Great God Almighty! I wonder what change of events this terrible day will bring! (*They exit, each on a different side of the stage.*)

END OF THE FIRST ACT

ACT TWO

(The frame for the tapestry has been removed. In its place stands a table, next to which a chair is placed. The curtain rises on LAPINEAU and LUCETTE.)

LAPINEAU. Ah! How quickly you run, Lucette. A rabbit couldn't pass you. Tell me. Tell me. I'm going to be on watch tonight. Do you want me to fly the coup?

LUCETTE. Oh! Leave me alone, Lapineau. Look here, I'm not in the mood for jokes. Go away. There's a lot of sadness and a lot of happiness around here. Leave me alone. I need to find Madame de Lormeuil, my mistress. She just sent word that she's waiting to speak to me. Ah! Go away, get out. There are a lot of new developments.

LAPINEAU. Ah! Then that's why I saw our young master looking sad and then a woman who seemed so happy to be with Mr. Volsange and then another young lady who was bawling her eyes out… crying so much that I thought she had lost her father and mother.

LUCETTE. It's exactly the opposite. She's discovered that Mr. Volsange is her father and… didn't I tell you there were a lot of new developments around here?

LAPINEAU. Tell me about them, Lucette. Do I ever keep anything from you? Do I? Just the other day, when my mother cracked a hard nut for me, didn't I come tell you right away?

LUCETTE. Well, my lad, the lady who arrived a little while ago, in spite of her simple appearance, is Mr. Volsange's wife. He had lost her years ago and lo and behold! All of a sudden, he's found her.

LAPINEAU. Give me the details, my dear Lucette, pretty please.

LUCETTE. Can you believe that Mr. Saint-Clair has been in love with the girl for a year now, the girl who came along with Mr. Volsange's wife. And just as he was about to ask his father's permission to marry her, lo and behold! All of a sudden, he discovers that she's his sister.

LAPINEAU. (*Surprised.*) She's Mr. Saint-Clair's sister?

LUCETTE. Yes. The lady named Pauline was the master's first wife. He was told that she had died, so he married somebody else.

This other wife died for certain and lo and behold! He finds his first wife alive with a young lady, his daughter. This concerns our young master since he wanted to marry the young lady.

LAPINEAU. Eh! What did the lady say to be discovered like that so quickly?

LUCETTE. That's what I'm going to tell you. You never listen to me. Imagine yourself in Madrid, where Mr. Volsange had taken the young lady and married her in spite of his father's objections. Madrid… do you know where Madrid is?

LAPINEAU. Eh, yes. It's there on the coast of Italy.

LUCETTE. No, numbskull! It's in Spain. It's obvious that I got better marks in geography than you did. Well, to make a long story short, no sooner had they been married when, lo and behold! They're separated from one another. Mr. Volsange was taken to one place, his son to another, and left to die in misery in Madrid were his wife and little daughter, the same one who's here now crying her eyes out because she's Saint-Clair's sister. You know very well that she can't marry him anymore.

LAPINEAU. So?

LUCETTE. So having fallen on hard times, the mother found a truly charitable woman who brought her to Paris. Since the woman was unable to care for the child as well, the young girl had to stay behind. A gentleman who had run away from France to elope took care of little Henrietta when her mother was taken away. After some time, when the mother, who is really Mr. Volsange's wife, as we discovered today… when she began to feel financially secure, she asked the gentleman to restore her child to her, which he did immediately. And to live with fewer expenses and more peacefully, they both came to this provincial countryside, where they lived close to our master without his knowing it.

LAPINEAU. Why didn't she recognize his name?

LUCETTE. Eh? Really. That's because he changed it. Our master was called Florval in his youth. But he said that name brought him bad luck, so he preferred to go by Volsange, the name of the territory he acquired several years ago.

LAPINEAU. Oh! How bizarre! Miss Lucette, I'm amazed at what you're telling me. How sad for Mr. Saint-Clair, discovering that the girl he wants to marry is his sister!

LUCETTE. Both of them are crying their eyes out. It breaks your heart to see them cry so.

LAPINEAU. Really! I can tell you that I'd be upset, too. They were so cute, the two of them, so well suited for one another. I would see them every day, I did, when I went hunting. Ah! Really, I wish that the happiness I pray to God for every day would fall upon them. Hush. I hear somebody.

LUCETTE. Don't say that I've told you about any of this.

LAPINEAU. Ah! Don't be afraid, Miss Lucette. Really! You're always telling me not to say a word and then I go to my watch, I do. Who do you imagine I talk to? The rabbits? (*He goes out.*)

LUCETTE. (*To VOLSANGE as he enters with PAULINE and HENRIETTA.*) Sir, may I go? I was just talking to Lapineau, who wanted to ask you about tomorrow's hunt. I told him that he was not to speak to you when you were busy.

VOLSANGE. Go to your mistress, my child, she may need you from time to time. Lucette, if people should drop in unexpectedly today, tell them I'm not at home. I absolutely refuse to see anyone today.

LUCETTE. (*Running out.*) Very good, sir, very good. I will not fail.

VOLSANGE. You see, dear girl, why you must help us conquer that young man's impetuousness. I'm afraid that, being excessively sensitive, he may be reluctant to return to the principles that virtue should inspire within him. If my beloved Pauline consents to it and if your heart, Henrietta, is in no way adverse to it, today must see you married to someone else.

HENRIETTA. (*Unsteady, preparing for the hysteria into which she is going to fall.*) Could you have imagined, Father, that your slightest wish would not be my command?

PAULINE. She is at your disposal, Volsange. I know her heart well enough to believe that you need not even question her obedience.

> (*HENRIETTA, overwhelmed by uneasiness, falls sobbing into the chair next to the table.*)

VOLSANGE. Ah! That's what I was afraid of. My happiness was certainly short-lived. (*He goes to HENRIETTA to comfort her.*)

PAULINE. (*Also by HENRIETTA's side.*) Daughter, my beloved Henrietta, pull yourself together. We're only looking out for your welfare.

HENRIETTA. (*With a weak voice, interrupted by tears.*) Ah! Let me die. Your unhappy daughter begs you for nothing but death. Don't try to bring her back to life. She isn't worthy of it seeing that she was able to betray, in a moment, the virtuous feelings that alone made life dear to her. (*After a pause, she gets up energetically.*) What am I saying! I will obey, Father. Forgive a moment of weakness. It's the last vestige of a star-crossed passion. I will learn to stifle it. (*Turning toward PAULINE with a trace of weakness.*) Alas, Mother, yesterday it was not a crime.

PAULINE. And your ignorance excused it. But as of today, it is, my girl.

VOLSANGE. You're going to accuse me of harshness, Henrietta. But the more you are unable to control your feelings, the more you must perceive how important it is to our mutual peace of mind that you take a husband quickly.

HENRIETTA. Command me, father, command me. My weakness will be redeemed at the price of my happiness. I sacrifice my life to you. To whom else should it be given if not to the people who gave it to me? I loved Saint-Clair. I make no secret of it. I loved him as much as I thought I could without committing a crime. The horror of that act, with which I would defile myself if I did not forget him immediately, would be an insurmountable weight upon my soul. I will replace a love most tender with a most reasonable friendship. (*Putting her hand into her father's.*) Here is my hand as a pledge. Dispose of it this very moment. I swear by the heavens, by you, my father, and by that sacred breast which nurtured me, that I will never again oppose your commands. I will give to the husband you choose for me, whoever he may be, this heart as pure as it was before falling in love with Saint-Clair.

VOLSANGE. (*To PAULINE.*) A soul like that was destined to be your daughter's. (*To HENRIETTA.*) I accept your oath, Henrietta. You've seen the man I've chosen for you… Valville, my son's friend.

HENRIETTA. (*With a kind of distress over which she has no control.*) Him, father?

VOLSANGE. He's the one.

HENRIETTA. (*As above.*) Is it also your command, mother?

PAULINE. My beloved daughter, I only ask for what will make you happy. You can be sure that your father wants you to be happy as much as I do.

HENRIETTA. Is there no middle ground between giving up Saint-Clair and marrying Valville?

VOLSANGE. None that will please us more. None that would as surely revive the calm in your soul… and your brother's. And, finally, none that would be a greater triumph for your virtue.

HENRIETTA. Good Lord, why not?

VOLSANGE. Because every other match would take time and under the circumstances, any delay would nourish the public's suspicions.

HENRIETTA. (*With controlled sadness.*) Very well, I will marry him. You have my word.

VOLSANGE. Yes, daughter, but that's not enough… neither for your happiness nor for the happiness of the husband I've chosen for you.

HENRIETTA. (*Firmly.*) What? You want more from me than obedience? Ah! Father, I'll only be a victim…

VOLSANGE. Eh! What do you think your mother and I would be if we thought you were unhappy?

HENRIETTA. Don't force me to do this.

VOLSANGE. What other recourse is there, my dear?

HENRIETTA. One of those sacred asylums.

VOLSANGE. A sad resource that puts neither your reputation nor conscience to rest. The vows that God wants never exist there. The sacrifices that the public demands never exist there. Today, no one is taken in by these forced retreats, the unique fruits of a father's greed or a daughter's dishonor. There, you are crushed by constant remorse and end your miserable life without having had the opportunity of correcting it.

HENRIETTA. (*Firmly.*) I thought it would be better to cry over your mistakes rather than erase them by a lie.

PAULINE. Between these two evils, Henrietta, it still is better to take advantage of mankind than to lie to God.

VOLSANGE. (*Quickly.*) Daughter, all marriages are not the work of love. Rather, they're made up of ties formed by interest and convenience. Little by little, duty triumphs over the estrangement. Logic comes to the aid of the heart and habit puts an end to the matter by lightening the weight of your shackles.

HENRIETTA. (*To her mother.*) Ah! You didn't tell me that one day I would stop taking care of you. Couldn't I simply continue to look after you?

PAULINE. Our circumstances aren't the same as they were, my beloved Henrietta, and that alternative would be less satisfactory than the other. Your miserable situation is beyond compare. We are very sure that you couldn't be guilty, but that's never enough. Eternal bonds must place you above suspicion.

HENRIETTA. It's impossible to bridle slander. If it can't leave the miserable Henrietta alone in her mother's lap, will it spare her more in the arms of a husband?

VOLSANGE. (*Continuing quickly.*) What a difference between them. The suspicion of adultery wrongs the guilty wife and the offended husband equally. The poison of slander is harder to spread around. People will have seen you fulfilling your obligations in other respects. The sacrifices people make in the public eye are hardly ever in vain. Don't worry, after that, you'll be rewarded. People will connect the false allegations of the first crime to the slander of the unjust accusation of the second.

HENRIETTA. So, Father, you've found your child only to sacrifice her to public opinion.

VOLSANGE. Say, rather, to her duty. (*Growing tender.*) Daughter, you're breaking my heart. You promised to obey me.

HENRIETTA. I renew my promise to obey you, but that's all I'm going to promise.

PAULINE. Virtue will accomplish the rest. I add your virtue to the vow you made your father.

VOLSANGE. Seduced by her heart, Henrietta doesn't know what she is capable of doing.

HENRIETTA. (*Firmly.*) Sacrificed by her father, Henrietta only promises obedience.

VOLSANGE. (*Passionately.*) Daughter, beloved daughter... do you want to see me beg? A last effort for your own good, I ask it in the name of all the affection I like to think you feel for me. The first step has been taken or so I believe. Your virtue satisfies me. But the second, beloved Henrietta, can't you at least promise me to work at it? I'm offering you a nice young man... full of wisdom and virtue. Though he had the misfortune of losing his parents when he was very young, they left him the master of a considerable estate and I'm giving you half of mine. Don't make me afraid that I'm only causing you misfortune when I'm only trying to look out for your welfare. (*Holding her against his breast, in tears.*) My child, my Henrietta. Your mother and I are going to prepare Valville for the news. Allow me to nourish at the bottom of my heart the sweet hope that soon I will find in yours something more than submissive obedience.

HENRIETTA. Go, Father. Go and remember that Henrietta will always offer you what sacrifices she can, even at the expense of her miserable life.

(*VOLSANGE goes out. HENRIETTA flies into PAULINE's arms, where she stays for a moment, covered with tears.*)

PAULINE. (*Going out.*) Oh, my child, how you disturb the happiness that I thought I recovered at last!

(*As soon as her parents have gone, she falls into the chair next to the table, holds her head in her hands, and surrenders to despair. Her sobs and sighs are audible. After giving full vent to her sorrow, she speaks.*)

HENRIETTA. (*Alone.*) Unhappy victim of duty and oppression, you are no longer allowed to keep them in balance without committing a crime. Oh, nature, are these the ideas about which the heart cannot be mistaken? If I wronged you in loving Saint-Clair, why did you allow me to love him without remorse? And if I can still love him without wronging you, what is this cruel duty, then, that men say emanates from you? Fatal passion, where did you lead me astray? Sacred laws, forgive me for having doubted your jurisdiction. My mistake is the fruit of that secret voice that people claim should belong to you. Ah, why then, at the moment of my surrender, do I hear myself speaking only of my love? (*She sinks again into misery. SAINT-CLAIR enters very quietly. She*

doesn't see him. He falls to his knees before her a little to the off-stage side. He hears her speak through her tears.) Saint-Clair, Saint-Clair, I will never see you again. Those wonderful moments of love and innocence have disappeared. They're gone forever. (*Hearing these words, he crawls toward her on his knees and utters a soulful cry. HENRIETTA, surprised, cries out.*) What do I see? Oh, heavens!
SAINT-CLAIR. Your beloved, Henrietta. Yes, your beloved at your knees.
HENRIETTA. Oh, God! (*She again falls into a state of complete depression. In tears, SAINT-CLAIR, still on his knees, squeezes her hand. A long silence, after which HENRIETTA continues with all the strength the situation allows her.*) Saint-Clair, we must part.
SAINT-CLAIR. (*Still on his knees.*) Henrietta, do these words come from your lips?
HENRIETTA. Duty and virtue impose their laws upon me. Remember who we are. (*Both of them get up. HENRIETTA rises first.*)
SAINT-CLAIR. To do that, I would have to forget as quickly as you who we were when love alone had fashioned our bonds.
HENRIETTA. Nature's bonds destroy them and I should not recall any others.
SAINT-CLAIR. (*Angrily.*) Very well! Enjoy the prize of your inflexible virtue by yourself and no longer delay the consequences of my despair. (*He starts to go out.*)
HENRIETTA. (*Stopping him.*) Alas, what are you going to do?
SAINT-CLAIR. Deprive you of a hideous sight.
HENRIETTA. (*Continuing to stop him.*) Stop, unfortunate man, yield to me. You must. I cannot be your wife, but let's not ruin the days to which friendship still leaves me a claim. Saint-Clair, we will love one another like two friends. I will no longer call you my beloved, but you will be my brother. You will no longer call me darling or dearest, like you used to enjoy doing so often, but you will call me your sister… your dear sister. All the tenderness of your passion can be wrapped up in this sacred bond which will join us for the rest of our lives. All that my passion can allow itself without committing a crime will express itself in the sweet name of brother that I will call you thousands of times. (*She weeps.*)

SAINT-CLAIR. (*Breathing heavily.*) No, you're not my sister. Remember when you were young. Carefully observe your mother's account. She lost sight of you for eight years. During this interval, you were in the hands of St. Fard, my father's companion in misfortune. At the end of this period, a child was sent to Pauline, a child she had not seen since infancy. Who can say that it's her own? Put together all these circumstances with the voice that speaks in the depths of our hearts… with the voice whose whisper is infallible and which never caused us to have anything to do with regret. No, I tell you. No, you are not my sister.

HENRIETTA. You're deluding yourself!

SAINT-CLAIR. You're not, I tell you. Stop it, Henrietta. Stop believing that we're united by bonds other than our love. Before this fatal discovery, did you feel any distress in calling me your beloved? Will you plead ignorance? Ah! Does the voice of nature change like our opinions? And can you convince me that nature wasn't instilled in our hearts yesterday as much as it is today? Let us yield to its inspiration rather than to things people tell us. The events that have produced such a serious change could be false. Nature never takes advantage of us. Let us listen only to nature, Henrietta, and let us flee a wretched country where people assume the right to interpret the voice differently than the way it speaks to us. Say the word. Everything is ready.

HENRIETTA. What are you suggesting?

SAINT-CLAIR. That you come with me to the ends of the earth… that we forget the titles we've known for only a day and which perhaps never existed. Henrietta, all laws are not the same. All countries are not alike. What does it matter where we live as long as your beloved takes you there and lives for you alone. If stricter ties frighten you and those fears cannot be conquered, I will respect them. I swear to you. We will live as pure in Asia as in Europe and there I will be certain, at least, that you will be mine alone and that my life can be dedicated to you without regret.

HENRIETTA. (*Trembling.*) Without regret!

SAINT-CLAIR. (*Firmly.*) Yes, without regret. Prejudice is what causes it. It no longer exists if our judgment is mistaken.

HENRIETTA. And if it isn't mistaken?

SAINT-CLAIR. I will consider you my sister as much as you believe it yourself.

HENRIETTA. What danger to virtue... what terrible anguish for love! To live forever between crime and destitution! Ah, Saint-Clair, either you would cease to love me or soon make me as guilty as yourself. Meanwhile, nothing would cast a new light on our frightening situation. We would only have uncertainty— doubts— to appease our regrets. Little by little, the strength of love, the only force behind these imaginary doubts, would diminish into a fear of the crime. Finally, we would only see the horror of it. Could you endure that, Saint-Clair? No. Your soul is as sensitive to virtue as mine. You would accuse me of weakness... I would curse your seducing me... and we would die from despair and regret, criminals engulfed by hate.

SAINT-CLAIR. Never, never!

HENRIETTA. (*Continuing energetically.*) Ah, I know you better than you know yourself. Let us have more strength and courage. It is a lot less frightening to separate today than to live as you propose. Go, my friend. The war is beginning. Go seek the glory that awaits you. It offers consolations for an unhappy love. I will never be insensitive to your success. You will keep me informed, Saint-Clair. That will continue to please the heart of your unfortunate beloved. Go, serve your country. Go merit a wife much worthier than I to enjoy the good things in life. (*She rushes into SAINT-CLAIR's open arms. They are both in tears.*) God does not want it, my friend. We were not born for one another. Let us respect nature's laws. (*In tears.*) Yes, you will inform me of your prosperity, my friend. It will soothe my misery. From now on, in you alone will I place the little bit of happiness I can hope for in the world... and heaven, which has prepared me in my youth for such a cruel future, at least cannot, in separating us, take from me the delightful pleasure of enjoying your good fortune.

SAINT-CLAIR. (*Carried away.*) Ah! Can you think that happiness can exist for me when I won't have you? Henrietta, come with me... or my death is certain. Come with me, Henrietta!

HENRIETTA. What do you want?

SAINT-CLAIR. I want you to love me!

HENRIETTA. I cannot at the expense of honor and virtue. I cannot when it results in a crime.

SAINT-CLAIR. (*Still carried away.*) Our love is more certain than the trifling crime you object to. Do as I do and only listen to love.

HENRIETTA. Your ideas disgust me.

SAINT-CLAIR. And your blind faith drives me to despair. Yes, I'll kill myself before your very eyes if you do not accept my proposal… and your gloomy virtue continues to make you prefer idle speculation to the voices of our hearts.

HENRIETTA. (*Passionately and firmly.*) I can no longer listen to you. Ah, Saint-Clair, I thought you were more sensitive than that. Is this what you call loving? You should be ashamed of your proposals. Return to your senses. Love has led you astray. Besides, you should understand the complete extent of our misfortunes. I am already spoken for.

SAINT-CLAIR. What's this I hear? Has your hand been offered in marriage?

HENRIETTA. Yes. My hand, but not my heart.

SAINT-CLAIR. To Valville, I suppose?

HENRIETTA. I'm being sacrificed to him, yes.

SAINT-CLAIR. (*With concentrated resentment.*) Good Lord! Why invest so much love when the heart is filled with lies!

HENRIETTA. What can you be thinking? That you have any rights? Don't you know that they've all disappeared because of the ties that bind us?

SAINT-CLAIR. (*In a violent state.*) How you love to remind me of them… and how you resist every possibility of their being false. It's over and there's no hope for me. (*Pulling himself together.*) I consent to your marriage, Henrietta. You couldn't wait to show those signs of slavery and obedience. Goodbye. It's time for us to part. Ah! I'm going to follow your advice.

HENRIETTA. (*Trying to stop him.*) Where are you going? Your eyes make me tremble. What are you planning, you unfortunate man?

SAINT-CLAIR. (*Pushing her away, overwhelmed by anger.*) My revenge! Let me go. I don't know myself anymore. All I recognize is my misfortune and my despair. Yes, I'm going to tear you from my heart. I will rip you out of it, cruel woman… but you will see that, tearing my heart to pieces with my hands, I will make the blood that I detest gush out all over you since it can join us in a way that's different from the ties of love. I will extinguish the bridal torches that burn for you with my blood. But don't think that my anger will spare your detestable husband. No. I will present you with that monster covered with blood and our bodies dying at your feet will create the altar where you will waste your faithlessness. It will be there, if he survives me, that you will betray our oaths. Let me go. Let me go, I tell you. It's a crime for me to delay. I must hasten to avenge myself.

(Unable to stop him, HENRIETTA gets in front of him. She throws herself on the ground and raises her arms to the sky to form a kind human barricade with her body.)

HENRIETTA. (*In the position described above.*) Look here! Here's your first victim. Strike this breast before you go any farther.

SAINT-CLAIR. (*He stops and looks at her. He is filled with emotion, begins to cry, and lifts her up.*) Henrietta, why have you betrayed me?

HENRIETTA. I did not betray you. The oaths made to my lover no longer exist because they were made to my brother. My despair is as great as yours. You know that perfectly well, cruel man. You have seen my tears flowing down my cheeks. Don't take advantage of my weakness any longer. (*As forcefully as possible.*) I do not love the man I'm destined to marry. I will never love him. See the shameful admission you've pulled out of me. It's the last victory you will have over me. It is time for sense to overcome a passion I renounce… a love I detest because it could be a crime. If you follow me… you will never see me again for the rest of your life. (*She goes out.*)

SAINT-CLAIR. (*Alone, distracted, wanders about the stage in a fury.*) Henrietta. Henrietta. She walked out on me. She doesn't want to see me anymore. Merciful heaven and you let me live! She's going to become Valville's wife and all of nature does not oppose it. I will see her in the arms of another man! Unmerciful God, who consents to this faithlessness, crush me if it succeeds, devour me if I allow it to happen. (*He starts to go out and, without being aware of it, lands in his father's arms.*)

SAINT-CLAIR. (*Still distracted.*) Father, is that you? Tear my life away. May it be to your hands that I owe this last duty. Why do you hesitate, Father? I am a monster, unworthy of life. Yes, I am guilty and I want to be. You're the one who must punish me. I don't deserve any mercy and I don't want any. You're the one, cruel father, who's responsible for my despair. She's left me. She told me that she hated me. I deserve it because I love her and will love her for the rest of my life. Well, aren't you going to stab me!
VOLSANGE. Oh, unfortunate boy. Come to your senses!
SAINT-CLAIR. No, no, I will love her until I breathe my last sigh. I want to fall to her feet. I want to show her that I have as much courage as she has. (*He throws himself into the chair next to the table. He is in the depths of sorrow.*)
LORMEUIL. (*Approaching SAINT-CLAIR.*) Oh, my friend, revive those feelings in your soul, which I always knew that you possessed. Recall them at this terrible moment when you must sacrifice everything to virtue.
SAINT-CLAIR. (*Beside himself.*) I don't recognize it any more. I no longer recognize duty, nor parents, nor laws, nor restrictions, nor nature. I know nothing anymore but my own despair and all I want to do is die. (*Seeing VALVILLE, he goes to him in a fury.*) What are you doing here, sir? Have you come to insult my sorrow? There's only one dishonest man around here capable of enjoying the state you find me in. Valville, do you know what I mean?
VALVILLE. I know nothing, Saint-Clair, but my friendship for you and I join with everyone who is dear to you to beg you to calm down. Follow me. Come see the state to which you've reduced a sister who loves you, but whom you offend.
SAINT-CLAIR. (*Shaking off VALVILLE, who tries to take his hand.*) Yes, I'll follow you. But do you know under what conditions? Your tricks will not deceive me. I want to be avenged!
VOLSANGE. (*To VALVILLE and MADAME DE LORMEUIL.*) Friends, don't abandon him in this terrible situation. Almighty God, did you make me a father only to experience sorrow?

END OF THE SECOND ACT

ACT THREE

LORMEUIL. I applaud your prudence, Valville. The true greatness of soul consists less in repelling injuries than in supporting, with a cool head, the inconsiderate outbursts of a man on the edge of despair. You have won the respect of everyone in the family by your conduct and you will become an even closer friend to Saint-Clair as soon as his senses calm his distracted soul.

VALVILLE. A gallant man can only be wounded by one who attacks him directly. Saint-Clair never knew what he was doing. I know him well enough to be sure that before long, he'll make up for his offences. From then on, he'll behave himself and all will be forgotten. His situation troubles me! Truly, Madame, I find that this business has proceeded too quickly. The wound is still too fresh and Mr. Volsange doesn't seem to have acted as wisely as he could have in all of this.

LORMEUIL. But, Valville, it was necessary to have acted quickly. Perhaps now things will move more slowly since it appears that my brother has decided that his son will go into the army. Henrietta will be given the time to return to her old self so that you can win her affection gradually.

VALVILLE. No, Madame. Mr. Volsange seemed very determined to conclude the matter tonight. I will not hide the fact that it took all the respect and affection that I have for your family to agree to such a setup. You will admit that this is all happening for me under the worst conditions.

LORMEUIL. I admit it. But my niece seems reasonable. I believe she has a good soul and I don't doubt that in time you will win her heart... and that you will deserve as many rights... (*VALVILLE makes a gesture indicating doubt.*) Sir, why should you feel an aversion to this marriage?

VALVILLE. It is useless, Madame, to try to hide the fact that this could be called a marriage of convenience in every respect... even if I venture to admit to you...

LORMEUIL. Could it be that you have another engagement?

VALVILLE. None, Madame. But you know the secret impulses of the heart. They're irresistible... they're fickle. Sometimes they carry us passionately toward an object that often isn't the least bit attractive. Sometimes they push us away, in spite of ourselves, from someone who ought to inspire eternal vows. How do you make sense out of these strange things? Alas, madame, the heart of man is a mystery to which nature alone has the key.

LORMEUIL. Here, sir, the situation explains it all. You see a young woman in love… a jealous friend who considers himself betrayed… resentment… anxiety… sadness… despair. Those are the causes of the situation in which you find yourself. But Henrietta will return to her senses and I find it impossible to believe that her second impulses won't belong to you entirely. You're the same age… with a similar fortune. It seems to me you're of the same mind. No doubt about it, Valville, Henrietta will make you happy. Now it's your responsibility to use every gift you have to bring her heart back to life. If you encounter certain obstacles, your victory will only be greater. You know, sir, love tests us with trouble. If we endure, it captivates us and it coyly entertains itself by only offering its pleasures to those who know how to confront its difficulties. So what did my niece say to you when you had the chance to speak to her?

VALVILLE. That she was going to obey, Madame… that she respected me, but doubted that she could ever feel anything more than that.

LORMEUIL. And you undoubtedly used all the charm and passion you know to persuade her that you would soon become worthy of leading her to something more pleasing to you.

VALVILLE. Not a word, Madame. I wanted to say all of those things, but I felt the words die on my lips. I looked at Henrietta. I found her beautiful… but I didn't feel anything. She acted as if she was surprised by my silence and what was especially unusual, she seemed to be the most grateful person in the world.

LORMEUIL. So, sir?

VALVILLE. Well, Madame, I'll marry her. I'll sacrifice myself for the happiness of a friend, for the good of all, for the peace of a family that is dear to me and which I totally respect. I expect that your nephew will not delay in making an appearance. I expect that on the eve of his departure, you will have some advice to give him. I don't want to find myself in a situation where my presence would still not be very pleasant to him. (*He exits.*)

LORMEUIL. (*Alone.*) What bizarre behavior in the quirks of fate! Two young people who seem to be made for each other are frightened by the idea of marriage; two others who adore one another, but whose blood-ties happen to interrupt their ecstasy. There's something very unusual in all of this. Really, it would almost make me believe in predestination! *(Enter Saint-Clair in a military uniform, but without a sword or cap.)*

LORMEUIL. Dressed to leave for the army, Saint-Clair! I like seeing you in such a haste to obey.

SAINT-CLAIR. It's certainly as much the result of my despair as my obedience. Honor opens up to me a career where, before long, I'll bury both my mistakes and my sorrows. I will guarantee the peace of the entire household. Henrietta will be married, Valville will be happy, my father will be calm. Isn't that all that matters, Madame?

LORMEUIL. Oh, wretched young man, your heart has yet to be where I would like it to be.

SAINT-CLAIR. It will never be there, Madame. You can't make demands of nature.

LORMEUIL. Do you dare to call upon nature when you have offended it so deeply?

SAINT-CLAIR. Who? Me, Madame? Offend nature? And what created the feeling that consumes me, if it wasn't nature? Where do I get these irresistible urges that draw me, against my will, to that cherished object… feelings that I will surrender only in death? Ah! If I offended nature, would this heart, the work of its hands, be enflamed with such a love that nothing will extinguish? Beside the most holy thoughts in my heart would I find the urge to adore Henrietta? Vainly will you quote me all the fallacies with which you fight the inclinations of nature. What I know… what I feel is that nature is just. It is the only light we have in the chaos of circumstances where fortune tosses us… and it is never its first impulse that lies to us.

LORMEUIL. Your love is leading you astray, Saint-Clair. It is preventing you from being able to see the justice of these holy impulses that you only interpret in terms of your foolish passion.

Where can this miserable inclination lead you? What are you hoping for? Where can you go for help? Doesn't the entire universe condemn you? Aren't all the laws against you?

SAINT-CLAIR. The law of my heart will endure.

LORMEUIL. What a help that is! When we've been deceived by our heart, we soon find it filled only with remorse and we end up crying for the rest of our lives over the fatal mistake of a single day. Believe me, Saint-Clair. Stop making Henrietta the victim of this mistake any longer if you don't want her to hate you. The first punishment of the offender is always the hatred of his accomplices. It appears that virtue seeks to avenge itself by the same means a person dared to use against it.

SAINT-CLAIR. (*For the rest of the scene he appears angry.*) Well, what do you want? I'm leaving and giving up Henrietta.

LORMEUIL. You owe her a better example of virtue. You must make her forget your love. You must encourage her marriage to your friend and be pleased with it.

SAINT-CLAIR. Me? I'm supposed to serve the happiness of a rival?

LORMEUIL. Couldn't you also consider him your sister's husband?

SAINT-CLAIR. My sister... my sister...

LORMEUIL. Isn't she?

SAINT-CLAIR. (*Abruptly.*) I don't know anything about it. That's what I was told, but I doubt it. They assured me... but I don't know.

LORMEUIL. That's how delusion always finds nourishment within itself. What idle fancy! Get rid of it, my friend. It will only continue your misfortunes and your offences. I'll leave you to ponder this. Think about your duty. Think about hurrying your departure, so unfortunately necessary to everyone's peace of mind. (*She exits.*)

SAINT-CLAIR. (*Alone.*) Yes, I will hurry this departure so necessary to everyone's peace of mind... and I will hurry it in the hope of finding certain death. Alas, she alone could put an end to such deadly misfortunes. What a difference a single day has made in my life! Yesterday, I thought I had happiness within my grasp and here I am today, certain that I'll never be happy again. God, here she is. What misery! I cannot control myself. (*He runs up to HENRIETTA, who is passing through the room to get to another. As soon as she sees him, she tries to flee.*)

SAINT-CLAIR. (*Delirious with misguided love.*) Henrietta, your virtuous heart should not object to this one last meeting. Grant it to me without fear. You will only see good judgment in me. And the love that displeases you, the love that I must not have anymore... I will lock it up in my heart so well that you will not catch sight of its slightest sparks. I must imitate your courage, Henrietta, and that fierce virtue which forces you to betray a lover whose only mistake is having adored you. Yes. I must imitate whatever force is necessary to suppress this passion which will lead me to the grave at whatever point it might explode against my will. I must not tell you that I love you... that I adore you and that I'm going to die for you. No, I must not say that to you and I will never say it again.

HENRIETTA. (*With continued interest.*) Are you leaving tonight, Saint-Clair?

SAINT-CLAIR. That won't be soon enough for you. Isn't that right, miss? You would prefer me to go immediately. Ah! But what does it matter since I don't love you anymore? It seems to me that is all that is necessary for your happiness. And as soon as the eternal impression you've made in the depths of my heart no longer exists... as soon as that love which continues to smolder is extinguished forever, am I right in thinking that there's nothing left you want?

HENRIETTA. (*To herself.*) How misfortune makes him unfair. (*Aloud to SAINT-CLAIR.*) Ah! My friend, I only want to see you at peace with yourself.

SAINT-CLAIR. (*Still contained, although in the greatest distress.*) Oh! I'm at peace. I've never been so calm. What could possibly disturb me? I'm leaving you happy. (*HENRIETTA sighs.*) That's all that I wanted. I only ever wanted you to be happy. That's right, my beloved Henrietta. When I was in love with you, I was trying to make you happy. My feelings for you were so passionate, so tender. And even though I no longer love you, I'm still trying to make you happy. Not being terribly successful at it, I want someone else to succeed at least. The thought of this, which, according to you, is very sweet, enables me to be content and to go away calm.

HENRIETTA. Not as much as I'd like!

SAINT-CLAIR. (*With a little less restraint.*) How do you want me to behave? Do you want me to say that I hate you like you said to me a little while ago? I can imitate your courage, but I will never repeat your insults. In a word, I'm leaving, miss. There now, you're free of that eternal trouble of trying to avoid me. From now on, I'm the one who's going to flee from you. And as I must restore peace to your soul by erasing the memory of our old mistakes I want to convince you of my indifference… to assure you that all that happened between us… before we became what people say we are… was only out of politeness, pure and simple.

HENRIETTA. (*A bit annoyed, though in spite of herself.*) Yes… oh, that's easy to believe!

SAINT-CLAIR. You believe it, don't you, miss? Yes… politeness, like we're supposed to treat all the girls.

HENRIETTA. (*Still annoyed.*) All the girls?

SAINT-CLAIR. Yes, but it isn't the least bit real. There's not even the semblance of real feeling with which nature would have stained our hearts. Along those lines, miss, not only do I not love you anymore, I never loved you at all. (*HENRIETTA turns to hide her tears. SAINT-CLAIR, fumbling through his pockets to find the letters of which he is going to speak, does not see her turn away.*) Look! Here are your letters… promises and other trifles for a moment's entertainment. I return them all to you. (*He offers them to her very reluctantly, dying of fear that she will take them.*)

HENRIETTA. (*Moved and in such a way not to show her face, which is still filled with tears.*) I will take them when I return yours. I don't have them here with me.

SAINT-CLAIR. (*Putting the letters back in his pockets very quickly.*) Well, yes. Or we'll each burn them on our own. Since I will not see you again. Oh, no! I will not see you again. This conversation is the last one of my life.

HENRIETTA. (*Restraining herself with the greatest difficulty.*) The last?

SAINT-CLAIR. Yes, the last. I'm exposing myself to certain danger and I will not escape it.

HENRIETTA. (*In the most frightening state, interrupted by her tears.*) Do you believe that there is no longer anyone who could care about you?

SAINT-CLAIR. I think that the only one who cared about me dearly either no longer cares or doesn't want to.

HENRIETTA. (*As above.*) Oh, God!

SAINT-CLAIR. (*In a perpetually contained delirium.*) They say the wedding is set for tonight, miss. Yes, they've sent for the notary. Oh! I know all about it. So tomorrow, you'll be Valville's wife and I'll disappear. Will you write to me, Henrietta? Don't you always want me to be your friend, your confidant? Those are a brother's rights. You will entrust them to me, Henrietta, you promised. How I will love those letters. I'll kiss them thousands of times. They'll be soaked with my tears. Not from love… oh, I have no more love! But since you will let me know in the letters how happy you are, that feeling of happiness will pass into my soul. And then the handwriting… the letters written by so sweet a hand. That will recall the old days when you used to write or speak of happiness directed toward me. You told me then that I was the one who made you happy. When I see the same words used to express feelings in which I have no part, I will perhaps feel a little sad… because friendship is as sensitive as love… but it's very different. If there's a battle, I'll write you about it. Yes, I'll write you. And if I'm killed, I will not send you my heart like Coucy[43] did to Gabrielle. No. I won't send it to you… I'll leave my heart on deposit in yours… but my last letter will be written in blood.

HENRIETTA. (*Unable to contain herself any longer, surrendering to all the frenzy of her passion and filled with confusion, she speaks in a low and serious voice throughout the rest of the scene.*) Say no more, cruel man, say no more. I can no longer sustain the condition your injustice forces upon me. Listen to me. Is your soul as strong, as courageous as mine?

SAINT-CLAIR. Do you doubt it?

HENRIETTA. I'm going to shock you, my friend.

SAINT-CLAIR. You can't if you're suggesting that we reunite.

---

[43] Le Châtelain de Coucy, a twelfth-century trouvère, whose heart was sent to his lover, Lady Fayel, who ate it at the command of her jealous husband.

HENRIETTA. Yes, but an eternal reunion. Answer me. Do you have the courage to undertake it?

SAINT-CLAIR. I understand. It's a horrible idea… worthy of the terrifying situation to which the barbarians have reduced us.

HENRIETTA. But, oh, my friend, can we offend the Supreme Being? I feel guilty already.

SAINT-CLAIR. Crime alone brings remorse and it's no crime at all to take the victim away from the executioner who's about to slay her.

HENRIETTA. If one of the two survived the other… if poorly aimed blows… oh! My friend, that moment would be frightening for the one who would be spared death.

SAINT-CLAIR. (*Bewildered.*) Guns. We'll agree on the signal. Don't be afraid. We'll die together.

HENRIETTA. What deadly effects of despair!

SAINT-CLAIR. (*Spoken at the same time.*) What holy resolutions of love!

HENRIETTA. Let's separate. At six thirty, in the forest next to the old oak tree, where you carved our initials…

SAINT-CLAIR. Good Lord, what a moment!

HENRIETTA. That's where we'll die.

SAINT-CLAIR. We have no other choice.

HENRIETTA. All the others are unlawful. That one alone…

SAINT-CLAIR. Is it as simple in your eyes as it is in mine?

HENRIETTA. Yes. Love, virtue, misfortune are forcing us to do it. It isn't wrong to kill yourself when it's only possible to live in misery or commit a crime.

SAINT-CLAIR. I fly to await you at the appointed place.

HENRIETTA. Ah! Saint-Clair, how different is this from what we used to do long ago under the same tree.

SAINT-CLAIR. We have to leave the house without a sound. People are watching us. We must escape their notice.

HENRIETTA. (*Cutting in quickly.*) We must escape life, Saint-Clair. Life, since it only brings us misfortune.

END OF THE THIRD ACT

ACT FOUR

(A forest next to the castle. An old oak tree stands at the front of a group of trees, right. The growth of trees, left, is somewhat thicker. Night is approaching slowly.)

LAPINEAU. (*Alone. Standing watch.*) Oh! I'm freezing. I've been here for three hours without catching anything. I get them right in my sights, but when I'm about to pull the trigger, there they go! They escape as if they suspected something. There's a good reason to freeze in this business. Really! My fingers are all numb. (*He gets up.*) Let's go take a look in the Blangis[44] forest to see if we can find some big animal. The proverb says: Seek and ye shall find. Nothing ventured, nothing gained. (*He goes out and takes his place at the watch. Enter Henrietta and Saint-Clair. Lapineau is out of sight, but at the watch close by.*)

SAINT-CLAIR. Henrietta, here it is. Here's the tree where we swore to love one another until our last breath.

HENRIETTA. Well, let it receive our last breath and we will not have betrayed our vows.

SAINT-CLAIR. Heavens! I will shorten your life! No! Let me die alone, Henrietta. It's the only favor I beg at your feet. The uselessness of an individual on earth excuses the plans he makes against himself. Henrietta, this way I can commit suicide without committing a crime. What good will I be to the world when I no longer possess you? Once I've lost you, could there be a duty I might fulfill? Could there be a pleasure I might enjoy? But you, beloved friend, you. How important are your virtues still to the world! In the name of all that is dearest to you, allow me to fulfill my destiny alone. It's the last sign of love. It's the most passionate expression that I dare to hope from you.

HENRIETTA. Man without courage and strength, did I come here to witness your sorrows? What happens to the virtues of which you think me capable when you're no longer either the cause or the object of them? Well, if you don't think your hand is steady enough to cut down your lover's hopeless life, let a signal, as you were saying, indicate the time of our mutual end. Death could take us together. Each of us could kill himself. There's a chapel dedicated to the Supreme Being in this forest. It's the

---

[44] The Duc de Blangis is a character in Sade's *The 120 Days of Sodom*.

custom at seven o'clock to warn men to collect their thoughts by ringing a mournful bell. Let the ninth ring be our signal. At the tenth, we will no longer exist.
SAINT-CLAIR. (*Offering her his hand.*) I accept. (*Both of them fall silent for a moment. They seem to be waiting for the hour to strike.*)
HENRIETTA. Does that cruel moment approaching us frighten you?
SAINT-CLAIR. It would frighten me less if I were dying alone.
HENRIETTA. Could you die with a clear conscience knowing about the restraints under which I would be forced to live if I lost you?
SAINT-CLAIR. That thought would certainly be horrible, but you would be alive and I would find consolation.
HENRIETTA. Ah! Saint-Clair, the death we are both embracing isn't as frightening as you think. My decisions have confirmed all of my intentions. I see death with a calm eye, full of hope in the goodness of God. I am far from considering Him a severe or dangerous judge. He has seen our misfortunes on earth. He can't blame us for wanting to end them. We are going to be reunited in Him, my friend. Reunited forever. Only in the eyes of a criminal is death a terrible thing. His guilt makes it seem frightening to him. But why should a virtuous man fear it since it takes away his sorrows and unites him with his creator?
SAINT-CLAIR. (*After a silence.*) Thus, in a few minutes, there will be nothing left of us except misshapen masses, devoid of feeling.
HENRIETTA. Oh! My friend, our love is eternal like our soul. Some deadly ties made that love a crime. Death rescues us. That inextinguishable feeling is purified and from then on, we can give way to it without committing a crime.
SAINT-CLAIR. (*Seeing night gradually cover the forest.*) The hour is ready to strike. When we hear the fatal bell, the shades of night will have covered the tops of the trees. It always happens this time of year. We'll hardly be able to see them. We'll never again see the star that just disappeared behind the trees. This is the last day its rays will shine on us. Take your lover in your arms, Henrietta. Swear that you'll love him… even after death.

HENRIETTA. Ah, as guilty as this oath might be, I take it without trembling on your heart. (*She embraces him.*) It's beating fast, Saint-Clair. You're trembling. Are you afraid of dying?

SAINT-CLAIR. I'd rather live to hold you.

HENRIETTA. Die then, since that is impossible.

SAINT-CLAIR. Thus these bloody hides will become the prey of the forest animals. Not even a single tomb will be able to shelter our ashes!

HENRIETTA. I'm going to write down a few words in my diary. It will rest on my breast. Will whoever finds it be able to excuse himself from carrying out our last wishes? (*She writes.*) Read what I'm writing.

SAINT-CLAIR. (*Reading.*) "Please bury the remains of two lovers, deprived of life, who, joined together by nature, were unable to be united by love."

> (*Both fall into each other's arms and wait for the signal. The clock strikes. They prepare their guns. At the third ring, the following scene opens and must proceed very quickly since the characters in the scene have to stop the suicides by the ninth ring.*)

LAPINEAU. (*Comes out of the brushwood opposite the two lovers and meets the TRAVELER, who is travelling along a path in the forest. To the TRAVELER.*) Oh, just heavens! Help me prevent the deaths of those two unfortunate young people. Let's separate them. Sir, let's separate them.

TRAVELER. (*About to do what LAPINEAU describes.*) What the devil's going on here?

SAINT-CLAIR. (*Distracted.*) Leave us alone. Leave us alone or you yourselves…

LAPINEAU. (*Quickly.*) Stop them, I tell you, stop them! I'm going to tell everybody at the castle. (*He exits quickly.*)

HENRIETTA. (*Very sharply.*) Whoever you are, go away and stop trying to save two unfortunates whose last resort is death.

TRAVELER. (*Taking them by the arms.*) Help me first, both of you… and the kindness of that action, perhaps reconciling you to life, will teach you to cherish an existence that can grow more beautiful with good deeds. I am poor… lost. Help me. Guide me. Heaven will reward you.

HENRIETTA. (*Quickly.*) Let us postpone our plans for a moment. Nothing will prevent their fulfillment, but a delay is necessary for us to help this wretched man.

SAINT-CLAIR. (*A little calmer.*) Who are you and what do you want from us?

TRAVELER. I'm a father deserted by my wife and children. A long voyage just exhausted my feeble resources. My needs are pressing. Guide me. Lead me to your house, my friends. I repeat, kindness is connected to life. I will tell you about my misfortunes. They will be of interest to you. You will tell me yours. You'll listen to my advice. My age and experience will make you respect what I say. Come, I tell you, dry those unhappy tears and you will no longer think about dying.

SAINT-CLAIR. He's right, Henrietta. We must help him. We must make him happy... and not die until we've dried his tears. (*They all exit.*)

END OF THE FOURTH ACT

ACT FIVE

(*MR. VOLSANGE's drawing room.*)

LAPINEAU. (*Running, totally distracted.*) Sir, sir. Sir, your son, Miss Henrietta, they were there in the woods. I saw them, sir, I saw them. They were going to kill themselves, I tell you. Really, sir, I saw them...

VOLSANGE. What are you saying? Are you crazy? Have you lost your head?

LAPINEAU. It's really more like they've taken it, sir, seeing that I tell you they were trying to kill themselves. If it hadn't been for me and a traveler who was passing by... really a decent man... well, sir, I tell you, if it hadn't been for us... me and this gentleman... your son and Miss Henrietta would be done for.

VOLSANGE. My friend, you must be exaggerating. (*He rings. A servant appears.*) Dubois, call my son. Tell him I insist on speaking to him. (*Seeing MADAME DE LORMEUIL enter.*) Ah! Sister, can you explain to me what's going on? Those wretched children will not give me a moment's rest. Leave, Lapineau. If Saint-Clair appears, send him to me immediately.

LAPINEAU. I'm going. I'm running, sir. I'd rather go find them for you in the other world than not send them to you immediately. Ah! I remember where I left them.

LORMEUIL. Don't worry in the least about your son, brother. He just returned with Henrietta and a lost traveler they met during their walk in the woods. The man must be an acquaintance of Valville's because they're talking together with a great deal of interest.

VOLSANGE. Ah, good, you set my mind at rest, sister. That imbecile got me worried. I hope the two of them are finally calmed down.

LORMEUIL. They ought to be, brother. Sense always resumes control of honest and sensitive souls. Really, it's Valville's situation that worries me the most now.

VOLSANGE. Indeed, I don't see him getting ready for this wedding as eagerly as I would have liked.

LORMEUIL. All I still see is hesitation.

VOLSANGE. It will come, sister. They are too deserving of one another for love and happiness not to be added to their gifts.

(Enter Henrietta, Saint-Clair, and Pauline.)

VOLSANGE. (*To the two young people he sees enter.*) Ah! My son. Henrietta. I am very happy to see you reunited. Who is this stranger they say you met in the forest?

SAINT-CLAIR. (*Disturbed.*) I don't know, father. Undoubtedly, Valville knows him. The two of them are having a heated discussion. The man's misfortunes are very peculiar.

VOLSANGE. Good, good, we'll hear all about that. Let's get down to business. We have to lay out the terms of the contract. I am very happy to see you calmer, son. Valville doesn't want to sign unless you're happy. He's become sensitive. So you'll sign. You'll embrace him. You'll hug your sister, your mother, your aunt, and myself. We'll all dine together and you'll leave tonight. The weather's good. How long will it take you to get the camp? Six days, isn't it?

SAINT-CLAIR. At least, Father.

LORMEUIL. Go on, go on, young hero. Go collect your laurels and then return to the care of your family where you will always find friends.

VOLSANGE. I want him to be made a colonel by the end of the war. Still, don't go and get yourself killed like an idiot.

SAINT-CLAIR. I promise I'll use my head as much as I can.

HENRIETTA. (*Aside.*) What a terrible moment!

PAULINE. Calm yourself, dear Henrietta.

VOLSANGE. Not with carelessness, but enthusiasm… not with false pride, but real bravery. Go to battle without fear. Laugh at every danger in the service of your country. Seek only honor in battle. Those are the laws written in the heart of every Frenchman and the only advice I give you.

PAULINE. (*To SAINT-CLAIR.*) Don't be sad on the wedding day, my son. The stranger here wouldn't know what it meant.

VOLSANGE. (*Continuing quickly.*) I'm grateful for his return to virtue. I was expecting it. I'm very happy to see that it filled him full of courage and strength.

SAINT-CLAIR. (*Growing impatient.*) Do you want me to go see what's keeping the traveler, Father?

VOLSANGE. No, no, stay, my friend. He's giving his regards to my son-in-law.

SAINT-CLAIR. I hear them.

VALVILLE. (*Leading the stranger by the hand and introducing him to MR. VOLSANGE.*) Here is a witness more necessary than you can imagine to the alliance we are about to contract. This is my father, sir. The happiest and most unusual events have just happened to me.

VOLSANGE. (*Amazed.*) Your father!

TRAVELER. Yes, sir. (*Seeing PAULINE.*) Madam, excuse me. Your face recalls to my soul memories as sad as they are sweet. Wasn't it in Madrid? There's no doubt about it. It's Pauline!

PAULINE. St. Fard, have I found you again?

ST. FARD. Yes, Madame, after much hardship. (*Noticing HENRIETTA's concern.*) What do I see? Is this the bride destined for my son?

PAULINE. Yes, she's my daughter… and we are very happy.

ST. FARD. (*Very quickly.*) Heavens! What are you doing?

SAINT-CLAIR. (*Together with HENRIETTA.*) What distress! I'm not myself anymore.

ST. FARD. (*Without hearing the reply.*) Ah, Madame, will you forgive the guilty mistake the tenderness of a wretched father has cast upon your sensitive soul? Henrietta isn't your daughter.

SAINT-CLAIR. (*Beside himself; together with HENRIETTA.*) Ah, I knew it! Good Lord!

ST. FARD. Henrietta, my beloved Henrietta, you are my daughter. (*He extends his arms toward her; HENRIETTA casts herself into them instinctively.*) After losing so tender a mother, have you any feelings left in your soul for a father who only deceived you for your own good?

SAINT-CLAIR. (*Still beside himself; to MR. VOLSANGE.*) Well, Father. (*He takes HENRIETTA's hand and kisses it.*) Ah! I knew it. I knew that you weren't my sister. Oh, nature, your inspirations are imprinted in the hearts of your children. They will never deceive them!

PAULINE. Sir, please explain.

ST. FARD. You recall, Madame, that Henrietta was a baby when you left her in Madrid in the care of my wife? Eight years later, you asked us to return her to you. Your daughter had died six years before. We decided to spare you the sorrow of knowing the truth and to shelter our daughter from the misery into which we had fallen. She was the same age as your daughter… with the same name… some facial resemblance. My daughter was the one who left. What terrible memories I must continue to recall to explain the mystery which led me to find a son and a daughter in this house at the same time! My wife left me, Madame, and passing by Segovia[45] where Valville was raised through the kindness of a friend, she kidnapped this sacred token of my love for her, which had been the only consolation in my life. Her reconciliation with her family at my expense, her childless marriage, her wealth, her death. That's all I was able to find out. Military service filled the few years that were left of my youth. Finally, tired of living as a stranger in the world, I came into this province where I once had relatives. How often I should thank heaven for this decision since I owe it all the happiness of this day. Henrietta, forgive me of robbing you of a mother and you, Valville, raised in wealth

---

[45] Segovia is a city in Spain north of Madrid.

and luxury, will you acknowledge a miserable father who lived for you alone?

VALVILLE. (*With great feeling.*) Oh, Father, this life only becomes valuable when heaven allows me to thank you for it. And about this fortune which I should have left when my mother dared to leave you, I give it to you, Father, happy if it can make you forget the sorrows that you received from the one who gave it to me.

VOLSANGE. Good, good, my friend. That's what I call a gentleman. (*To ST. FARD with tenderness and good humor.*) Sir, don't think that you're stealing Henrietta away from us. We do not concede you our authority so easily. (*Joining SAINT-CLAIR and HENRIETTA together.*) Here's the first thing I'll do with what authority I have left. (*To the young people.*) You forgive me this time.

HENRIETTA. Ah, sir, how sweet it is to be able still to call you father.

VOLSANGE. (*With good-natured irony.*) Yes, yes, but you agree that it's better this way than the other.

SAINT-CLAIR. (*Transformed.*) Oh, Father! (*To ST. FARD.*) Sir, aren't you also my father? You agree to everything, don't you?

ST. FARD. (*To SAINT-CLAIR.*) Be happy, young man. And may the lesson you learned today teach you never to despair of heaven's goodness. You were ready to offend it.

VOLSANGE. How so?

ST. FARD. You'll hear all about it, sir.

SAINT-CLAIR. Valville, I'm not jealous anymore. Please forgive an impulse that was too strong for me and always be my friend.

VALVILLE. I only ever listened to your heart, Saint-Clair. It's the only place where friendship should be heard.

VOLSANGE. The security of your children is my only concern, sir. If you caused us to lose a daughter, it isn't right that Valville should lose a wife. I will take it upon myself to get him the heiress I had picked out for my son. Come on, my old comrade in misfortune. Let's go forget so much misery in the lap of friendship and beneath the eyes of love.

LUCETTE. (*To MR. VOLSANGE.*) Sir, since you're in such a good mood today, is it all right for me to marry Lapineau? You know I've been in love with him for a long time.

LAPINEAU. Oh! Yes, sir, I beg of you. Really! If you give her to me, we'll both dedicate the rest of our lives to you.

VOLSANGE. Yes, my friends. I will join you together. I want to celebrate today with the happiest events possible. Oh, unfathomable providence, must it always be at the price of the cruelest misfortunes that you reward man with the little happiness you give him on earth!

END OF THE FIFTH AND LAST ACT

A Select Bibliography

Bloch, Dr. Iwan. *Marquis de Sade: His Life and Work.* Translated by James Bruce. N.p.: Brittany Press, 1948.

Bremmer, Jan, ed. *From Sappho to De Sade: Moments* in *the History of Sexuality.* London and New York: Routledge, 1991.

Cleugh, James. *The Marquis and The Chevalier.* New York: Duell, Sloan and Pearce; Boston: Little, Brown and Company, 1952.

Dawes, C.R. *The Marquis de Sade: His Biography and Writings.* New York: The Macauly Co., 1927.

Dictionnaire Dramatique, Contenant L'Histoire des Théâtres, les Règles du genre Dramatique, les Observations des Maîtres les plus célèbres, et des Réflexions nouvelles sur les Spectacles, sur le génie et Ia conduite de tous les genres, avec les Notices des meilleures Pièces, le Catalogue de tous les Drames, et celui des Auteurs Dramatiques. Three volumes. Paris, 1776; reprint, Geneva: Slatkine Reprints, 1967.

Du Plessix Gray, Francine. *At Home with the Marquis de Sade: A Life.* New York: Simon and Schuster, 1998.

Endore, Guy. *Satan's Saint.* London: W.H. Allen and Company, 1966.

Foster, Annetta. "The Place of Theatre and Drama in the Life of the Marquis de Sade, *homme de lettres extraordinaire.*" Ph.D. diss., University of California, 1975.

Gorer, Geoffrey. *The Devil's Disciple: The Revolutionary Theories of the Marquis de Sade.* Paris: Collection "Le Ballet Des Muses," 1933.

———. *The Life and Ideas of the Marquis de Sade.* New York: W.W. Norton and Company, 1963.

Hartman, Janine Cey. "The Politics of Decadence: The Political and Social Ideas of Sade, Gautier, Baudelaire, and Flaubert." Ph.D. diss., University of Illinois at Chicago, 1986.

Hayes, Julia Candler. "The Representation of the Self in the Theater of La Chausée, Diderot, and Sade." Ph.D. diss., Northwestern University, 1982.

Horace. *Satires, Epistles, Ars Poetica*. Translated by H.R. Fairclough. Cambridge, Massachusetts and London: Harvard University Press, 1991.

Howarth, William D., ed. *French Theatre in the Neoclassical Era, 1550-1789*. Cambridge: Cambridge University Press, 1997.

Kennedy, Emmet. *A Cultural History of the French Revolution*. New Haven and London: Yale University Press, 1989.

Laborde, Alice M. *Correspondances du Marquis de Sade et de ses proches enrichies de documents, notes et commentaries*. 27 vols. Geneva: Editions Slatkine, 1997.

Le Brun, Annie. *Sade: A Sudden Abyss*. Translated by Camile Naish. San Francisco: City Light Books, 1990.

Lély, Gilbert. *Vie du marquis de Sade*. Paris: Mercure de France, 1989.

Lernig, Walter. *Portrait of de Sade: An illustrated Biography*. Translated by Sarah Twohig. New York: Herder and Herder, 1971.

Lever, Maurice. *Donatien Alphonse François, marquis de Sade*. Paris: Fayard, 1991.

Manceron, Claude. *Age of the French Revolution*. 5 vols. Translated by Patricia Wolf. New York: Simon and Schuster, A Touchstone Book, 1989.

Marchand, Henry L. *The French Pornographers: Including a History of French Erotic Literature*. New York: Book Awards, 1965.

Pauvert, Jean-Jacques. *Sade Vivant*. 3 vols. Paris: Editions Robert Laffont, 1986.

Rodmell, Graham F. *French Drama of the Revolutionary Years*. London: Routledge, 1990.

Sade, Donatien Alphonse François, Marquis de. *Lettres inédites et documents retrouvé par Jean-Louis Debauve*. With a preface by Annie Le Brun. Paris: Editions Rams*ey, Jean-Jacques Pauvert, 1990*.

———. *Oeuvres complètes*. 16 vols. in 8. Paris: Cerde du livre précieux, 1966–1967.

———. *Oeuvres complètes*. Vols. 32-35 Théâtre. With a Preface by Jean-Jacques Brochier. Paris: Jean-Jacques Pauvert, 1970.

———. *Selected Letters.* With a preface by Gilbert Lély. Translated by W.J. Strachan. Edited and with a new introduction by Margaret Crosland and with an afterward by Jeremy Reed. London: Peter Owen, 1965.

Schaeffer, Neil. *The Marquis de Sade.* New York: Alfred A, Knopf, 1999.

Schama, Simon. *Citizens: A Chronicle of the French Revolution.* New York: Alfred A. Knopf, 1989.

Smith, Daniel T. Jr. "Libertine dramaturgy: Reading obscene closet drama in eighteenth-century France. Ph.D. diss., Northwestern University, 2010.

Thomas, Donald. *The Marquis de Sade.* New York: Citadel Press, 1992.

Toepfer, Karl. *Theatre, Aristocracy, and Pornocracy* New York: PAJ Publications, 1991.

Wilson, Colin. *The Misfits: A Study of Sexual Outsiders.* New York: Carroll and Graf Publishers, Inc., 1988.

www.ingramcontent.com/pod-product-compliance
Lightning Source LLC
Chambersburg PA
CBHW060556230426
43670CB00011B/1844